We Build the Road as We Travel

Roy Morrison

Essential Book Publishers

Warner, NH

Essential Book Publishers

Warner, NH

Copyright © 1997 by Roy Morrison

All rights reserved. If you want to reprint, reproduce, transmit in print, electronically or by recordings all or part of *We Build The Road As We Travel*, beyond brief excerpts used in book reviews, please contact the publisher for permission:

Essential Book Publishers
P.O. Box 114
Warner, NH 03278

ISBN #: 0-9658903-0-9. (Paperback). Price $19.95.

Publication history:

First published by New Society Publishers, Philadelphia, PA, 1991.

First Essential Book Publishers edition, 1997.

Printed in the United States of America on partially recycled paper by R.C. Brayshaw & Co., Warner, NH.

Cover Design by Anne Breault, Pizzazz Publishing,
Map by Jan Schaffer. Table and Charts by Roy Morrison. Figures 1-2 and 1-3 by Adam Auster. Book design by Tina Birky.

To order please contact:
Essential Book Publishers
Toll Free number: 1-888-874-6904

Preface
–the Essential Books Edition

The Mondragon Cooperatives in the Basque region of Spain, at more than fifty years of age, remain the world's outstanding example of building a cooperative social system within the context of a now global market economy. This effort is foremost an adventure. It's an expression of individual and collective energies and dreams, as well as the requisite careful business practice of tens of thousands of cooperators engaged as social entrepreneurs.

What's most exciting, for me, about the Mondragon cooperatives is their daily wrestling with the dynamic tension between freedom and community —between the needs, rights and imperatives of the individual, and the similar, and often conflicting, imperatives of the group. Mondragon's greatest social innovation and contribution has been the understanding, developed through hard work, sometime troubling experience, and innovative practice, that freedom and community are fundamentally interdependent and indivisible.

You cannot have true freedom without community; you cannot have true community without freedom. This means that at all times a balance must be found and struck between these essential, sometimes at odds, but ultimately complementary imperatives. Open discussion and democratic practice is the means to find this balance between the individual and the group, between one cooperative and the cooperative system, between the cooperative system and the Basque region, and so on. The cooperators have called this democratic process, this wrestling with the hard questions the pursuit of *equilibrio*—the search for dynamic balance and the heart of the matter. It is this process of struggle and discovery that is the engine for social change, the root of new prospects and possibilities, not just for the Mondragon cooperators, but for all of us.

This is the importance of the Mondragon experiment. It reflects one group of people's creative struggle with the dynamic of freedom and community, what Gandhi called, in his own terms, an experiment with truth. Mondragon, as an experiment, and as a human creation is certainly not without faults. It's not just to be copied. Beyond the specific lessons and fine grained context of the experience of the Mondragon cooperators, we can learn the crucial importance and power of engaging the fundamental questions of freedom and community that can open the door toward building a democratic and liberatory future.

The Mondragon cooperatives have often been dismissed or given up for dead over the years, but have endured and adapted to changing circumstances. In a small way, this book with a new publisher now shares that attribute of endurance. The original publishing house, New Society Publishers, reorganized, and decided not to reprint *We Build The Road As We Travel* when the first printing sold out. With that, the idea for the Essential Books edition was born. And idea has become reality.

I welcome letters and comments from readers on their own work and struggles with the questions raised in this book.

Roy Morrison, June 1997

Roy Morrison can be reached at:
P.O. Box 114, Warner, NH 03278

Contents

Acknowledgements v
Author's Note vii
Preface ix
Introduction 1
1. Mondragon 8
2. Mondragon's History and Development 35
3. Cooperation: The Basis of the Mondragon System 61
4. Caja Laboral Popular: The Creation and Use of
   Social Capital 85
5. An Encounter with *Homo Oikonomia* 103
6. Cooperative Entrepreneurship: A Key Social Innovation 111
7. Social Structures: The Elaboration of the Mondragon
   Experiment 135
8. Economic Performance: Considering Mondragon's Record 167
9. Economic Transition and the Mondragon Response
   to Change 183
10. Mondragon and Reimagining Future Society 219
11. Mondragon Is Perspective 243
Appendix 1-1. The Mondragon Cooperatives in Detail 247
Appendix 1-2. Spanish Inflation Rates and Conversion
   to Constant 1985 Pesetas 258
Appendix 1-3. Regional Cooperative Groups 259
Appendix 2. Resources for Forming Cooperatives 261
Bibliography 265
Index 271

Charts, Figures and Tables

Table 1-1.	Types of Cooperatives	13
Figure 1-2.	Mondragon Cooperative System	17
Figure 1-3.	The Ideology of Industrial Modernism	24
Table 2-1.	Industrial Cooperatives' Expansion, 1961–84	53
Chart 2-2.	Number of Cooperators, 1965–87	53
Chart 3.	Mondragon Cooperative Organization	75
Table 4-1.	Growth of CLP Net Financial Resources	88
Chart 4-2.	CLP Resources and Total Mondragon Sales	90
Table 4-3.	Distribution of CLP's Assets	91
Chart 4-4.	CLP's Own Funds as a Percentage of Total Resources	92
Table 4-5.	Distribution of CLP's Surpluses, 1986	93
Chart 4-6.	Individual Capital Accounts as a Percentage of CLP's Own Funds	94
Chart 8-1.	Mondragon Annual Sales, 1970–87	171
Table 8-2.	Sales per Cooperative Member	176
Chart 8-3.	Growth of Mondragon Sales and CLP Total Resources	176
Table 8-4.	The Balance of Mondragon Cash Flow and Investments	177
Chart 8-5.	Growth of Sales per Cooperative Member, 1970–87	178
Table 9-1.	Ularco Formula for Adjusting *Anticipos*	194
Table 9-2.	Mondragon Unemployment Policies	199
Chart 9-3.	Mondragon Exports, 1970–87	207
Table 9-4.	Fagor Group—1987	211

Acknowledgements

My work has depended upon the kindness of both friends and strangers. I wish especially to thank (in no particular order or protocol):

Allen Kaufman of the University of New Hampshire for his provocative conversation and bibliographical assistance for the nonacademic; David Schweikart, philosopher, for his early encouragement and help; Jan Schaffer, union organizer and my life partner, for sharing her insights into the dynamics of the world of workers and bosses and for her patience and support; Gotzón Ormazábal, Merche Palacidos, Yolanda Palacidos, and Igor Altuna Azuargota for their friendship and invaluable assistance during my stay in Mondragon; Joaquín Meoqui, Justina Larrea, Juan Leiber, Mikel Alzola, María Asún González, José Antonio Zabaleta, and Nick, Pedro, Felix, and all the others I spoke with in the Basque country for their willingness to discuss their perspectives on the cooperative experience; Luis Iriondo and Izaskuna Arana of the Caja Laboral Popular for their help in obtaining information on the cooperatives and for the cover photographs; David Ellerman of the Industrial Cooperative Association and Tufts University for his assistance, conversation, and insight, which have been essential for my own analysis; and Joshua Hornick of the Bank for Socially Responsible Investing for current information from Mondragon.

Also, my thanks go to T. L. Hill of New Society Publishers for his energy, belief, and help as publisher and as editor; Peter Solomon for his wit, insight, and skill as the final editor; Peter Ladd, repatriated Warner, New Hampshire, native, logger, homesteader, and Thoreauvian original, for his pithy and challenging comments and conversation; Arnie Alpert for his reading of the draft manuscript and for his many useful suggestions; Bob Bower, farmer and logger, progenitor of the Sugar Bush Revolt, for his encouragement and provocation; Judy Elliott for her help in translating some difficult materials from Spanish that had exhausted my interpretive abilities to the last *palabra*; Joanne Landy of the Committee for Peace and Democracy East/West for her perspectives on Europe in transition (a transition in which she contributed to no small extent as courageous activist and writer); Doug Newton and Nancy Ladd for their interest and encouragement; Howard Hawkins and Guy Chichester for lively discussion on the relationship between Mondragon cooperativism and the Green movement; Steve Bellantone, Glen Hipple, and Joe Horton for their support; Nancy Schaffer, for her anthropologist's reading of Chapter 2 and for her challenging comments on the idea of deep social structures; Adam Auster for for his graphic work on charts detailing the ideology of industrialism and Mondragon cooperative organization; and Andrew Davis of New Society Publishers for facilitating *We Build the Road as We Travel*'s entry into the world.

Roy Morrison, Sam and Sparky

Author's Note

This book is, in part, a result of my personal and political involvement since 1976 in the grass-roots struggle against the Seabrook nuclear plant in New Hampshire. This was a struggle I did not seek; *it* came to *me*, as things often do in a technological age. A New York City expatriate, I was living in my best approximation of nineteenth-century rural splendor with hand pump, outhouse, garden, and no car on a farm in southern Maine. My idyll was suddenly compromised by the attempt to build what would have been the world's largest nuclear power project thirty miles away.

Thus began my involvement with the Clamshell Alliance, and it has transformed me; I no longer believe in the efficacy of social or personal attempts to escape the reach of modern industrialism. I am much more aware of the possibility for dramatic social change and of the sometimes relentless and thankless work involved.

Politics led to practice, and advocating energy conservation and renewable energy resources became my vocation as an energy consultant in 1981. In 1984, I wrote a book proposal for David Albert of New Society Publishers (whom I had met in Clamshell). The thesis of "Owning the Sun" repudiated the idea that mere choices of technological forms could determine the nature of society. That book would never see the light of day. But in the proposal, the Mondragon cooperatives were used to exemplify democratically controlled social, economic, and technological development.

On Dave Albert's initiative, my new proposal for a book on the Mondragon cooperatives (and their implications for social change) was transformed into a cooperative project with Terry Mollner and Will Flanders of the Trusteeship Institute of Shutesbury, Massachusetts. Their work focused on the formation of cooperative firms based on the Mondragon design. The result of our collaboration was the manuscript "Mondragon: Beyond Capitalism and Socialism." When it became clear that Terry and Will's broad philosophical interests transcended the scope of a work focused on Mondragon and diverged from my beliefs, we decided to end our collaboration, and I began an entirely new work on the Mondragon cooperatives.

While *We Build the Road As We Travel* is my own work, it emerges, in part, from my discussions and collaboration with Terry and Will; from the prior efforts of the group of Mondragon scholars and researchers including David Ellerman, William Foote Whyte and Kathleen King Whyte, Ana Gutiérrez-Johnson, Christine Clamp, Henk Thomas and Chris Logan, Robert Oakeshott, Jacques Kaswan and Ruth Kaswan, Keith Bradley and Alan Gelb, Davydd Greenwood, and Steven Curtis Jackobs; from the scars and occasional insights of my experience of political struggle; and from my life as urbanite and reborn countryman.

In this regard, it is worth recalling that individual authorship has rather recently emerged as a social phenomenon accompanying the mass production of books. With the printing press, books became an item bought and sold, raising the attendant questions of income, celebrity, and the intellectual property rights of authors. (See McLuhan and Fiore 1967, pp. 122–23.) In reality, as the comments above and the acknowledgments to follow suggest, *We Build the Road As We Travel* is not simply the result of the efforts of a solitary author, but is the product of a social matrix of thought and conversation. This book is offered as a contribution to the effort for social change and renewal, which, by its nature and by necessity, is the work of many hands and many voices.

Preface

The world surprises. The astounding transformation of Communist Europe and its global implications have changed everything except the way we consider the possibilites for the future. Both right and left seem to have lost their historic compass, their sense of destiny and confidence. The right wields power as though it believes that the political changes of 1989 and 1990 did not happen. The left in the face of revolution is cowed.

The time has come for us to reshape our imaginations in light of dramatically changed circumstances. The collective hesitation in the face of the sudden and grand collapse of Stalinism and the Cold War and a gathering global environmental catastrophe is not merely an ideological and public-relations problem. It reflects the underlying instability and weakness in the foundations of the industrial state itself—and its inability to deal with the real issues as the screen of Cold War antipathy dissolves.

This book considers the Mondragon cooperatives as a model for a democratic, labor-managed social system. The fundamental global task we face is to re-form the conduct of industrial civilization as a whole, to establish democratic, just, and ecologically sustainable societies. The Mondragon model can help provide a basis for dramatic social transformation where existing capitalism and socialism have failed.

After the revolutions have ended and the dust of reality begins to settle, it will be unavailing for those newly freed from the yoke of Stalinist tyranny merely to recapitulate the forms and errors of capitalism. Mondragon has demonstrated that there is another, and I believe better, way to build democratic market economies. The "market" need not mean capitalism as we have known it.

The Mondragon experience suggests that building a dynamic and just market economy does not require the stock markets or absentee owners that have been fundamental (and largely unexamined) features of industrial capitalism. The existence of a labor-managed, democratic-market alternative is a matter of global relevance that does not merely apply to the new European democracies, or only to advanced industrialized states.

The real choice now is between building labor-managed systems or the more-or-less painful adoption or prolongation of traditional capitalism. The choice, by and large, is *not* between a market economy or a planned socialist economy; the challenge is to change the conduct of industrial society, not merely the nature of its management. The ecological devastation wrought by socialist industrialism under Stalinism is a painful reminder of the practical convergence of existing capitalism and socialism in action.

The tension animating the crisis of industrialism is not the opposition between "freedom" and "planning." Mondragon's practice reflects an understanding that freedom and community are indivisible—the embracing, in ecological terms, of unity in diversity—and that new democratic social choices must be made to reconstruct the nature of industrial society if it is to survive.

The writing of this book was largely finished by the end of 1989. As I wrote, the post-World-War-II era suddenly drew to a close, and the issues and themes considered in this book suddenly moved from theory and the margins of practice to matters of fundamental concern for millions. I believe that the Mondragon model and its implications are most relevant to those now looking at the world in new ways.

Dedicated to Helen and Leo Morrison, my mother and father
and in memoriam to my cousins
Harvey Morrison and Paul Morrison

Introduction

The Mondragon cooperative system in the Basque region of Spain is a creative and renewing response to the agonies of industrialism. The Mondragon cooperators have found the way to make new social choices that provide revolutionary and constructive solutions to the common problems of industrial society. This book examines these social choices and the prospects they hold for human renewal.

The questions we face are fundamental, sometimes stark. The modern era—the era of industrialism—is ending. The essential tension is no longer between existing capitalist and socialist worlds, long since resigned to their existence as industrial states. We are increasingly preoccupied with the intertwined environmental, social, and political themes of exhaustion and uncertainty, for which the mainstream of industrial modernism can provide few solutions. The optimism that predicted the emergence of a perhaps conditionally utopian postindustrial world through the ministrations of technology has faded.

The Mondragon system exemplifies the ability of new social choices to influence and shape the nature of the transformation away from an unsustainable industrial modernism. Mondragon demonstrates that these currents of change carry the potential for social reconstruction and are not merely a venue for decay and chaos.

Mondragon suggests that we can act creatively within our own communities to build social systems that embrace freedom, justice, and ecological sanity. Mondragon has something to say to us, not because it is exotic or distanced, but because it arose from the smoldering, boiling heart of industrialism itself, from the workers in the Unión Cerrajera steel mill of Mondragon.

Industrial Modernism

Before we attempt to glimpse the future, we need to untangle the intricacies of the present and place it in context. The first flowerings of modernism arose with the dramatic series of world-shaping changes of the fifteenth, sixteenth, and seventeenth centuries, which included Francis Bacon's articulation of the scientific method and Rene Descartes's disquisition on the separation of mind and body. Baconian science, with its reductionist manipulation, combined with the analytic spirit of Cartesian dualism to serve a new world of commerce, of reason—and then, by the end of the eighteenth century, a world of enlightenment, with its faith in technical progress and revolution.

Revolution came in the political struggles of the Americans and the French against monarchy and for popular rule. It also came with the rise of the factory and the machine, an industrial revolution that began in Great Britain and (in influence and impact) rapidly surpassed the contemporary political struggles. Industrial modernism arose with entrepreneurial zeal in the latter part of the eighteenth century and swept all before it. The next century saw the triumphant consolidation of capitalist industrial modernism as the dominant world system.

And what a leviathan industrial modernism has proved to be. Its practice has been so powerful and successful that its ideology (based upon the steel triangle of progress, hierarchy, and technique) has largely consumed the energies of socialists as well as capitalists: both march under the banner of an industrialism that has more to do with production and power than with liberation.

The metaphor of leviathan, the marauding beast, clearly is a recourse to an archetype of primal fear. We are facing a monstrous social megamachine of our own creation: a machine that is not merely steel, plastic, and silicon, but flesh; a machine we serve not just as master and servant, but as working parts.

As the twentieth century draws to a close, the destructive legacy of industrial modernism, in both its capitalist and socialist manifestations, is all too apparent. A recourse to more of the same, to the further ministrations of bureaucratic technocracies, is a commitment to follow a trajectory leading to catastrophe—climatic change and global poisoning, precursors to ecocide and mass starvation; to social collapse; to nuclear obliteration.

Saving change, fundamental change, must come from below, from the social practice of people fully engaged and in struggle with the forces of industrial modernism. The Mondragon cooperatives are an example of changes from below. While they are not the "answer," they are a relevant example of the kind of path we can choose to follow, a path that leads away from the abyss and toward personal and communal freedom, dynamic social revitalization, and ecological sanity.

Mondragon

From its beginnings in the 1940s as a training school for apprentices, the Mondragon cooperatives have become the world's most significant cooperative system in an industrialized market economy. Once hidden in the Cantabrian Mountains of Guipúzcoa Province, today the Mondragon co-ops are a prominent element of the economy and society of the semiautonomous Basque region of Spain.

The Mondragon system of more than 170 co-ops, including 100 cooperative businesses, has grown steadily, often spectacularly; it has developed and used sophisticated technologies and has responded effectively to the exigencies of the business cycle. The Mondragon cooperative system includes schools, houses, stores, clinics, foundries, robots, factories, and banks, but its center is the industrial cooperatives and the system of cooperative entrepreneurship.

Mondragon's economic success, wrought by ordinary people with no significant material assets and living under the tyranny of Francisco Franco, is impressive; but even more significant, Mondragon's social success is a response to industrialism itself. Social development has been an absolutely essential element in its economic development. While erecting factories and producing goods, the Mondragon cooperators were also creating from below a cooperative social reality. At the heart of the system is the solidarity that they have built, sometimes painfully, among themselves and between themselves and their communities, a solidarity that is a result of an inclusive, ongoing, and gradually expanding evolutionary process.

The Mondragon response to industrial modernism includes:

1. Democracy and self-management that works by one member, one vote

2. Personal and collective risk taking through cooperative entrepreneurship that focuses and amplifies the cooperators' energies creatively, dynamically, and humanely
3. An enduring community-centered nature: the co-ops are community institutions owned by their cooperators, but an individual's interest cannot be sold
4. Earnings related only to a person's own work
5. The ability and will to make social choices that can limit the destructive conduct of industrialism while strengthening the community socially and economically
6. Above all, a many-voiced, spirited, and democratic pursuit of what the cooperatives call *equilibrio*. This means not just equilibrium or balance, but also implies harmony, poise, calmness, and composure. Equilibrio is a vital process that harmonizes and balances a diverse and growing community of interests: those of the individual and the co-op, the particular co-op and the co-op system, and the co-op system and the community and environment.

Ecological Postmodernism

Mondragon cooperativism is not a machine. It is not merely the material fruits of cooperative entrepreneurship, but the result of a complex social reality. The pursuit of equilibrio pervades all aspects of the life of the Mondragon cooperatives and gives vitality, direction and human value to the experiment. And while some organizational intricacies may be peculiar to the Mondragon setting, the pursuit of equilibrio is decidedly transferable and can be the basis for fundamental social transformation in any setting.

The Mondragon cooperative system is informed by an essentially ecological consciousness. Ecology, conventionally defined as the relationship of living things to their environment, is understood here to encompass social as well as biological reality and their interaction. Today, Mondragon's ecological consciousness is manifested not primarily through environmentalism, but through the practice of a social ecology: the pursuit of equilibrio is fundamentally connected to the basic ecological principle of diversity and unity, or, in social terms, freedom and community. Its promise is basic change that will harmonize both social life and the relationship between the social and natural worlds.

The Mondragon system represents the emergence of what I call an ecological postmodernism, a possible splitting in the path of social development away from the self-destructive processes of industrial modernism and toward the revitalization of human society and the integration of a sustainable social and natural ecology.

This represents not merely a separation from the "cultural logic of late capitalism"[1] but a departure from industrialism as a whole in its capitalist or socialist manifestations. It is the process of healing the estrangement between people and nature (expressed socially through domination and oppression, and within ourselves by the separation of mind and body) that has reached its apotheosis with an industrial modernism now poised on the verge of self-destruction.

The democratic pursuit of equilibrio is a healing art. The ethics of an ecological postmodernism, developed through social choices and social practice, can replace the ideology of industrialism. Through our practice, we can embrace self-management, freedom and democracy instead of hierarchy, evolution and renewal instead of mindless progress, empathy instead of technique.

The ethics and social choices of an ecological postmodernism are conditioned by the complexities of the living world and its social systems. In the view of social ecologist Murray Bookchin, "An ecological nature—and the objective ethics following from it—can spring to life, as it were, only in a society whose sensibilities and interrelationships have become ecological to their very core."[2]

Process

This book examines the building of the Mondragon system and the dynamics that inform its conduct. It pursues and weaves together three lines of inquiry. First, it investigates the development of the Mondragon system, with special attention to the broader applicability of some of Mondragon's responses to particular, but common, events and conditions. Second, it explores the characteristic and exemplary elements of the Mondragon social system, focusing on the ways they interact and change in a living and evolving community. Third, it considers the larger social forces at play in the transition from an afflicted industrial modernism to a postmodern world, using Mondragon as an example of an emerging ecological postmodernism.

The first two narratives are based upon what is palpably at hand (if in the process of change), and their interpretation is to some extent bracketed by the evidence. But the third, including as it does claims about the possibilities of social transformation, is bolder. I hope it will spark animated discussion, but I also hope that even those who are skeptical about Mondragon as a model will remain open to the more straightforward lessons it teaches.

Names and Places

Mondragon is the name of the town where the cooperatives began, but it has also become synonymous with the whole of Mondragon cooperativism. In these pages, "Mondragon cooperatives" or "Mondragon" refer to the entire group of associated cooperatives in the Basque provinces of Alava, Guipúzcoa, Navarra, and Vizcaya in Spain. In their published material the co-ops sometimes refer to the "Mondragon Cooperative Experiment" and often just to "our cooperative experience" or to the "Cooperative Group."

There is a bit more to the name question. Mondragon is the Spanish name for the town. In Euskara, the Basque language, its name is Arrasate. A visitor sees that the name Mondragon has been painted over with Arrasate on many older road signs, and anyone attempting to navigate the confusing and serpentine mountain road network soon learns that it is at least marginally easier to ask for directions to Arrasate than to Mondragon. Still, there does not seem to be a move toward using the name "Arrasate Cooperatives."

Many co-op publications are written in both Spanish and Euskara, but cooperatives and their structures are usually named in Euskara. As the co-ops become increasingly involved in international trade, use of English (the lingua franca of commerce) is emerging, so that, for example, the annual report of the co-op bank now appears in both Spanish and English.

Conclusion (and Beginning)

The Mondragón cooperative experiment is not perfect. More voices need to be fully admitted to the search for equilibrio. I am not saying, "I have seen the future and it works." Mondragón makes no such utopian claims for itself, nor do I.

What is most appealing about Mondragón is its sweaty humanity. Mondragón is social transformation in process. In their day-to-day experience and hard-won accomplishments, the cooperators, responding to the common conditions of industrial modernism, have created a social system that deserves our attention.

Notes

1. Jameson 1984, pp. 53–92.
2. Bookchin 1982, p. 276.

1
Mondragon

The Mondragon cooperatives, because of their established and intertwined economic and social success, are a mature model for people interested in both economic development and social change. Much more than a lonely cooperative business attempting to stay afloat in the capitalist sea, Mondragon challenges us to rethink our images of typical cooperatives.

Overview of the Cooperative Social System

The scale of Mondragon is impressive. As of the start of 1988, the system included 166 cooperatives with 21,000 workers. In 1987, the cooperatives' sales were $1.6 billion, including $310 million in exports. Constituents of the group include a bank, the Caja Laboral Popular (CLP), with $2.9 billion in total assets and 180 branches; Ulgor, Spain's largest appliance manufacturer; Lagun-Aro, a social security and insurance system; Eroski, a retail co-op with more than $360 million in annual sales; Hezibide Elkartea, a collection of schools ranging from the elementary grades to universities and adult education that serves more than forty-five thousand students; and Ikerlan, an advanced technology research center.[1]

Mondragon is a dramatic departure from past social and organizational practice. The cooperatives reflect the development and application of the social innovation I call cooperative entrepreneurship, informed by the pursuit of equilibrio. More than a tool or an organizational technique, this entrepreneurship is a process that allows ordinary people to shape humane, democratic, and prosperous societies.

The Mondragon system clearly transcends conventional cooperative efforts now familiar in the United States, such as those in which workers buy out failing companies to save jobs, or employee stock ownership plans (ESOPs), which allow owners to sell their businesses and receive substantial tax benefits but often grant the worker-owners little control of "their" company. Mondragon is basically different from the small (and usually undercapitalized) service, retail, or light industrial co-op.

The difference is not one of motivation or courage. Cooperators around the world work hard; they are practical idealists willing to make sacrifices in their struggle for dignity, self-determination, and community. Nor is the difference geographical: conditions in the Basque country are not remarkably different from those elsewhere in industrial society. In fact, Mondragon is inspiring precisely because it has grown out of familiar conditions and because its basic elements are accessible to working people. Mondragon's forty-year history is one of endurance and the triumph of human community; Mondragon provides practical hope.

Mondragon and Social Change

On the surface, the Mondragon accomplishment is clear. The cooperators have created an economically strong, democratic, and revolutionary social system from the most slender resources. While they have built up impressive material and capital assets, the essential wealth of the system is its community. The cooperators have long been acutely conscious of the importance of community to their experiment, and in 1987, at the first Cooperative Congress, they took the time to articulate and debate the precise wording of the basic cooperative principles that guide the Mondragon experiment.

The 350 cooperators sitting in the congress were neither bureaucratic functionaries nor a founding elite; they were women and men elected by their peers, people from the shop floor, from co-op schools, from management. This congress and its debates fulfilled the social goals of democratizing knowledge and power. This democratization runs deep. The Cooperative Congress's decisions remain largely advisory; they do not bind a particular co-op unless they are ratified by that co-op's general assembly. This is characteristic of the pursuit of equilibrio: the search for consensus and empowerment of both individuals and groups.

Alfonso Gorroñogoitia, one of the five founders of Ulgor, the first cooperative, and now chair of the governing council of the cooperative bank, said in a 1975 interview: "What surprises other entrepreneurs is the poetic-philosophical vein that we have as entrepreneurs.... We could not be pure technocrats who know perfectly the process of chemistry or physics or semi-conductors but nothing more. We have never been pure technocrats. We see the development of these firms as a social struggle, a duty."[2]

But what is that struggle, that duty? The cooperators' experiment began as a social response to the poverty and disempowerment that they faced as Basques and as workers under Franco and the owners of various large mills. Basic to Mondragon is the struggle to continue to make free choices that advance the cooperators' idealism in practical ways, a process that continues today as they engage the remnants of Franco's legacy and the common conditions of industrial modernism in crisis.

The Ten Cooperative Principles

The principles codified at the 1987 congress are a guide; the cooperators are well aware that disparities exist between theory and practice. As *Trabajo y Unión*, the co-op magazine, notes: "The reality of our cooperative practice differs somewhat from the formulation of the basic principles. But this difference constitutes a spur, a motivation to overcome the difference between the ideal and the possible, the desirable and the real."[3]

The principles are not legalisms or ideological statements, but an articulation of cooperative and participatory values that have developed over the forty years of the Mondragon experiment. They are essentially labor-based and communitarian, rooted in a variety of movements and experiences: aspects of Basque cultural institutions and industrial heritage; the Catholic church's social doctrine; and socialist, communist, and anarchist ideas. The principles affirm the freedom and empowerment of working people and at the same time provide limits, characteristic of the pursuit of equilibrio, in the interest of community. This tension between centralization and autonomy is fundamental to Basque political life and a significant characteristic of industrial modernism. The Mondragon system represents, in part, a creative resolution of this tension.

In their preamble, the cooperators note that the proclamation of the Mondragon cooperative principles takes into account the universal Rochdale cooperative principles, as modified by the International Cooperative Alliance; their own thirty years of practical experience; and the open and dynamic character of these axioms, which change and evolve to meet the needs of the cooperators.

Open Admission

The cooperative system is open to all who agree with the basic cooperative principles without regard to ethnic background, religion, political beliefs, or gender.

Democratic Organization

The cooperative system is based upon the equality of owner-workers (*socio-trabajadores*). Aside from limited and special circumstances all workers must be members. The cooperative is democratically controlled on the basis of one member, one vote; its governing structures are democratically controlled and are also responsible to the general assembly or other elected body.

Sovereignty of Labor

Labor is the essential transformative factor of society. The cooperatives renounce wage labor, give full power to the owner-workers to control the co-ops, give primacy to workers in distribution of surpluses, and work to extend the cooperative choice to all members of society.

Instrumental Character of Capital

Capital is basically accumulated labor and a necessary factor in business development and savings. The co-ops pay a just but limited return on capital saved or invested, a return that is not directly tied to the losses or surpluses of the co-ops. Their need for capital shall not impede the principle of open admission, but (after an initial trial period) co-op members must make a substantial, affordable, and equal financial investment in the cooperative. At present, this membership contribution is equal to a year's salary of the lowest-paid member.

Self-Management

Cooperation involves both collective effort and individual responsibility. Cooperation "is the development of the individual not against others but with others." Democratic control means participation in management and the ongoing development of the skills needed for self-management (*autogestion*). There must be clear information available on the co-op's operations, systematic training of owner-workers, internal promotion for management positions, and consultations and negotiations with all cooperators in organizational decisions that affect them.

Pay Solidarity

The co-ops will practice both internal and external pay solidarity. Internally, the total pay differential between the lowest- and the highest-paid member shall not exceed a factor of one to six.[4]

In addition, compensation is comparable to that prevailing in neighboring conventional firms. A new institution, the F.I.S.O. (see p. 19), constitutes, in effect, a third level of co-op solidarity, in this case solidarity between the individual co-ops.

Group Cooperation

Co-ops are not isolated entities. Cooperation exists on three levels: among individual co-ops organized into groups; among co-op groups; and between the Mondragon system and other movements.

Social Transformation

Cooperation in the Mondragon system is an instrument for social transformation. As José María Arizmendiarrieta, a founder of the movement, wrote, "Cooperation is the authentic integration of people in the economic and social process that shapes a new social order; the cooperators must make this objective extend to all those that hunger and thirst for justice in the working world."

The co-ops reinvest the major portion of their surpluses in the Basque community. A significant portion goes toward new job development, to community development (through the use of social funds), to a social security system based on mutual solidarity and responsibility, to cooperation with other institutions (such as unions) advancing the cause of Basque workers, and to collaborative efforts to develop Basque language and culture.

Universal Nature

The co-ops proclaim their solidarity with all who labor for economic democracy, peace, justice, human dignity, and development in Europe and elsewhere, particularly with the peoples of the Third World.

Education

Education is essential for fulfilling the basic cooperative principles. It is fundamentally important to devote sufficient human and economic resources to cooperative education, professional training, and general education of young people for the future.

The Mondragon Cooperatives Today

The seven basic types of Mondragon cooperatives are listed in Table 1-1.

Table 1-1. Types of Cooperatives

	Number of Co-ops
Industrial	86
Agricultural	8
Service-Sector	4
Educational	46
Retail	1
Housing	15
Second-Degree and Support	6
	Total: 166

Source: CLP annual report (1987)

From their origin in the town of Mondragon, the cooperatives have spread throughout the four Basque provinces (there are twelve co-ops in Alava province, eighty-nine in Guipúzcoa, ten in Navarra, and fifty-four in Vizcaya). But since several of the co-ops—such as Eroski, the retail co-op, and CLP, the bank—have branches throughout the Basque country, they actually are even more widespread, and even more a feature of Basque life, than these figures indicate.

The Co-op Menagerie

The cooperatives vary enormously in nature, size, and complexity. They range from the 6-member agricultural co-op of Artxa in Alava Province; to Goiti, a manufacturer of computer-controlled machine tools in the city of Elgiobar, with 51 cooperators; to the giant Ulgor in Mondragon, an appliance manufacturer with more than 2,000 cooperators; to the Caja Laboral Popular (CLP), with 180 branch offices and 1,234 cooperators.[5]

There is no fixed minimum or maximum size for cooperatives. For industrial start-ups, the goal is at least 40 members within five years; experience suggests that 400 to 500 members is the maximum, since beyond that size bureaucracy almost unavoidably intrudes and attenuates cooperative intimacy and solidarity. Where feasible, and to avoid diseconomies of scale, large co-ops hive off divisions to form new associated cooperatives. But the business co-ops are not simply a collection of companies. While integrated into a supportive network, complete with

14 *WE BUILD THE ROAD AS WE TRAVEL*

service co-ops, they maintain their independence—and the entire structure is governed democratically.

Cooperative Types

Of the seven types of cooperatives in the Mondragon system, six are described below. (The seventh type, second-degree cooperatives such as the bank and the social insurance co-op, is described on pp. 18-19.)[6]

Industrial Cooperatives

Although there is a great diversity of cooperative types, the majority of jobs (16,020, or 76%, of 21,000 total positions) are in the industrial cooperatives. In 1986, these co-ops had annual sales of $1.18 billion. Much of the Mondragon system has been based upon the surpluses produced by the industrial cooperatives.

The eighty-six industrial co-ops are divided into five basic groups:

1. casting and forging (heavy primary metalwork), seven co-ops
2. capital equipment (tools and finished goods for industrial and commercial use, ranging from sophisticated machine tools and electronic controls to hydraulic presses, excavation equipment, buses and small ships), twenty-seven co-ops
3. intermediate goods (parts and components of many types and materials for industrial use, from valves to molded plastic to copper wire to electronic components), thirty co-ops
4. consumer goods (such products for the retail market as refrigerators, water heaters, furniture, stereos, bicycles, eyeglass frames), sixteen co-ops
5. construction (a broad range of supplies and tasks, including design, manufacture, and assembly of all types of steel structures, greenhouses, and housing construction and promotion), six co-ops

Agricultural Co-ops

The eight agricultural cooperatives have about 250 owner-workers. In 1986, sales were $30 million, with a surplus of more than $1 million. These co-ops are involved in such traditional pursuits as dairy farming and hog and sheep rearing, as well as greenhouse horticulture, animal-feed production, and agricultural marketing.

Service-Sector Co-ops

There are four service-sector co-ops in the Mondragon system, although a number of the industrial co-ops also offer services. These range from the low-tech Auzo-Lagun, which provides institutional food and cleaning services and subcontracts assembly work, to Uldata, which designs data-processing systems.

Retail Co-ops

Eroski, the retail cooperative, has 270 stores spread throughout the Basque country. It carries a full range of consumer goods, has more than 1,600 cooperators, and its 1987 sales exceeded $363 million. Its sophisticated democratic structure combines the input of owner-workers and of customers. Eroski also has an extensive consumer education program.

Housing Co-ops

There are fifteen housing co-ops with about one thousand apartments. The cooperative system has also been active in urban and land-planning issues.

Educational, Training, and Research Co-ops

The cooperative system began with a training school for industrial apprentices organized by José María Arizmendiarrieta, and the co-ops have continually elaborated their educational basis and mission. As Arizmendiarrieta wrote, "It has been said that cooperativism is an economic movement that uses education; we can also alter the definition, affirming that it is an educational movement that uses economic action."[7]

The Mondragon co-ops' broad educational concerns extend from day care, to primary education in Basque-language schools, to university training at Eskola Politeknikoa in Mondragon, to a wide range of continuing-education and postgraduate courses. The educational work of the co-ops takes several forms.

Hezibide Elkartea (formerly the League for Education and Culture) coordinates educational co-ops and associated institutes and training programs in the region around Mondragon. There are about sixty-five hundred students in degree programs that culminate in college-level programs at the Eskola Politeknikoa and thirty-five hundred students in other types of training courses. The special training institutes associated with Hezibide Elkartea include:

1. Institute of Industrial Design—assists the Mondragon co-ops and other Basque businesses
2. Goier—coordinates and promotes postgraduate engineering and technical studies abroad
3. Iranukor—offers continuing education courses both for general subjects and to meet specific co-op requests
4. Iraskale Eskola—teacher training
5. Saiolan—worker training in new technologies

The *Ikastolas* are Basque-language primary schools; more than forty are associated with the Mondragon system, with about thirty-five thousand students in the four Basque provinces. They now have a relationship with the Basque government. The growth of the *Ikastola* movement has been strongly linked with the Euskara cultural renaissance and with the Mondragon co-ops.

Alecoop is a unique co-op factory in Mondragon, largely staffed and run by students, that produces parts for other industrial co-ops, while offering students a mix of part-time work and vocational training.

Ikerlan is a high-technology research cooperative in Mondragon with a staff of about one hundred. It works closely with the co-ops and other Basque businesses on research projects in electronics, computer science, mechanical engineering, and production systems. Ikerlan is involved, for example, in developing flexible manufacturing cells that use a combination of robots, CAD-CAM systems, and self-guided vehicles for automated production modules.

Finally, the Ikasbide training center provides postgraduate management training for prospective co-op managers, training for co-op members, and multilingual programs for education about the Mondragon system.

Cooperative Structure

The Mondragon cooperative system is a complex and evolving network that supports the cooperators and their families, the individual cooperatives and the system, and the communities and society of which the co-ops are part. The structure is decidedly dynamic, capable of making both major and minor changes in response to the lessons of the cooperative experience.

Organizationally, the support structure functions on three levels. Each individual cooperative has a broadly similar internal structure of operation and democratic control that is in accord with agreed-upon cooperative principles. A variety of second-degree cooperatives and support structures provides a wide range of assistance to the co-ops, cooperators, and the community on all levels. Finally, the new, democratically elected Cooperative Congress and the Council of Cooperative Groups afford forums for open discussion and democratic consideration of the most basic issues affecting the Mondragon cooperatives.

Within this system, each cooperative and cooperative structure makes additional democratic decisions and may decide to associate voluntarily with other co-ops and cooperative structures in ways that respond to their mutual needs. Most important, this means that no Mondragon co-op is alone: while each is independent and under the direct democratic control of its members (who are at financial risk), individual co-ops are also embedded in a supporting structure that provides financial, business, technical, educational, philosophical, and social support.

Figure 1-2 depicts the constellation of the components of Mondragon's organizational structures. It is a challenge to present the relationships between the Mondragon structures graphically, since they do not form a typical pyramid or a flowchart, but are more like a dynamic web of shifting nodes of communication and cooperation, the levels always interacting.

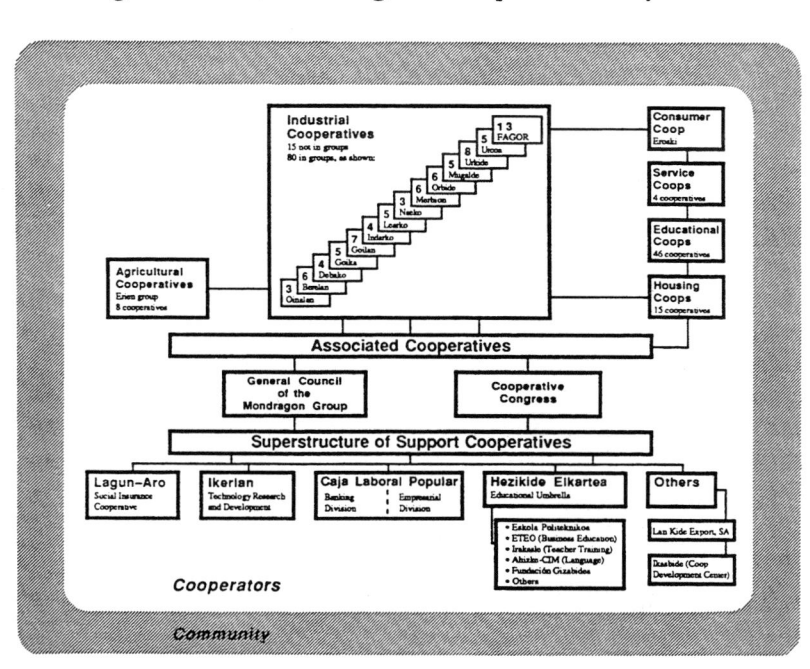

Figure 1-2. Mondragon Cooperative System

Individual Cooperatives

Each co-op is a legally separate cooperative corporation organized under Spanish and Basque law. Called *sociedades cooperativas* (S. Coop.), they are distinct from the conventional, stockholder-owned corporations, *sociedades anónimas* (S.A.). (In Spanish, *anónima* means "anonymous," a particularly apt description of conventional corporations.)

All co-ops share some basic organizational structures, designed to ensure democratic control and the ability to function flexibly, dynamically and durably. These allow for the distribution, and monitoring, of power and authority: for example, managers are generally free to manage, in the sense of coordinating the co-op's energy and creativity, to meet the goals of the mutually agreed-upon business plan. The individual co-ops are built to human scale and their structures rely on face-to-face relationships; they could not be used to reform enormous bureaucracies unless the bureaucracies were first broken up into human-sized pieces.

The basic structures of the individual co-ops have six common features. First, all owner-workers are members of the general assembly, which has ultimate authority for all co-op decisions and operates on the basis of one member, one vote. The general assembly meets at least yearly.

Second, the governing council (junta rector), elected by the general assembly, is in charge of the day-to-day implementation of cooperative policy. It meets at least monthly, makes decisions by majority vote, and is responsible for hiring senior co-op management.

Members of the social council, the third common structure, are elected by the cooperators, usually as representatives of groups of close coworkers or of a formal work group; they make decisions about personnel issues, including pay, health benefits, and safety. Fourth, the account control board (watchdog council), elected by the general assembly, audits the books and monitors co-op operations.

Fifth, the co-op manager, and sometimes other senior managers, are hired by the governing council. Managers are expected to show initiative in implementing the co-op business plan. They are, of course, co-op members, with one vote in the general assembly. Finally, the management council, an informal advisory body, is composed of top managers and co-op officers. It meets at least monthly to discuss co-op operations and policy.

Second-Degree Cooperatives and Support Structures

The Mondragon system continues to develop a variety of support structures and second-degree cooperatives to meet the cooperators' and cooperatives' needs. These include the bank, some resource organizations, the social security co-op, and the various groups meant to facilitate planning and collaboration between related cooperatives.

The operations of the Caja Laboral Popular (the Working People's Bank; literally, the "Bank of People's Labor") are now central to the operation and development of the co-ops. The economic component of the Mondragon cooperatives can be most quickly understood as consisting of the bank and the associated cooperatives.

The Caja Laboral Popular is a second-degree cooperative, a co-op of co-ops. It is controlled by both its owner-workers and members—in this case, cooperatives that have signed a detailed contract of association. The

Caja Laboral Popular is divided into financial and business (Empresarial) divisions. The former conducts banking operations and works to meet the needs of the associated cooperatives; the latter supports the planning and start-up of new co-ops and provides ongoing technical assistance and support for existing ones. The bank's assets are based upon the savings of local citizens and the recycled income and surpluses (profits) produced by both the associated co-ops and the bank's own operations. By using this money, and offering expert assistance to associated cooperatives, the CLP has effectively freed Mondragon from dependence on capitalist financiers, whose view of cooperatives is often jaundiced both by business prejudice and by ideological hostility.

Under Spanish law, the co-ops are exempt from normal social security taxes and benefits, so the cooperators started the Lagun-Aro social security and insurance system to provide a full range of retirement, disability, health, insurance, and other social benefits to cooperators and their families. In 1987, Lagun-Aro had 140 member co-ops with 18,055 member-cooperators and had paid health benefits to 46,333 people. Lagun-Aro is actively involved in studying general and specific worker health and safety concerns.

Cooperative groups provide an intermediate level of organization and additional flexibility and resilience in the face of economic and social changes. They also encourage individual cooperatives to work together, rather than seeing themselves as islands in a sea of conventional firms. There are now fourteen cooperative groups with a total membership of about eighty co-ops. They are based on geographical proximity or on similarity of activities. While maintaining its individual identity, each co-op in a group participates in planning and coordination and shares in some or all of the group's profits or losses.

In 1987 the co-op groups established the Intercooperative Solidarity Fund (F.I.S.O.) to provide resources beyond those available from the CLP to aid economically distressed member cooperatives. The F.I.S.O. will be funded over five years by member co-ops at a rate of about $600 per co-op member; this will provide an endowment of about $13 million. In effect, co-op members are paying for employment insurance, but unlike most unemployment plans, F.I.S.O. is preventive: it assists co-ops in distress and strives to prevent job loss.[8]

Cooperative Congress and The General Council of Cooperative Groups

The third level of co-op institutions includes the new Cooperative Congress and the General Council of the Mondragon groups. The congress meets at least once every two years to consider issues of broad concern to the system. All co-ops send at least one democratically elected representative; the 350 seats in the congress are apportioned based on the number of owner-workers in each co-op. The congress has a president and a vice-president, as well as a permanent commission to follow up on its decisions.

The new General Council is designed to improve operational planning, coordination, and cooperation among the co-ops. It includes senior representatives of cooperative groups and second-degree co-ops.

Mondragon and the Challenge to Industrial Modernism

The Mondragon project is nothing less than the creation of a new reality. It is an attempt to rescue reason from instrumentalism, from the tyranny of technique and power that has shaped the world of industrial modernism at the price of mangling the human spirit and devastating the biosphere.

Mondragon is an example of evolutionary change, not an attempt to sweep all away in a single revolutionary stroke. It builds a new reality through social practice; hence we can proceed from reality to theory. Our task is not to spin utopian webs, but to clarify and explain what is already in process, what is implicit in a complex reality. An examination of Mondragon, then, is a search for a new realism—for a system that enables us to analyze and understand both the problems addressed by Mondragon and the solutions the cooperators have proposed.

Industrial modernism is much concerned with questions of knowledge, and of science as a method to obtain knowledge. Research is the privileged pursuit. In reality, however, knowledge is only a gloss on the true text of power: "basic" research into the nature of matter is followed by "applied" research into the use of thermonuclear weapons.

The counterpoise to knowledge is often held to be a focus on the nature of being itself. But the substitution of ontology (the study of the nature of being) for epistemology (the study of the nature of knowledge) does not resolve the modernist conundrum. While being simply "is," the modernist approach to ontology is first to agree with the mystical connotations of "is-ness," and then to probe and dissect the nature of being—to attempt to use the customary tools of modernism to answer the question: "Is what?" The dominant approaches to defining and understanding knowledge and being should be viewed as subsets of the ideology of industrialism.

Mondragon offers the possibility of a constructive response to the centrifugal forces at work within advanced industrial society; it represents an alternative I call ecological postmodernism. Postmodernism is generally associated with cultural disassociation, a radical mixture of styles and a collapse of tradition in discourse and social values. The resolution provided by ecological postmodernism is to understand and experience being in the context of becoming—a process in which our participation, our values, and our ethics are inseparable.

Mondragon cooperators' dynamic and democratic search for balance—equilibrio—is conditioned and mediated by clearly articulated cooperative principles and agreements. Mondragon's participatory reality is not simply shaped from ideas or concepts, categories or language; its meaning is found in the living world, where social and natural orders are inextricably linked and relations are supremely relevant. Mondragon belongs to the logical category of social systems, not of economic or nationalist organizations. It has been built using cooperative forms, many of them new and almost all of them still evolving. The challenges facing Mondragon cannot be considered in terms of conventional economics or sociology; understanding that system requires particular conceptual tools. Thus, the themes shaping Mondragon examined in this book include:

1. The nature of the social choices made in the name of cooperation and informed by a democratic pursuit of equilibrio, and how they limit the conduct of industrialism
2. The essentially ecological protocols and ethics of Mondragon social practice, with its embracing of diversity and unity
3. The engagement and change of deep social structures through social practice
4. The tension between centralization and autonomy—energies creatively harnessed by the pursuit of equilibrio
5. The freeing of social practice from the ideology of industrialism
6. The diverse and yet converging paths that inform the reimagination of future society now in progress

The Mondragon system represents a constructive challenge to industrial modernism, an act of re-creation in the process of building a new and liberatory social system. Mondragon's accomplishments cannot simply be measured in dollars or rhetoric, but must be considered in terms of social practice. The importance of Mondragon lies in the promise it holds for social change, for the transformation of reality.

The Ideology of Industrialism and Postmodernism

This book is predicated on a belief that more of the same will not work, that constructive change will not be found along well-trodden paths. José María Arizmendiarrieta wrote of Mondragon that "we build the road as we travel [*se hace camino al andar*]."[9] We must not only alleviate the symptoms of industrialism, but engage and change fundamental social structures.

Here, it will be helpful to reexamine the ideology of industrialism. This not only reveals the dynamics of industrial modernism, but casts light upon the genesis and nature of the Mondragon challenge to business as usual. The enormous power of industrial modernism is not limited to the ability to create or to destroy in the present; it can also use, to an astounding extent, the social forces of reason, creativity, and aspiration to perpetuate and re-create its power. Industrial modernism cannot be overthrown merely by critique or by the revolutionary replacement of rulers; it can only be toppled by creation of a new reality through social practice.

Such a task is not simply a matter of exercising "free will." We are faced not only by the repressive power of industrial modernism, but by the durability of its ideology, which pervades the world view of those who attempt to change industrialism from within. This ideology validates and legitimates the industrial system. It also encourages the maximization of power, however it is defined (as money, authority, possessions, and so forth), and therefore encourages the growth—in quantity, in intensity, and in geographical extent—that is a principal aspect of the behavior of industrial modernism.

The meaning of Mondragon is to be found in a profound process of social reconstruction that has political, economic, and social implications. We must ask how and why the social means and social product are used, not merely who owns them. For our purposes, "social means" include social organization, as well as technology and knowledge; "social product" includes both physical and functional results of use.

Under industrial modernism, social behavior and the nature and use of the social product are shaped by factors that go beyond class, as described by the Marxist paradigm, and beyond the "rational" pursuit of self-interest posited by classical capitalist economists. (Of course, many capitalists and socialists may want to avoid any serious examination of the ideology of industrial modernism and the nature of the industrial state.) To deny that class is the central and primary issue in social and historical change does not mean rejecting the notion of a struggle for social change—indeed, the pursuit of equilibrio involves both hard work and active opposition to power; this may be nonviolent and evolutionary, but it is, nevertheless, a struggle. Mondragon is the product of such an experience.

The Socialist Alternative and Who Is To Blame

Industrial modernism puts us in a fundamental dilemma. We have embraced technology—yet technology, rather than redeeming us, seems to be driving us relentlessly toward an apocalyptic moment. Those within the industrial system propose the steady elaboration and growth of a global technocracy as the only way to avoid extinction. The alternative posed by *existing* socialism too often appears to be no alternative at all: changing the ownership of the means of production has not definitively transformed the nature of its use. Social ownership by itself may change the hand on the rudder of industrialism, but it will not alter its course.[10] Stalinism and socialist bureaucratic states cannot simply be defined away in retrospect. The point is neither to demean the prospects of socialism by identifying it facilely with Stalinism, nor to exalt capitalism in action, but to recognize the hard lessons of the communist experience and its version of "social" ownership and industry.

To be sure, the liberatory impulses that animate the broad socialist project are essentially consonant with Mondragon's desire to develop a democratic, self-managed society. The British socialist Raymond Williams, for example, advocates a process quite similar to the pursuit of equilibrio when he calls for including working people at every stage in the development of "a concept of a practical and possible general interest, which really does include all reasonable particular interests [and which] has to be negotiated, found agreed, constructed."[11]

Nor does a critique of industrial modernism mean abandoning a critique of capitalist or socialist exploitation, an embracing of wage labor, or a repudiation of humane ideals. It is completely clear that capitalists still exploit workers and operate with astounding disregard for the community and nature—but so do the overlords of bureaucratic socialism. The central concern is not to determine who is worst, or what comparisons are valid; this is not an attempt at liberal evenhandedness. Rather, a critique of industrial modernism holds that, in practice, both capitalism and socialism can best be understood as divergent parts of a single global system. This system is characterized by a minority in the industrialized countries inflicting (deliberately or not) environmental and social havoc on the whole world, prospering through exploitation at home and through a largely unseen (and therefore even crueler) exploitation of the majority of the world's people who live in the so-called Third and Fourth Worlds.

To say this is not to deny any of the evils of capitalist or socialist practice, or to imply that they bear equal responsibility; nor is it meant to impeach the work of any person or group for peace, social justice, and ecological sanity. It does suggest, however, that industrialism, as such, is self-destructive. Consider nuclear power, the paradigmatic technology of industrial modernism: there are no good socialist nuclear plants contrasted with bad capitalist nuclear plants, or vice versa; the purposes and values that inform the political economy of the nuclear industry are simply grotesque and terrifying. The Chernobyl disaster in 1986 was a global catastrophe of industrial modernism.

Those who reject the notion of an ideology of industrialism should consider the historical proposition that socialist industrialism was the creation of capitalist industrialism. The faults of existing socialist industrialism are not a result of bad theory but of the fact that the practice of socialist industrialism does not represent a complete or a sufficient departure from that of capitalist industrialism.

The Steel Triangle of Industrialism

The ideology of industrial modernism is composed of three themes: progress, technique, and hierarchy (see Figure 1-3). Progress is associated with change and informed by the notion of scarcity; technique is associated with science and with knowledge; and hierarchy is associated with order—it is the state cult of industrial modernism, and consumption is its profaned sacrament.

Figure 1-3. The Ideology of Industrial Modernism

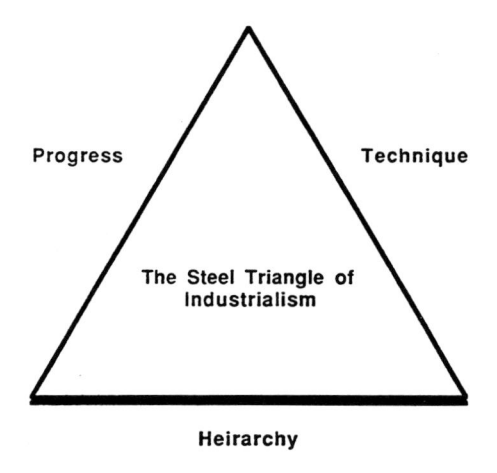

```
              /\
             /  \
            /    \
   Progress/      \Technique
          /        \
         /  The Steel Triangle of  \
        /       Industrialism       \
       /                              \
      /_____\
                  Heirarchy
```

Industrial modernism is perhaps best understood as a system, an ensemble of social relationships and material objects shaped by the dynamics of technique–hierarchy–progress and pervaded at all levels by an attempt to maximize power. This is power unlimited, power that is essentially antiecological; power manifested through the industrial state, the interlocking pervasive and global bureaucracies. Under industrialism, our human energies are consumed with maintaining and expanding human inequality and separateness.

Technique

Technique is crucial for the ideology of industrialism. It mediates between the aspirations of progress and the order of hierarchy. Through the instrumentalities of technique (science, technology, industry, bureaucracy), we have built a culture that is capable of transforming the landscape, climate, and biosphere, produced abundant wealth (for some) and technological marvels—and perfected nuclear militarism.

Technique, even more than the machine, is central to the practice of industrial modernism. Technique is systematized and rationalized means and method. A machine may be "pure technique,"[12] but the human meaning of technique, like that of capital, is ultimately a matter of power. Technique and the power of hierarchy establish the boundaries of the social landscape. In this way, technique both reflects and shapes deep social structures; it is nearly as integral to our sense of ourselves as is our language, and this makes it hard for us to wrestle with it directly, even in our committed struggles for liberation.

Technique, freed from the ethics of social mutualism, becomes a means for dividing things, events, and people. It breaks down operations into discrete parts that can be manipulated, reproduced, and optimized. Such a process is inherently antiecological, as Barry Commoner points out, since "the ecosystem cannot be divided into manageable parts, for its properties reside in the whole, in the connections between the parts."[13] Technique as a tool of power encourages difference to be turned into hierarchical order.

The antiecological effects of technique—the rationalization and optimization of human activity—creates (or reproduces) capitalist social relationships in the workplace and in the community, whether they are nominally capitalist or socialist. An ecological society must treat the use of technique as a basic ethical question, conditioned by explicit social choices. Aspects of technique, such as the elimination of waste (conservation) and the improvement of the ratio of outputs to inputs (productivity), can be considered in accord with ecological ethics.

Technological decisions thus should be made in a political and ethical context, and we must understand these broader issues. But we cannot deal effectively with technology, let alone with technique, merely as an abstract thing: creating an ecological society is predicated upon an ongoing stream of democratic decisions rooted in everyday practice that encompasses issues of technique and technology.[14]

The Mondragon cooperators are not technophobes—indeed, they are intimately involved with industrialism—but they are struggling to re-form it from within through the pursuit of human, not machine, values. They understand that while some technical issues are important, fundamental social change is not reducible to questions of technique—of choosing, for example, "hard" or "soft" energy paths. The real issue is the ensemble of social choices that define the nature of technology and its uses.

Mondragon is not simply the sum of an interrelated series of technical fixes that work to resolve some of the contradictions inherent in industrial modernism. Its social and mechanical innovations are not attempts to maximize some hypothetical efficiency, but are informed and shaped by new social choices made by the cooperators—choices that limit the conduct of industrialism while strengthening the cooperative community. The structures and dynamics of Mondragon social institutions are noteworthy and informative, but this does not fully explain Mondragon cooperativism as social reality.

Power and Hierarchy

The exercise of unlimited power by industrial modernism is cloaked by our acquiescence, our willingness to identify with our social position, and legitimated by an ideological concept of order that embraces hierarchy as a basic state of nature. Power is the lifeblood of this system. The oppression of industrial modernism transcends the denial of material sustenance and political liberty; it includes a variegated assault upon our humanity and social potential.

The hierarchy of industrial modernism is exquisitely delineated. Its purpose is not so much to keep individuals fixed in a social role, as in traditional societies and caste systems, but to define a generic division of labor and status. People can circulate, to a greater or lesser extent, along the paths of power defined by the hierarchy. Our motivation, after obtaining minimal social necessities, is to increase our security, to gain access to more material objects and to a greater array of the newly monetized services that have invaded the domain of what were once social, vernacular, and free activities. "Needs" are manufactured with as much deliberation as the products they ostensibly represent.

Thus, hierarchy is supported both by the unadorned imposition of power and by an internalized acceptance of its values: an underlying belief that the hunt for security and for things is justified by material scarcity—a notion that remains generally serviceable in even the richest industrialized states, despite the fact that we are literally choking on our own garbage. In this atmosphere we find flourishing such pseudoscientific notions as social Darwinism—the idea that an "evolutionary" hierarchy of fitness applies not only to nature but among humans as well—and such pseudohistorical notions as progress.

Progress Lost

Progress is the call to action that justifies the practice of domination. It blesses the act of applying the destructive powers of technique as another step in the war upon scarcity. Progress is the "go code" for industrial modernism; combined with social Darwinism, it provides a nearly seamless rationale for greed and cruelty, the idea that competition and self-aggrandizement were not social creations of capitalism but part of the rootstock of human nature.

As the historian J. B. Bury notes:

> *The Origin of Species* led to the third stage of the fortunes of the idea of Progress. We saw how the heliocentric astronomy, by dethroning man from his privileged position in the universe of space and throwing him back on his own efforts, had helped that idea to compete with the idea of a busy Providence. He now suffers a new degradation within the compass of his own planet. Evolution, shearing him of his glory as a rational being specially created to be lord of the earth, traces a humble pedigree for him. And this second degradation was the decisive fact which has established the reign of the idea of Progress. . . . If it could be shown that social life obeys the same general laws of evolution as nature, and also that the process involves an increase of happiness, then Progress would be as valid a hypothesis as the evolution of living forms.[15]

Progress as a credo, as part of the ideology of industrialism, is a commitment to feed the endless appetites of the industrial machine by identifying change as good. That is why such measures as gross national product include the cost of cleaning up toxic chemical spills, the fees of the lawyers who defend the companies responsible for the spills, and the medical bills of those poisoned by them all as positive contributions to the national wealth. Both capitalism and socialism claim to be superior in fostering progress, in overcoming scarcity and satisfying human needs. But industrial modernism's war against scarcity can never be won: it has become an open-ended commitment to a ceaseless orgy of production and consumption, of creating and then satisfying limitless needs. The problem cannot simply be laid to capitalism's instrumental need to stimulate demand. Sociologist Alvin Gouldner, in discussing Marx's views on scarcity and industrialism, notes that "wants are in part induced socially, but oddly, never restrained socially. There is an undertow here of a conception of human insatiability. . . . Satisfaction recedes even as production increases."[16]

Under industrial modernism, capitalism and socialism are both committed to limitless growth. But in its decline, industrial modernism has undermined the idea of progress. Our media, our visions, our nightmares are filled with images of destruction and decay, of nuclear armageddon, of longing not for the future but for the simpler and clearer days of the past. Even in the popular post-nuclear apocalypse movies (from the middle-class melancholia of *The Day After* to the slaughter and barbarism of the "Mad Max" series), the survivors almost never try to find a new beginning. Instead, amidst the wreckage, they despair of being able to re-create "real" life. The Las Vegas strip (and the nearby Nevada test site, with its hydrogen-bomb "pumped" X-ray lasers) are real; nuclear power plants, the secret police, such computerized bureaucracies as the Internal Revenue Service, dioxins, desertification are real; poisoned air, water, soil, food are real—and freedom, community, peace, health, love, and sanity must be illusion.

Equilibrio and Ecological Postmodernism

In just two hundred years, industrialism has brought us to the brink of rendering the planet uninhabitable and has extinguished life on a scale once the exclusive province of natural forces and geological time. In the midst of this great dying out, with its corollary social disintegration, it is not surprising that we see ourselves as caught in perpetual crisis. We want to act; yet we feel overwhelmed by the power of the megamachine. To regain our sense of time and change we need to act not only for today, but for the next generation, and for ages undreamed—act as the Native Americans counsel, with humility, and for the seventh generation. But how? Prescriptive morality, ideas, logic, and ethics seem unable to change the course of industrialism substantially—abstractions cannot stop locomotives or influence the conduct of computer networks. Our prospects for social change must rest upon our actions. We must work to develop societies that re-create a sustainable social and natural ecology; societies that choose self-management and democracy, not hierarchy; evolutionary change, not a blind commitment to progress; empathy, not a reflexive reliance upon technique. This is a path to build social systems where community and freedom are indivisible: in the words of Murray Bookchin, "ecological wholeness . . . is a dynamic unity of diversity."[17]

A sane future is not something distant or dependent upon the seizure of state power, but is essentially in our own hands. For Mondragon, that has meant the search for equilibrio; William Foote Whyte and Kathleen King Whyte call equilibrio the first of the basic guiding principles that pervade the life of the cooperatives:

> In discussions of important decisions, the word *equilibrio* appears again and again as a justification for any action proposed. The basic idea is that life in a cooperative should not be carried on as if it were a zero-sum game in which some win and some lose. There must be a balancing of interests and needs; we hear it said that technological imperatives must be balanced with social objectives and that the financial needs of the firm must be balanced with the economic needs of the members.

The word *equilibrio* appears prominently in discussions of relations within groups—between one cooperative and another and between member cooperatives and the management of the cooperative group. It also appears in discussions of relations between a cooperative or cooperative group and a support organization. We find it further in discussions of relations between the cooperative and the community in which it is located.[18]

For individuals, the experience of equilibrio in action may be called a sense of freedom and community. This is in marked contrast to the freedom to pursue an isolated "self-realization"—a goal that is too often consistent with the pursuit of power and property. The search for equilibrio makes attaining freedom and community a matter of social practice, of personal experience and individual and social responsibility, not simply an idea.

As Judith Plaskow notes from a Jewish feminist perspective,

> The individual is not an isolated unit who attains humanity through independence from others or who must contract for social relations. Rather, to be a person is to find oneself from the beginning in community—or, as is often the case in the modern world, in multiple communities. To develop as a person is to acquire a sense of self in relation to others and to critically appropriate a series of communal heritages.[19]

In this context, unity in diversity, freedom, and community are best understood not as things, ideas, or categorical definitions (e.g., freedom as lack of restraint), but as values. These are principles informed by ethics that have meaning as the result of social practice. We have, as yet, no word that clearly describes a society, shaped by dynamics, that creates and re-creates unity in diversity, the sense of freedom and community. "Ecological" society is a reasonable designation. The practice of such a society will differ fundamentally from that of industrial modernism.

The material bounty and productivity of industrial modernism has neither eliminated poverty nor facilitated the creation of unity in diversity. Our prescription for the future cannot simply call for redistributive justice combined with more production. The industrial system continues to spend trillions of dollars on weapons while millions of children starve, continues to pour billions of pounds of poison into the environment. The essential problem is not an existential scarcity, but scarcity created through the exercise of power and hierarchy; not "bad" technology, but technology created to serve the interests of the megamachine and its masters.

There is a shared and growing search, from a variety of political perspectives, for freedom and community. Feminist philosopher Susan Griffin observes that "we must now make a distinction between the libertine's idea of liberty, 'to do as one likes,' and a vision of human liberation."[20] The conservative social philosopher Robert Nisbet maintains,"No more inspired words on behalf of the individual, his needs, his emotions, his mind, are to be found in Western literature than in Plato's *Republic*. But it is the very essence of Plato's method to place this individual in the liberating and also reinforcing contexts of the political community."[21]

Mondragon's central significance is that the democratic pursuit of equilibrio is a way to integrate human freedom and community. Ecological postmodernism is not merely a substitute for notions drawn from social interpretations of nature, such as social Darwinism or sociobiology: applications of "value free" science that typically justify power and hierarchy. Human societies are, of course, a subset of nature, but ecological postmodernism does not rest upon the need to see social development as in thrall to the supposed dynamics of natural systems.[22]

It is suggestive and pertinent to characterize Mondragon's functioning as being in accord with the ecology of living systems; however, the two need not share common purposes. We can try to reach deeper understandings that lead toward a harmonious synthesis of society and nature, but we must proceed with caution and humility. Similarly, ecological postmodernism represents more than simply an idea; it is a matter of social practice, not the result of an ecological determinism reflecting the "true" nature of human society or simply the adoption of an ecological ideology.

The Mondragon accomplishment, so far, has been the creation of a cooperative economic sector and convivial social institutions. Economically, it reflects a practice of controlled and deliberate growth; the internal measure of its success has been the rise of an enduring system, not the maximization of sales, profits, or membership. The creation of a community-based cooperative system is not merely another manifestation of growth. It is precisely such a system that can place industrialism on the rack. The pursuit of equilibrio can allow us to raise relevant questions of value; teaching by example, Mondragon encourages us to extend our sense of what we can do.

The Dynamics of Ecological Postmodernism

By its nature, the search for equilibrio operates in accord with a logic that can be called dialectical but makes decisions in terms of "both/and" rather than "either/or"; it tries to incorporate and adapt, not exclude. This approach suggests an evolutionary method that is not driven by progress or determinism, but instead reflects the dynamism of living systems.[23]

In social action, the logic of equilibrio inclines not only toward seeking consensus, but toward applying it to the full range of social relations.

This process reflects an understanding of both the natural and social worlds as functioning on complementary levels, without hierarchy. It contrasts with the "either/or," "off/on" logic of machines and computers. An inclusive "both/and" logic is essentially capable of unlimited gradations, able to reflect the infinite variety of meanings that can be conveyed by living systems. This means the behavior and protocols of ecological postmodernism are rendered with all the complexity and nuance of human language, and are rife with ambiguity—and therefore with possibility for human choice and agency.

Unity in diversity, the outcome of the successful pursuit of equilibrio, has three characteristics that contribute to the seamless integration of dynamic living systems—keeping in mind that one must proceed cautiously in ascribing "scientific" virtue to analogies between social and natural ecology.

First, unity in diversity values the importance of both the individual and the group—the species and the ecosystem—as parts of a living whole. Our lives are only possible and meaningful within a community; however proud and solitary and predatory we may see ourselves as masters of industrialism, we are no more free of social life than the eagle is free of its prey, and of the mosaic in which both prey and eagle exist.

Second, unity in diversity recognizes the integrity and validity of varying levels of responsibility. Each level of social or natural life is part of a living system, with its own area of competence and responsibility. Thus, each cooperator has rights and responsibilities, as does every work team, co-op, co-op group, co-op superstructure group, and each collective decision-making body. All are interconnected; there is no privileged standpoint. Similarly, in the natural world we find various levels of functioning: subatomic, molecular, electrochemical, cellular, organismic, community, biospheric, planetary.

Finally, unity in diversity recognizes the differences among degrees of organization in scale, time, and intimacy. Thus Mondragon has limited the size of individual co-ops to help maintain communication, intimacy, and trust among members and to avoid the growth of bureaucracy.

As individuals, we see that which appears to be "below" us (or smaller or simpler in structure) as a tumult of noise and motion; but this apparent chaos is, in fact, the murmurings, stirrings, voices of life. What appears to be "above" us (or larger or more complex) looks implacable and unchanging, a source for reference and reverence. These grand structures are, in fact, a reflection of our aggregate being and behavior. They are also in motion, with dynamic and living rhythms.

This is the reality behind unity in diversity. The health of social and natural systems is reflected in the functioning, integrity, and interrelations of all of their components. Power in such systems reflects a facilitating freedom, an interactive potential whose apotheosis is love—a "power to" that is constrained and responsive, and can exist fully only within an ecological context.

The search for equilibrio on all levels leads to social choices that limit the conduct of industrialism. These boundaries are not imposed by some authority or chosen as acts of self-denial, but developed as part of the democratic decision-making process—as we shall see, the greatest internal crisis for the Mondragon co-ops was the result of management's assertion of "legal" power against cooperators.

Looking Forward

The Mondragon system is self-regulating and not self-destructive. This is not the self-regulation of Adam Smith's invisible hand that supposedly transmutes greed into social benefit, nor is it the self-regulation of a centralized and bureaucratic technocracy. Mondragon has demonstrated the possibilities for democratic self-management not merely of a firm but of a social system.

Its lessons are broadly applicable, but not as mass-produced copies. The pursuit of equilibrio means adapting to local conditions. The development of self-regulatory mechanisms on national and global levels will, of course, involve many diverse and hybrid forms—using existing institutions and structures, and creating new social organs that proceed through their own evolution, driven from below, as part of a dynamic and responsive interaction of the whole system.

Whatever the future may hold, the Mondragon system is an important demonstration of the possibilities and dynamics for constructive change. The cooperators have learned through the pursuit of equilibrio the intimate relationship between grassroots democracy, work, and social change. We must discover our own piece of the truth. Our small and local acts of social reconstruction can be part of a great movement for social transformation from below. As José María Arizmendiarrieta knew, we need more than words and ideas to change our lives and our communities. We need to understand and we need to act.

Notes

1. Monetary figures throughout are generally converted from pesetas (Ptas) to dollars at the exchange rate of 115 pesetas per dollar to make the amounts more relevant to readers in the United States. Actual exchange rates fluctuated widely between 1985 and 1989: from 175 pesetas per dollar in 1985 (or 1 million Ptas = $5,714) to 115 pesetas per dollar (or 1 million Ptas = $8,696) after the October 1987 stock market crash (the dollar has since strengthened and then weakened again). This made the Mondragon cooperators relatively rich in dollar terms, but since exchange rates are driven by speculative fevers and central bank policies, as well as by underlying economic condi-

tions, it would be a mistake to make too much of this sudden appreciation of Mondragon assets. To account for the (often high) rates of Spanish inflation, historic figures are expressed in constant (1985) pesetas before being converted to dollars (see Appendix 1-2). Thus dollar values do not reflect the "real" value of either the peseta or the dollar but are offered to indicate relative changes in real co-op performance and the general scale of its operations. Data on Mondragon for 1987 come from the Caja Laboral Popular annual report for 1987 and from the co-op magazine *T. U. Lankide*. Co-op publications do not agree precisely on the total number of cooperators. At the end of 1987 there were 18,262 cooperators in the business co-ops and 1,234 in the bank; adding those in the research, social insurance, and educational co-ops, 21,000 seems fairly accurate.

2. Quoted in Whyte and Whyte 1988, p. 229.

3. "Principios Básicos de la Experiencia Cooperativa de Mondragon," in *T. U. Lankide*, May 1987, p 4; translation by Roy Morrison and Judy Elliott. Information on the Mondragon Co-op principles is from the preceding article and from one with the same title in *T. U. Lankide*, October 1987, pp. 11–13. This is the amended version approved by the co-op congress, which modified and strengthened provisions on solidarity, self-management, and education.

4. As of January 5, 1987, pay ranged from $11,915/year (level 1.000) to a maximum of $53,617/year (4.500). However, workers receive pay above $41,702 (3.500) only under special circumstances that require extraordinary overtime, skill, and travel. Pay rates are from Caja Laboral Popular, "Anticipos Laborales Según Índice, 1/5/87." Recently, after considerable debate, the maximum pay grade has been raised to 6.0 for certain positions.

5. Data from *Caja Laboral Popular* (Bilbao: S. Coop. Elkar, 1987), a glossy and well-illustrated compendium of recent information about the Mondragon cooperative system, and from Caja Laboral annual report, 1987.

6. Appendix 1-1 lists in some detail the specific industrial, agricultural, service, and retail co-ops, using 1985 data. (Summary figures used in the text of this chapter, however, are based on 1987 data.)

7. "Principios Básicos de la Experiencia Cooperativa de Mondragon," *T. U. Lankide*, May 1987, p. 6.

8. "Fondo Intercooperativo de Solidaridad," *T. U. Lankide*, May 1987, pp. 10–11.

9. Translation by Ana María Pérez-Girones in Whyte and Whyte 1988.

10. One could weigh liberatory socialist theory against capitalist practice, or dismiss the Soviet Union and other existing socialist states as deformed examples of state capitalism, but this would be historically dishonest.

11. Quoted in Ryle 1988, p. 33.

12. Ellul 1964, p. 4.

13. Commoner 1972, p. 185.

14. Webster and Lambe 1986, pp. 63–64, is an excellent examination of the question of dealing with specific technological choices, and not abstract technology, though it tends to view the subject in terms of machines and their social implications rather than considering broader questions of technique.

15. Bury 1952, pp. 335–36.

16. Gouldner 1980, p. 200.

17. Bookchin 1982, p. 24.

18. Whyte and Whyte 1988, p. 259.

19. Plaskow 1990, p. 77.

20. Griffin 1982, p. 110.

21. Nisbet 1982, p. 10.

22. Concerning the perils of analogies: taking a break from writing, I walked outside and stood in front of massed late-summer flowers. What is the relationship between the

buzzing of dutiful bees gathering pollen and the petrochemical buzzing of a chain saw perhaps a half-mile away? As I stepped closer, I saw swarms of tiny flies diving into the flowers, searching perhaps for nectar or pollen or bee droppings, and avoiding, if they could, the webs of small spiders hung between leaves and petals. What place have the flies in the drama shared by human and bee preparing for winter?

23. Gutiérrez-Johnson 1982, especially chapter 2.

2
Mondragon's History and Development

> It is necessary to rise above the penury of ideas which emerges from spirits lacking in generosity and place our stakes on the good of others.
> —1986 Annual Report, Caja Laboral Popular

This chapter examines the roots of Mondragon in Basque culture and history, provides a capsule history of the co-ops, and examines the underlying tensions between centralization and autonomy in Basque society and in the industrialized world that informed Mondragon cooperative development.

The Roots of the Mondragon Cooperative Experiment

Upon first consideration, it seems strange that the Mondragon system of cooperative entrepreneurship arose in an obscure industrial town in the baleful aftermath of Franco's victory in the Spanish civil war. Mondragon in the 1940s was a town in which many of the community's leaders had been killed or fled into exile to escape the vengeance of Franco.[1]

Unions were outlawed, and the mill owners, allied with the Spanish fascist state, maintained tight and repressive control. But social dislocation proved to be a necessary concomitant for creative change. Hard times and the goad of necessity provided the impetus for social experimentation.

The privation and desperation of the people, combined with their knowledge and traditions, catalyzed by José Arizmendiarrieta and a small group of his students, started a process that continues to evolve more than forty years later. Gradually, the people of Mondragon discovered that through their collective effort they could solve not only the problems of poverty, but also the larger problems of community and social health.

Yet, while the Mondragon cooperative system grew out of a unique historical and cultural environment, it is not relevant only in the Basque context: it arose and still develops in response to conditions that exist throughout the industrialized world; it is a creative and successful adaptation to universal problems.

The Land

The Basques are an ancient European people who inhabit the Pyrenees Mountains and their western extension, in the Cantabrian Range. The mountains rise quickly from the rocky coastline of the Bay of Biscay to the north, forming the rugged heartland of the Basque region. From the south flank of the Cantabrians, the Basque country extends southward into the fertile plains of Navarra and Alava, ending at the river Ebro.

Euzkadi, the Basque nation, today consists of seven provinces, four in northeastern Spain and three in the Biscay and Pyrenees area of southern France. The international border dividing Euzkadi in half was fixed in 1512—a date more mourned than celebrated. Most Basques live in the Spanish provinces; since the death of Franco in 1975, they have gained limited autonomy from Spain. Mondragon is in the Basque province of Guipúzcoa, and the cooperative system is limited so far to the four Basque provinces (Guipúzcoa, Vizcaya, Alava, and Navarra) in modern Spain (see map on p. 6).

Much of Euzkadi is mountainous. The climate is temperate, moderated by the cool breezes sweeping in off the Bay of Biscay, with significant rainfall. The rain, the mountains, and the sea are three central influences on Basque culture and history.

The rain has permitted a sustainable agriculture based upon small independent farms and stable peasant villages. Further to the south, heat, drought, and crop failures encouraged the development of huge estates and grazing lands, *latafundia*, often owned by absentee landlords and worked by impoverished laborers.

The mountains, which in their wild beauty are sometimes compared with those of Switzerland, also provided the Basques with refuge from the many invading armies (Romans, Visigoths, Franks, Moors, Castilians, the Napoleonic French, and finally Franco's forces) that periodically swept across Iberia. While the Basques were not able to defeat the vastly stronger invaders, the land and the people's spirit enabled them to maintain some degree of autonomy.

Over the centuries, the mountains also encouraged self-reliance. Although the climate made it possible for small farmers to grow crops and pasture animals, the mountains represented formidable obstacles to what are quite ordinary activities elsewhere. Mountaineers in any setting by necessity understand the value of cooperation and innovation.[2] The mountains also provided the Basques with rich deposits of iron ore. Combined with plentiful coal from the mines of Asturias to the west, this led to the early development of metallurgy and an iron industry, then to the production of steel.

Finally, the rich waters of the Bay of Biscay spawned a tradition of fishing and shipbuilding. The sea was a window on the world; it facilitated the entry of the nascent Basque industries into trade and commerce and, over time, the Basques became heavily involved in international trade.

Writing in 1943, the historian Gerald Brenan noted:

> The Basques, with their large industrial capital at Bilbao, their mercantile marine and their active commercial relations with foreign countries, are the most European of all Iberian races. Their language is the only primitive thing about them. Though conservative in a political sense, their conservatism is that of an active commercial race such as the English, which believes in individual effort. Their Catholicism, too, is modern; if one wishes to see monks who are not engrossed in political propaganda, well-educated clergy, unfanatical bishops, this is the part of Spain where one is most likely to find them.[3]

Basque Language and Cultural Identity

The Basques are a gritty, proud people with a unique culture and a history of resistance and endurance. Euskara, their ancient, singular, and singularly difficult language, is thought to be unrelated to any other Indo-European tongue and has long been a key ingredient of their cultural identity.

Such is Euskara's importance to the Basques that the victorious and vindictive Franco forbade its use. Since his death, there has been a renaissance of the spoken and the written language, manifest in the rapid proliferation of literary efforts, films, and *ikastolas* (primary schools teaching in Euskara). For example, more literary works were published in Euskara (generally in Euskara Batua, the unified literary dialect) in 1984 than in the previous two centuries.[4] It is no accident that both the Basque cultural renaissance and the Mondragon cooperatives arose in Guipúzcoa, the mountainous rural heartland of the region and of Basque nationalism, where the speaking of Euskara had remained alive under Franco.

Through the centuries, the Basques have struggled constantly for at least a degree of political independence, and nationalism remains a central feature of Basque life, whether expressed culturally or politically. Basque political agendas range from moderate demands for strengthened autonomy within Spain and self-expression within France to the armed struggle of ETA (meaning, roughly, "Basque Nation and Freedom") for an independent and united Euzkadi. The pride of the people and their commitment to Basque cultural identity and independence seems to be considerably more important than conventional political labels.

The development of the Mondragon cooperatives is, to some extent, another indication of Basque self-assertion, one more way of proclaiming their common identity in spite of the Spanish state. But the Basque rebirth seems to be as much or more a flowering of long-repressed impulses for cultural self-expression than simple nationalist self-assertion. As the grip of repression gradually loosened, Basque strength, patience, and determination grew into confidence that anything might be possible, that it was time to search for new forms, whether literary, political, or organizational. The Mondragon cooperatives thrived in this climate.

The Basque country achieved a conditional level of autonomy in the parliamentary democracy of post-Franco Spain. The Basques elect their own regional parliament in addition to the representatives they send to the Cortes in Madrid. The regional government can pass laws and levy taxes and has its own police force, who wear distinctive Basque berets. The police powers of the government, however, do not extend to political questions. The feared Spanish Guardia Civil and Policía Nacional remain a largely unwanted presence in the Basque country, focused on the activities of ETA. The Spanish army is also very much in evidence.

Basque Industrial Heritage

The Basques have an ancient metalworking tradition. Guipúzcoa was a major participant in the medieval iron trade, and by the 1500s the Basque provinces were producing about one-sixth of Europe's iron ore.[5] The town of Mondragon in particular was long known for the manufacture of swords, anchors, and chains. The Basques traded widely with Europe and with Spain's colonies in Latin America.

In more recent times, the Basque region became the focal point for the development of industrial and finance capitalism on the Iberian peninsula. Its low-phosphorus iron ore was in high demand for Bessemer process steel mills, so the Basques developed an active bilateral trade with Britain, and the ships that carried iron ore north often returned with high-quality Welsh coking coal for the steel mills of Vizcaya and Guipúzcoa. British capital helped finance modern Basque industry in the last quarter of the nineteenth century. The rise of industrial capitalism tended to undermine communalist and cooperativist Basque traditions. For example, iron ore, once communally owned, became private property; artisan industry gave way to mills and factory production; and tensions between capitalists and workers grew.[6]

In the 1850s, when new Spanish laws allowed the organization of modern railway, mining and finance corporations, Basque capitalists organized a number of banks, such as the Banco de Bilbao, which are still among the largest in the country (four of the "big seven" Spanish banks today are either Basque or have strong Basque links). These institutions were in the tradition of the merchant banker, acting as both industrialist and financier. As we shall see, Mondragon's Caja Laboral Popular acts much like these early banks, with the critical difference that it is democratically controlled and combines industrial and financial efforts for the benefit of the community rather than for individuals or families.

As capital grew, Basque financiers soon took the lead in developing hydroelectric resources and the electrical distribution system. They also profited handsomely from the mineral trade of officially neutral Spain during World War I. By the 1920s, Basque capitalists were ascendant and confident. Robert Graham observes:

> The crowning symbol of this confidence was the suburb of Neguri which had, and still has, no parallel in the rest of Spain. Neguri was sited away from any sight or smell of the grime of Bilbao, yet close enough to monitor daily how the banks, factories and shipping were performing. The early 1920s mansions, toned down versions of Victorian vulgarity, stand today as a monument to the triumphant affirmation that Basque wealth was on a par with that of the England it admired so much. In the 1920s, this wealth was split between no more than 30 families and their offshoots. These families, with their distinctive sounding names (Echevvarrieta, Oriol, Orbegozo, Urquijo, Ybarra), were at the core of Spain's modern industrial development.[7]

Such developments and concentration of wealth led to a response from the workers whose efforts supplied the wealth. In Mondragon, a 1916 strike at the Union Cerrajera steel mill lasted three months, ending when hunger forced the workers' return to work.[8] But although this strike and others were broken, the spirit of the working people of Mondragon was not. During the 1934 revolt of the socialist miners in Asturias (brutally repressed by Spanish army forces led by Franco), Mondragon sent the only armed support to come from outside Asturias. And during the Spanish civil war, three Mondragon battalions fought on the side of the Spanish Republic and Basque autonomy (one socialist, one Basque nationalist, one unaffiliated).[9]

Franco's victory in the civil war led not only to political repression of the Basques but to increased economic repression of the workers and their unions. The Basque region was taxed to help finance the economic development of the rest of Spain, and the weight of this unfair economic burden fell most heavily upon the workers. The Francoist economy was characterized by a corrupt and despotic bureaucracy that linked government and capital within a debilitating and impoverishing structure of regulations, protective tariffs, currency and import restrictions. Its tendency was to enrich private interests through a sort of fascist "lemon socialism," whereby either state-run monopolies (with private interests) or a state-run industrial holding company (Instituto Nacional de Industria, INI) would involve itself in partnership with private interests. Salvador de Madariaga gives a good sense of the Francoist economy:

> The INI is a byword of incompetence. Grandiose schemes ... are launched with no particular inquiry into their financial, economic or commercial viability. A horde of public figures, with one leg on politics and the other on finance, cluster round councils and directorships, fostering all kinds of semi-public, semi-private enterprises. A complicated system of controls, regulations and inspectorates overlords capital issues, material supplies, labor questions, markets, quotas and tariffs; so that at every turn a political sleight-of-hand becomes necessary in order to squeeze through all these bureaucratic toll gates. As all this happens behind the opaque curtain of paper raised by a "His Master's Voice" press, corruption is rife from top to bottom of the state.[10]

By the mid- and late 1950s, Franco's political and economic grip was beginning to loosen. He kept himself rather aloof from the struggles and intrigues that swirled around him—a stance that allowed him to concentrate on maintaining his power—and he permitted a series of reforms advocated by a group of technocratic modernizers, many of whom belonged to the lay-Catholic organization Opus Dei. They removed many existing economic controls, instituted an economic stabilization plan in 1959 to deal with the inflation caused by earlier economic policies, and generally redirected the country along a path of economic liberalism that was perfectly in tune with the worldwide economic expansion led by the United States. By the 1960s, the Spanish economy was growing at an average rate of 7 percent a year, with real wages increasing by 6 percent annually. This unprecedented level of growth provided the context for the birth of the Mondragon industrial cooperatives.

Basque Church and Community

Underlying the conflict between the Basque desire for autonomy and the power of the Spanish state (which, in various guises, has been a fundamental force in Basque politics and history), is a dynamic relationship between church and state, and church and community. Historically, these tensions helped form (and reflected) the cultural and philosophical setting of the autonomy-centralization drama, and they helped define the nature of capitalist industrialism and socialist reaction in the Basque country.

While the Spanish clergy historically tended to be preoccupied with their vast tracts of agricultural land and with the country's most conservative elements (with whom they vied for power), the Basque clergy had different concerns. With its stable agriculture based upon small plots, Basque society developed a number of cooperative and democratic social structures. The Basque church was a supportive and integral part of both this village culture and Basque nationalism. Historian Hugh Thomas notes that "[s]ince the church here remained close to the land, the churches stayed the center of civic life. Local councils customarily still met in verandahs on the side of these squat buildings."[11]

Particularly in the countryside, the Basque church remained in close touch with the people and their land. The oppressive, feared, and hated state was normally a distant presence, and both people and church excluded it from their affairs whenever possible. The church, with some conditions, made common cause with Basque nationalism, supported the democratic rights of Basque farmers and workers, and approved of the responses of the still pious Catholic workers to the growth of Basque industry. Indeed, as late as 1936, when most Spaniards had stopped going to church, more than half of the Basques in the industrial areas, and nearly all in the agricultural ones, were practicing Christians.[12]

This relationship with the church was strained but not dislocated by industrialism. The leading Basque trade union, ELA-STV, maintained a cordial relationship with the church before the civil war, in contrast to the anticlerical attitudes of the giant Spanish national unions, the socialist UGT and the anarchist CGT. From its founding in 1911 to the Nationalist rebellion in 1936, ELA-STV generally organized craft and skilled workers and played a role broadly analogous to that of the conservative American Federation of Labor in the United States.[13] Moreover, because it was resolutely nationalist, the ELA-STV found itself allied with the clearly middle-class Basque Nationalist Party, PNV.

Before 1936, then, Basque Catholicism criticized some of the excesses of industrial capitalism and supported Basque nationalism, but typically tried to avoid overt struggles with power. The church was sympathetic to the reformist efforts of its working class parishoners, but with reservations, reservations based in part on its natural opposition to the revolutionary atheism of the Spanish socialist and anarchist movements. But the political and economic turmoil of the 1930s pushed the Basque Church to overt involvement in political affairs. The deep passions of Basque Catholicism, which had produced such men as St. Ignatius of Loyola, founder of the Jesuits, and St. Francis Xavier were turned toward the social agenda.

The Spanish civil war, La Guerra Civil, is central to modern Spanish and Basque history. A complex web of tensions and divided loyalties collapsed into this bloody conflict, which began in July 1936 with a Rightist uprising against the elected government and did not end until April 1939. For many, the defense of the Spanish Republic was a test of the opposition to fascism by an alliance of liberal democrats and the Left. For the Basques, beyond being a struggle for democracy against tyranny, the war was a battle for autonomy and ethnic identity against the forces of Spanish monarchism and Nationalist conservatism.

When events forced the Basque church to take sides during the war, it resisted the overtures of the conservative Spanish cardinal Gomá to assist the Rightist uprising. Instead, most of the clergy in Guipúzcoa, Alava, and Vizcaya supported Basque nationalist forces that chose the path of autonomy and fought along with the Left in defense of the Spanish Republic. It was no small shock to generals Franco and Mola that both the middle-class Basque nationalists of the PNV and the supposedly reliable Basque Catholic hierarchy opposed their rising against the Republic.

A complex series of political maneuvers in the summer of 1936 ended with the Basque provinces of Guipúzcoa, Alava, and Vizcaya joining with the Republic under an autonomy statute passed by the Republican Cortes, while Navarra, the center of ultrareactionary Carlista sentiment and the armed Carlist Requetés militia, joined with Franco to fight against Basque nationalism and for the restoration of a centralized monarchy that would attempt to turn back the hands of time.

Thus, while in the rest of Spain the civil war was characterized by widespread violence against churches and priests by the revolutionary Left and Republican forces, in the Basque region a large part of the clergy and the pious laity allied itself with Basque nationalists and their Leftist allies to defend the Spanish Republic. Indeed, the Basque clergy became a particular target for reprisals and repression by Franco's armies: in October 1936, military authorities executed a dozen Basque priests, including "a priest deservedly famous locally for his piety, Father Joaquín Arín, arch-priest of the little steel town of Mondragon."[14]

Bishop Múgica of Vitoria angrily told Cardinal Gomá that it would have been better if Franco and his soldiers had kissed Father Arín's feet instead of shooting him. In Rome, Bishop Múgica succeeded in intervening with the Catholic hierarchy to stop the excommunication of priests who supported the Basque nationalists and in discouraging further executions.[15]

As the war raged, one young and religious Basque who served as a dedicated journalist for the Basque forces was José María Arizmendiarrieta.

The Role of Don José María

José María Arizmendiarrieta was born April 22, 1915, on a farm in the mountains of Vizcaya, about thirty miles from Mondragon. He left his tiny village of Marquina in 1928 and entered Catholic seminary in Vitoria. Recalling the cloistered isolation of this period, Arizmendiarrieta wrote of the danger of being "removed from the reality of practical life."[16] But his years in the seminary exposed him both to Catholic social thought and to such people as the Basque writer Agustín Zubikarai, the director of the Bilbao newspaper *Eguna* during the civil war. Arizmendiarrieta, who wrote and edited for *Eguna* during the war, was imprisoned at its end to await perfunctory trial and likely execution. A visitor to the small museum in the Ikasbide training center in Mondragon today can see his list of jail inmates—one by one, he crossed off their names as they were executed. But the conquerors' bloodlust abated, and Arizmendiarrieta was spared. He then returned to the seminary and stayed until 1941, when he was assigned to Mondragon, where he would live until his death in 1976.

Arizmendiarrieta's ideas were a distinct departure from the rather conservative social Catholicism taught at the seminary. In many ways, they prefigured points raised in Pope John Paul II's 1981 encyclical *Laborem Exercens* ("On Human Work"). But in fact Arizmendiarrieta transcends these ideas and makes a clearly humanist break with the world of technique that underlies "On Human Work" and Catholic social thought.

Arizmendiarrieta was a pious Catholic, a person of great modesty and little personal ambition. But he was more than a dedicated servant of his parish and his church—he was both an intellectual and a supremely patient and practical thinker who had an extraordinary ability to meld, over time, theory and practice into the development of the Mondragon cooperative system.

Although he cast his socially revolutionary practice as an appreciation and reaffirmation of fundamental church principles, Arizmendiarrieta went far beyond current doctrine. For example, the reasoning in "On Human Work" follows from the biblical injunction to "subdue the earth." Work fulfills this command, and technology is one result. John Paul II declared, "The expression 'subdue the earth' has an enormous range. It means all the resources that the earth (and indirectly the visible world) contains and which, through the conscious activity of man, can be discovered and used for his ends."[17] Clearly this conception is central to the development of the world of technique and domination, redeemed in Catholic theology by the free moral choices of human beings.

But Arizmendiarrieta's ideas were not hobbled by this vision of conflict and violence. Instead, he undertook a sensitive examination of the complex dynamics of creating a humane cooperative community, one for which love is a generative principle and that is informed by the desire to act as "servant/steward rather than conqueror/consumer."[18] He rejected the notion that work was a matter of suffering ordained by the biblical command for humanity to toil following the expulsion from paradise. Rather, it was a means of individual and collective human renewal, of building community. "Work constitutes a good, renewable day by day . . . the antidote to correct social and mental imbalance. . . . Work was, then, well-being for him [Arizmendiarrieta], calming, friend, medicine, and the best means in the search for social peace."[19] Arizmendiarrieta focused on the development of democratic cooperativism, "the best resource to choose for self-government."[20]

Arizmendiarrieta was distinctly Basque. He shared in the amalgam of tensions and tragedy that shaped his people's struggle for self-rule and independence and had access, as well, to the progressive tradition of the Basque church and its reservations about industrial capitalism. From this base his mind ranged widely, freely, and creatively to find lessons to be adapted to the development of Mondragon cooperativism. Something of his character is revealed in an anecdote related by Robert Oakeshott:

> What struck me most, when I was lucky enough to meet him, was his commitment to the values of freedom as well as to the importance of work and of technical skill. His emphatic preoccupation with the second had seemed to me to align him rather with Mao Tse Tung. I can still remember the amused delight in his eyes when I suggested the parallel. He opened a locked drawer at the bottom of his desk and proudly produced for my inspection a copy of the Spanish translation of the Little Red Book. On the other hand, I was all the more surprised when he repudiated Mao's reliance upon compulsory productive work. The context, I hasten to add, was not labour camps, but the inclusion in the curriculum of schools and colleges of sessions of compulsory productive work. Fr. Arizmendiarrieta had just described—and de-

scribed with obvious satisfaction—how students at the professional and polytechnic school were able to cover their required contribution to school fees by taking part in productive work for the market—but he insisted that they must be free not to do that if they so wished."[21]

Mondragon and Basqueness

Mondragon is strongly identified with Basque culture and self-assertion, but it is not merely a Basque institution: open admission, regardless of ethnicity or nationality, is a basic principle. Similarly, while Arizmendiarrieta's social Catholicism was the inspiration for Mondragon's development, it was secular from the beginning.

The cooperatives' success is often attributed to some exotic "Basqueness" in order to somehow diminish their significance, as if their accomplishments were contaminated by certain cooperative and entrepreneurial values foreign to the cultures of industrial modernism. In this way, the Basques' particular history is used to deny the possibility that Mondragon's example might challenge the reigning ideology. But the importance of Mondragon is not its antecedents, but its relevance to our future. Considering the meaning of Basque traditional *fueros* (autonomous rights) for Mondragon, José María Arizmendiarrietta observed:

> *Fueros* is a term of useful historical sound; although the only valid revolution—the one which can satisfy us—must be made looking ahead, at the future. However, we cannot, and should not, start at the "zero point" without history, without ties to a past in which we have, no doubt, carried out deeds which attest to our spirit and strength, but which also holds memories that do not honor us. We don't deny our lineage, our culture, our parents; we are neither anonymous nor of unknown parentage. However, those of us who know by experience the devastation of our past collective psychoses—which have engulfed us—have to alert ourselves to the possible return of similar events in the present. . . . We must remember that nothing is made, nor can be made starting from the zero point; but, also, that everything needs to be made current. The most fertile and promising renewal is that which can be trusted to personal and community conscience, which can reject both immobility and adventurism, and which can find its support in the free and permanent participation of the people.[22]

This commitment to the free and permanent participation of the people, to the exercise of freedom in the building of community, informs this book. One lesson of Mondragon is that our lives can be more about democratic process, about becoming, than about the immutable solutions and abstract truths presented by authority.

The Development of the Mondragon Co-ops: The Early Years

Ordained as a priest at twenty-six, Arizmendiarrieta was assigned to the obscure, war-ravaged town of Mondragon in February 1941. Given his interest in social problems, the new assistant curate was named counselor to the lay group Acción Católica. At the time, the only opportunity for advancement for the town's young people was a small apprentice-training school operated by the Union Cerrajera steel company. It admitted the children of employees, plus twelve other local youths (about 15% of those who might have been interested in attending). Arizmendiarrieta soon became an instructor in religious and human values at the school. He proposed expanding the enrollment, but the firm refused, despite his offer to help raise funds.[23]

Rather than acquiescing, Arizmendiarrieta took action. He went to the people of Mondragon with a proposal and placed ballot boxes on street corners where people could indicate their willingness to support an independent training school. There were about six hundred responses pledging support in cash or other contributions, and in October 1943 a new, community-run training school began operation with twenty pupils.

The contributors elected the school's management committee, and the students played an important role in fund-raising efforts. Thus, from the beginning, Arizmendiarrieta turned toward members and participants for self-governance and self-financing. He avoided the easier path of placing the school under Acción Católica or the church. Over the next forty-five years, the school for apprentices evolved first into the League of Education and Culture and then into the comprehensive and complex Hezibide Elkartea educational cooperative with approximately forty-five thousand pupils in programs ranging from elementary school to adult education.

In many ways, Mondragon's schools were the foundation of the cooperative system; they provided both technically trained workers and the basis for today's specialized co-ops. But the training was more than technical. It included social and ethical education that, in part, led pupils to begin the cooperative enterprises and helped guide future choices. Before starting the first co-op, the early students spent up to eleven years in a milieu that valued cooperative ideas. By the time the industrial cooperatives opened, there was a core of trained young people with shared values and ideas who could move very quickly—a pool of would-be cooperators ready to see the advantages of the emerging system.

But in the sad days of the 1940s, such developments were not part of Arizmendiarrieta's intentions. From the beginning, the Mondragon system was based on the needs and visions of the participants in their particular situations, and not on a detailed plan. Mondragon's history is marked by an ongoing series of inspired adaptations to changing circumstances and sudden opportunities. This is not to say there was, or is, no planning, but it is planning in the context of democratic and collective risk taking. Arizmendiarrieta, and such people as Ormaechea and Gorroñogoitia, provided crucial leadership and inspiration along the way, but Mondragon has always been more than the sum of the work of its leaders. From the outset, Mondragon cooperativism has been a collective and self-renewing process, developed and guided by the pursuit of equilibrio.

The apprentice school was a success and expanded. By 1948, Arizmendiarrieta had organized the League of Education and Culture to encourage and coordinate educational efforts on all levels for children and adults. As the league could not offer more than middle-level technical training, he arranged for some of the senior students to continue their studies at night (after work) and to take the engineering examinations at the University of Zaragoza.

In 1952, eleven Mondragon students passed these exams. Among them were five young men (Usatorre, Larrañaga, Gorroñogoitia, Ormaechea, and Ortubay), the first letters of whose names became the name of the first industrial cooperative—Ulgor. Four of the five worked for Union Cerrajera; their technical training and motivation brought them naturally into managerial positions. Their intention, shared with many other graduates of Arizmendiarrieta's school, was to reform and democratize existing capitalist firms from within. But they soon discovered that management was not inclined to reduce its control.[24]

In 1954 the five decided to try to buy a small bankrupt factory near Vitoria. Its major asset was an existing license to manufacture paraffin cooking stoves; this freed the five from the need to deal with the Francoist bureaucracy. However, they had little personal capital, a not terribly adequate product, and no solid notion of a legal form for their new enterprise, though it was clear that the existing Spanish cooperative law did not meet their needs. Jesús Larrañaga remembers that "[t]his was no ambitious and well-considered project; what we needed was to start something, to wake up, to see what would be the outcome."[25]

So the Ulgor founders turned to the community and to their own creativity. Most of the needed original capital (roughly $100,000, though accounts vary) was obtained from one hundred people in Mondragon, particularly from friends and associates who were members of the *"chiquitos,"* the town's private dinner and social-drinking clubs. The loans had no guarantee beyond the personal integrity of the founders.

After operating briefly in Vitoria, Ulgor moved to Mondragon and built a new factory in 1956. The firm employed twenty-four workers to manufacture an Aladdin space heating stove. (They had bought one of these stoves in France, disassembled it, and copied it—without regard to patent rights—and then obtained the Spanish patent rights.) Demand for the appliances proved strong, and soon Ulgor was designing its own stoves, buying an existing foundry and casting shop to free itself from outside suppliers (in 1965, these shops were hived off to become part of the Ederlan co-op), manufacturing a line of electrical equipment under a foreign license, and building a new factory to produce butane cookers under the brand name Fagor. By the end of 1958, Ulgor had 149 employees.

Ulgor's early success ignited similar cooperative efforts in Mondragon and nearby towns in the late 1950s and early 1960s. These included Arrasate in Mondragon, which began by producing lawnmower parts (and would eventually become one of Spain's leading machine tool manufacturers); Comet, a steel foundry formed from two existing capitalist firms in Guipúzcoa (later to become Ederlan, meaning "good work"); Funcor, a foundry in Vizcaya; Ochandiano Talleres, a manufacturer of food handling equipment; Tolsan, a foundry in Vizcaya; and a retail co-op store, the first of what would become the Eroski chain.[26]

Until 1959, none of the cooperatives had a fully developed organizational and legal structure. Each operated informally along democratic lines on the basis of one worker, one vote. Arizmendiarrieta worked diligently with outside legal experts to develop a durable and flexible legal structure. He recalled:

> In effect, formulas were found by which our enterprise's essential basis could be brought into line with current legal precepts, enabling the first industrial cooperatives to be set up in Mondragon. . . . To do this, we had to overcome more than legal difficulties. . . . From the beginning we bore in mind the needs of a modern enterprise, and a formula was adopted which would make its development viable from all points of view: economic, technical, social and financial; not as a second rate entity suitable for only a limited field of activity, but one which would be appropriate across a wide sector of the economy.[27]

But the problems facing the growing cooperatives went beyond the need to find a suitable legal structure. As they attempted to expand, they began to run into the difficulties that co-ops typically confront in a capitalist world: they found their access to capital and financial markets severely restricted, which usually limits co-ops to the role of isolated, undercapitalized, and marginal "dwarf fish" in the capitalist sea of major corporations.[28]

A conventional corporate structure was clearly out of the question. Although Arizmendiarrieta had developed, with assistance, mechanisms that he believed could accommodate the need for enduring, effective, and democratic cooperatives under Spanish law, this law placed severe financial obstacles in the path of development. Specifically, it blocked outsiders who might be willing to invest in a fledgling firm from any equity participation (buying a share of ownership), and it limited the use of co-op property as collateral for loans. In addition, banks and other investors were hesitant to finance worker cooperatives, which reflected both skepticism about the co-ops' long-term economic viability and hostility toward worker ownership. The law also excluded co-ops from the Spanish social-security system, which left members without protection for health, disability, or retirement.

This was the moment of truth in the development of the Mondragon cooperatives. Some economists argue that co-ops tend to be undercapitalized not simply because traditional capitalist markets are hostile, but because owner-workers tend to value maximizing short-term income over both capital reinvestment and the creation of more jobs. Thus they could survive only in one of two ways: by a commitment to growth, which would ultimately lead to adopting the traditional capitalist mode of development and operation, becoming co-ops largely in name only; or by remaining small, isolated, and marginal, cut off from the opportunity for effective change. Either course would drain the cooperators' early energies and aspirations.

But the Mondragon co-ops broke the rules and created their own solution. First, they developed and formalized a comprehensive series of organizational and operational principles for each individual co-op. These rules, or Social Statutes, established a durable and democratic governing and operational structure. By detailing such things as basic cooperative principles, the rights and responsibilities of owner-workers, and the organization of cooperative self-management, the Social Statutes established the mechanisms for creating structures based on the central co-op principles of openness, solidarity, and social responsibility.[29] (The co-ops' internal structure will be discussed further in Chapter 3.)

The cooperators' second, and decisive, break with convention was to create the cooperative bank, the Caja Laboral Popular, as a second-degree cooperative. The bank made it possible to consolidate and use productively the social capital produced by the cooperators' labor, thus incorporating capital into the system. Establishing a successful cooperative bank tipped the economic scales in Mondragon's favor.

The Caja Laboral Popular adds a truly revolutionary dimension to Mondragon's handling of wages, surpluses (or profits), and losses. Co-op "wages" (actually advances, or *anticipos*, against the cooperative's income) are set according to the principle of wage solidarity, so the base wage is roughly comparable to that of similar workers in neighboring Basque industry. Each year, after meeting all expenses, including these "wages," at least 10 percent of the co-op's annual profits are donated to social or charitable institutions. The remainder is used to help finance the operation of the co-op and the entire co-op system: 20 percent (or more) of total profits is held in a reserve fund; the remaining 70 percent (or less) is distributed to the owner-workers' personal internal capital accounts, apportioned according to number of hours worked and salary grade. Internal capital accounts are adjusted for inflation and can be used as collateral for personal loans. Interest is paid yearly on these accounts and can be withdrawn, but the principal cannot be removed until the owner-worker retires or leaves the co-op.

For individual cooperatives, this means that approximately 90 percent of the annual surplus is effectively saved, not just the 20 percent nominally kept as a reserve. All these funds are potentially available to help finance the whole cooperative system. The creation of internal capital accounts and the reserve fund provides the basis for a durable solution to the problem of undercapitalization, but creating a cooperative bank to administer and consolidate these accounts is what really frees the cooperative system from the usual capital restraints.

The bank solves a number of problems. It makes it easy for the co-ops to save and to reinvest their capital in co-op operations. Because it is organized like a credit union, the bank can also attract savings accounts from the local population, thus enormously expanding the pool of available capital. Moreover, the bank offers the infrastructure for a cooperative social-insurance system. Finally, it provides ever more sophisticated management assistance to existing co-ops and to start-ups. In effect, the Caja Laboral Popular closes the circle of power between the co-ops and their communities: it pools cooperative and community income to support the cooperatives and facilitate community development.

Although the bank now provides all this, the early cooperators were quite skeptical when Arizmendiarrieta first proposed the idea. One Ulgor founder recalls: "We told him, yesterday we were craftsmen, foremen, and engineers. Today we are trying to learn how to be managers and executives. Tomorrow you want us to become bankers. That is impossible."[30] The structure that Arizmendiarrieta chose for the bank was termed a "second degree cooperative" under the co-op law. As such, the Caja Laboral Popular could include a combination of the Mondragon cooperatives and the bank's own owner-workers—those employed by the bank were themselves members of a co-op. They were not only responsible for helping manage the financial affairs of other cooperatives, but also individually at risk for the success of both their own co-op (the CLP) and the entire system. Individual co-ops sign a "Contract of Association" with the bank that formalizes their financial relationships and defines the duties and responsibilities of both (see Chapter 4).

The organization of the Caja Laboral Popular was approved by the Spanish government in July 1959, and the bank began operations that year in borrowed office space. From the first, its growth has been dramatic.

The Rise of the Industrial Cooperatives in Context

Between 1956 and 1959, an extraordinary burst of entrepreneurial energy led to the creation of the essential elements of the Mondragon system, including the core cooperators of what would become the Ulargo group and the CLP. By 1964, Mondragon had twenty-seven cooperatives and 2,620 owner-workers. Clearly, the young cooperators were energized by Arizmendiarrieta's developing vision of a democratic, cooperative society. Their accomplishments also withstood the test of the capitalist marketplace, leaving a durable and flexible foundation. Best of all, the early cooperators' efforts quickly developed into a cooperative entrepreneurship that built community health, wealth, and solidarity, rather than mere personal riches—and did so in the face of the ongoing threat of Francoist repression.

Of course, the cooperators had their share of luck. The dictator probably overlooked what was happening in Mondragon in the late 1950s, in part because he faced direct challenges to his authority elsewhere, such as the anarchist CNT's metalworkers strike in Barcelona in 1956 and the birth of the Communist Party-associated Confederation of Workers Committees in Asturias in 1958.[31] In addition, the idea of co-ops as such was not inconsistent, in principle, with whatever tattered and distorted populist inclinations still adhered in the Francoist state, the legacy of the Left wing of the Spanish Falange, the Juntas de Ofensiva Nacionalista Sindicada (JONS), which was sympathetic to worker empowerment—albeit through a lens of militant nationalism, bigotry, repression, and fierce opposition to Basque autonomy.

In addition, the cooperators clearly benefited from the economic boom of the 1960s, which included tremendous demand for industrial goods and consumer durables of the sort produced by the mushrooming co-op system. But there is almost always some sort of economic opportunity—strong demand for consumer durables is not essential for developing a cooperative social system. Under different circumstances, the cooperatives would have followed a different path, for the Mondragon system is not just a creative response to a boom but to the underlying tensions between centralization and autonomy. These strains are at once a fundamental theme in Basque history and a characteristic of the forces at work within industrial modernism. Thus the cooperators brought social resources—cooperative entrepreneurship and the search for equilibrio—to bear on some of the common problems of industrial society.

In other words, Mondragon was not simply possible only in one place at one time. Rather, given the conditions of industrial modernism, Mondragon (or something like it) was bound to develop. Furthermore, the co-ops' history encompasses not just the great expansion of the 1960s and early 1970s, but the worldwide recession of the mid-1970s, and the stagnation and moderate growth of the 1980s—which suggests that the system is a robust one, capable of surviving and even flourishing in hard times. Economically, the Mondragon co-ops grew rapidly during the boom, more slowly during the recession, consolidated in the early 1980s, and had begun to grow rapidly again in the late 1980s. The cooperatives' responses to cyclical economic crises and structural transformation have included technical economic adjustments, forming new cooperative democratic structures, and creating new jobs to help ease Basque unemployment. (The record is considered in detail in Chapters 4, 6, 8, and 9.) Table 2-1 and Chart 2-2 detail the patterns of Mondragon growth.

With the latest expansion, Mondragon seems to have progressed through the first cycle of the classic S curve of economic growth (start-up, rapid growth, slowing growth, renewed expansion). That this newest growth takes place even in a time of economic difficulty for Spain and the Basque region (during 1988, Spanish unemployment was 20%) is a further tribute to the strength of the system. Of course, expansion and growth in and of themselves are not necessarily beneficial, and the Mondragon cooperators have contributed to the destructive effects of industrialism. But they have also shown an impressive ability to recognize the consequences of their actions and to take steps toward rectifying them.

Mondragon has also proven its flexibility and durablilty in responding to the dramatic political and social transformation of the post-Franco years: the social values of the cooperators did not evaporate when the going got rough.

Centralization-Autonomy and Development of the Co-ops

A basic theme of Spanish history has been the conflict between regional groups such as the Basques or the neighboring Catalans who want independence, or at least autonomy, and centralizers—whether monarchists or modernizers. For the Basques, this struggle has been heightened

Table 2-1. Industrial Cooperatives' Expansion, 1961–84

Year	Co-ops Founded	Year	Co-ops Founded
1961	4	1973	1
1962	6	1974	6
1963	11	1975	3
1964	3	1976	2
1965	4	1977	3
1966	4	1978	2
1967	7	1979	0
1968	1	1980	5
1969	3	1981	4
1970	0	1982	1
1971	2	1983	4
1972	0	1984	5

Sources: Oakeshott (1978) and Caja Laboral Popular, Materials Prepared for *Visit of Kenneth Clarke, Minister of Employment for the United Kingdom*, September 10, 1986.

Chart 2-2. Number of Cooperators, 1965–87

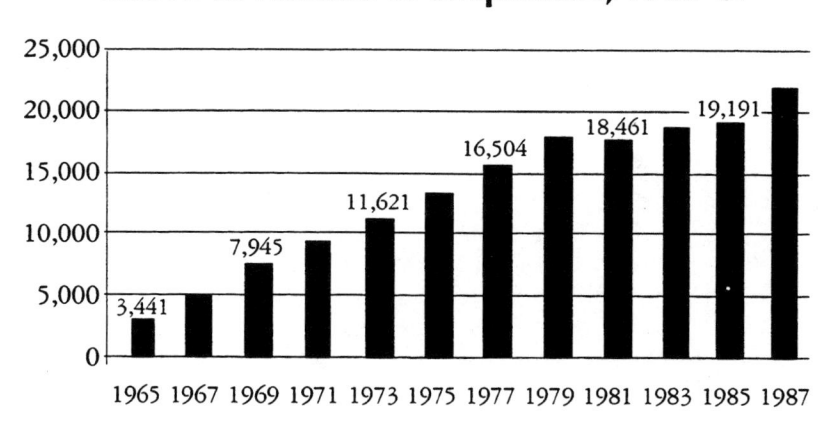

Year	Cooperators
1965	3,441
1969	7,945
1973	11,621
1977	16,504
1981	18,461
1985	19,191

Source: CLP annual reports
Number of cooperators, 1987 = 21,000

by tensions between towns or villages and the Basque feudal aristocracy. In modern Spain, it has generally been expressed in terms of conflict between the forces of liberalism and conservatism.

Spanish liberals have been intent on encouraging the development of a modern industrial and capitalist state; they have been nearly as hostile as the feudal monarchs to the traditional *fueros* (local rights and powers of self-government) that are dear to many Basques. For the liberals, local tariffs and regulations, as well as regional taxation and commercial customs, have seemed a grave obstacle to the growth of national economic power. Paradoxically, the nationalist and separatist Basques, along with the Catalans, have been leaders in the development of Spanish industry and banking. Still, they have had little use for a bureaucracy based in Madrid that often casts a covetous eye upon their resources.

Socialists have also been among the most vigorous proponents of centralization. This attitude is complicated by the relative lack of antipathy between Basques and the Catholic church—a cordiality that made it easy for the Left in the rest of Spain to suspect all forms of Basque nationalism, however innovative or democratic.

What may be broadly defined as conservatism in Spain has been not simply an alliance between the large landowners, the reactionary church hierarchy, and some industrialists (who benefited in the Basque country by a tariff policy favorable to their interests). Conservatism also attracted some Basques with strong commitments to the local *fueros*, as well as small independent farmers and merchants fearful, for good reason, of the central government's power.

Some Basques, particularly in Navarra, were among the fiercest partisans of the reactionary Carlist cause (a fixture in Spanish politics since the nineteenth-century War of the Spanish Succession) and played a major role in support of Franco in the Spanish civil war. They joined the Carlistas for the sake of God and a pretender to the throne who embodied both their hope for the good life of the past and their rage at the dislocation and corruption of modernity. But most Basques fought against Franco, the fascist Falange, and the Carlistas and on the side of the Republic and for Basque autonomy. Some of them developed the Mondragon cooperatives.

Without delving much further into what Gerald Brenan has described as the "Spanish labyrinth," it is clear that Mondragon grew out of an extremely complex and divided social and political situation. Mondragon cooperative entrepreneurship, with its pursuit of equilibrio, was a creative resolution of the centralization-autonomy dynamic of division and social stress. Beyond the specific Basque context, it can be seen as an example of the kinds of positive changes potentiated by the emergence of postmodernism. The singular importance of the cooperatives is their ability to bring to a world characterized by centrifugal forces of social change a creative solution that harnesses and harmonizes many of these energies. As such, Mondragon demonstrates a developing ecological postmodernism, able to place limits on the destructive conduct of industrialism.

Mondragon and Postmodernism

As the pace of historical change appears to accelerate under the influence of modern communication technologies, global media folkways, and integrated high technologies, events that are separated by decades, or even by a few years, begin to seem unrelated. We are bid to regard the past as curio or as nostalgia. This is the postmodern illusion: we have separated ourselves from our own history, not just as individuals, but as peoples. Yet embedded in that history are the realities of our particular culture, of our existence as real human beings, not just as consumers or as soldiers.

Human choice and human history are parts of our lives: we need to remember who we were in order to understand who we are and to make informed decisions about who we will become. The swirl of history conditions, but does not foreclose, our choices. Without memory, our choices fade into illusion, and we respond without awareness to historical forces we do not see.

Mondragon and its development is part of, and a commentary on, the postmodern condition—it is essentially an experiment in social reconstruction through cooperative community. Although spawned amidst the historical context that produced both Carlistas and militant Basque separatists, the Mondragon cooperators have chosen a radically different path, one that helps them begin to transcend the general conditions of industrial modernism and the more particular forces of Spanish history (they have, for example, avoided entanglement with the politics of Basque separatism while successfully advocating Basque autonomy).

The pursuit of equilibrio is what enables the cooperators to choose. This pursuit requires them to pay attention to their history, to the economic, natural, political, and social context, and to the desires of all parts of their community. Equilibrio is many-voiced and inclusive; it bids us to build and participate in a new, liberatory, and kaleidoscopic consciousness. Its promise is to dissolve industrial modernism's division of the world into self and other, master and slave.

The trajectory of the new consciousness and the practice of ecological postmodernism is to reclaim vernacular knowledge from the domination of the ideology of industrialism. Vernacular knowledge is community knowledge, the product of social practice. In the name of progress, science, and power, industrialism wars against this knowledge; for example, over centuries of practice the indigenous organic agriculture of Indian rice farmers developed thousands of plant varieties. This diversity is now relentlessly assaulted by a chemical-based agriculture—genetically homogenized plants requiring synthetic fertilizers, pesticides, fungicides, and herbicides. This is the agriculture of Bhopal and famine.

Vernacular knowledge is not limited to premodern cultures, as Mondragon's innovation of cooperative entrepreneurship demonstrates. The cooperators are not cloistered primitives; they walk an eminently practical path, and have an informed and sophisticated awareness of the ironies and contradictions of the postmodern moment.

The promotional film for robotics from Ikerlan (the research co-op) uses as background music a song from the movie *The Wall* by the British rock group Pink Floyd. As the robot works, the words to the music (which are not heard) are the angry "We don't need no thought control . . . Teacher, leave those kids alone" of alienated British youth. The film is a wry and knowing commentary on machine "workers" that subtly poses some of the questions and contradictions rasied by an emergent postmodernism. Are we watching the path of liberation of people from service to the machine or the apotheosis of technique and a manifesto for human redundancy? The answers are to be found in social practice.

The process of re-creating equilibrio gives the cooperators the means to resist the postmodern illusion, to transform postmodern disintegration into community, to create their own center. The pursuit of equilibrio gives the cooperators a constructive, effective, and responsible way to use the enormous and terrifying freedom that is central to the postmodern condition. Mondragon suggests that we can strive for more than mere survival or for power. By exercising our freedom we can build community.

Deep Social Structures

An important element in the cooperators' attempts to create a new social system was Arizmendiarrieta's emphasis on practice. He realized early on that transforming society from below takes more than moral values or revolutionary enthusiasm. By focusing on action and participation, he (and the cooperators) engaged what I call "deep social structures"—not social structures in an anthropological sense of kinship, but in the sense of socially constructed reality.

These structures are the nearly invisible cultural and social patterns that shape our consciousnesses, our perceptions, our reality. They are a product of current and past experience and of our interaction with the environment. These patterns are so deeply embedded, so much a part of who we are, that they are essentially transparent. They are also much more fluid and plastic than the architectural words "structure" or "pattern" might suggest. As structural anthropologist Claude Lévi-Strauss writes of the dynamic and protean nature of social being, "We are dealing with a reality in process, a reality which is perpetually under attack from a past which ruins it and a future which changes it."[32]

As hard to see and to hold as they are, deep social structures nevertheless condition our beliefs (and behavior) about what is desirable, attainable, and even real. Discussions of structure are typically associated with placing constraints upon human action, sometimes in a rigidly deterministic way. But if deep social structures are seen as reflections of the plasticity and protean nature of people and society, human choice may be able to effect dramatic change. Such a view keeps structure embedded in the human relationships that constitute society and the human actions that constitute history. For reality is social, not an abstract creation or category. In the words of sociologist Alvin Gouldner, "Social 'situations' are not regions in which persons act; they are the recurrent and collective actions of persons."[33]

The relevance of deep social structures to social change is informed by two basic themes, and they provide the context in which the Mondragon cooperatives can be viewed.

First, the existence of deep social structures is a consequence of the nature of the human organism as a part of a living world. There is no inherent separation between human development and nature—belief in such an estrangement is a result of the deep social structures of civilization. As living beings, as animals, we are inextricably tied to the creation of our perceived reality. In this participatory world, where knowing is doing and where there is no privileged outside observer, there is an unavoidable convergence between being and becoming. This is an essential condition of a world of change, an ecological world whose nature seeks dynamic equilibrio.

Deep social structures are not simply ghosts. They have both a physical property and an informational property and are expressed (exist) through human consciousness. Our collective consciousness is our social reality; we accept it as a given, but it includes perception, memory, emotion, and symbolic forms and patterns that are ordered and transformed in the conscious mind. It is a basic characteristic of our species, as well as a necessity for survival, that there is the capacity for rapid feedback and change within this system of consciousness. This accounts for the incredible variety and flexibility of human social and cultural forms.

Our capacity for learning underlies the nature of deep social structures that I believe reflect the basic physical ordering and development of human neuronal pathways in response to experience. Gerald Edelman suggests that such pathways are "selected" within the brain on the basis of use, a view that provides strong support for the idea that human behavior is flexible, that freedom and culture mean much more than "hard wiring" and sociobiological reflexes.[34] But the physical basis of social organization is not limited to the brain. Physiologist Candace Pert has found receptors for neuropeptides, hormones crucial in the processes of emotion and feeling, throughout the body. She concludes: "I can no longer make a strong distinction between the brain and the body. . . . A mind is composed of information, and it has a physical substrate, which is the body and the brain; and it also has another immaterial substrate that has to do with information flowing around."[35]

Thus the phrase "deep social structures" is not used here to describe innate, fixed, and presumably genetically determined operators in the brain. They are not mental molds waiting to be filled by content[36] nor are they limited by the nature of language. They are the form of human experience internalized and remembered: through accretion and accumulation they have a fundamental influence on the content of our "human nature." As the stuff of human history and experience, deep social structures connect the personal and the political; they draw together human experience (which is always individual) with the experience of human society, without which individual experience would be meaningless and "inhuman." They are both an expression of human history and the substance that shapes the processes of historical change.

The second underlying theme is that the formation of deep social structures begins no later than the moment of birth, and probably earlier: the birth moment, the slap on the bottom of a baby, reverberates with the impact of thousands of years of human culture and social choices, but that slap is not the first experience; much has already happened in the womb. But in the industrial modern world, the child awakes not simply to the "outside," but to cool fluorescent light and stainless steel, to ceremonially gowned and masked figures. Its awakening scream is the moment of initiation into the collective consciousness of industrial modernism. It is a pattern-establishing moment, the beginning of the rush of learning that makes us American or Chinese, a woman or man. It is a moment before language, but not before understanding. It is the beginning of a relentless accretion and patterning of experience, of deep social structures.

These patterns define the nature of the hegemony of society over knowledge and consciousness. This is an optimistic view, one that sees possibilities for change, because the need to re-form human society is central to the question of human survival. This is at once an absolutely personal and an absolutely social process. It requires making new social choices and building new social realities—not in the abstract, but in the everyday actions of individuals and groups.

We are all the lonely children of industrial modernism; our survival and our humanity are absolutely determined by our connection with and love for others. As lonely children we face the postmodern challenge of human community or catastrophe. There is no separate individual solution. The path to survival, the path of possibility, to the ecological postmodern world must be a social one, a crowded one.

Developmental Indeterminacy

Mondragon demonstrates that the deep social structures that shape and influence our individual and collective consciousness can also facilitate liberatory transformation, such as the creation of an ecological postmodernism from the agonies and ashes of industrial modernism. Mondragon demonstrates that our future choices are governed—or not governed, really—by what I call developmental indeterminacy. Both evolutionary and dialectical processes are indeed part of history, but the changes they predict or explain are not irrevocable: history is not yoked to fixed mechanisms of progress or to cyclical fluctuations, whether technological, social, or economic. Change can be dramatic, nonlinear, revolutionary, and unpredictable.

Human choices and social relations, operating in the context of a living environment, are central to the changes we call history. The living environment, including both human consciousness and the material world, provides a framework of chance and necessity. It imposes limits on knowledge: not knowing everything, we are free to choose, free to experiment and to learn. This ability means we are not fated to pursue paths either to utopia or apocalypse, or that the only alternatives are ecological postmodernism or global technocracy. Rather, we act in the realm of uncertainty; our actions can affect our trajectories. So we can choose to try to build ecological communities, which may free us from hierarchical and exploitative models of power, progress, and scarcity. But we cannot make these exhilarating, terrifying choices alone. The real issues raised by history as we address the future are not those posed by the evolution of machines and the technological imperative, but those posed by the evolution of societies.

Notes

1. Thomas and Logan 1982, p. 16.
2. I have found clear affinities between the Basques and the native mountaineers of Vermont.
3. Brenan 1960, p. 97.
4. Mintegi 1986, p. 3.
5. Nef 1964, p. 114.

6. Thomas and Logan 1982, p. 15; Graham 1984, pp. 70–73.
7. Graham 1984, p. 73.
8. Oakeshott 1978, p. 167.
9. Ibid., p. 168.
10. de Madariaga 1967, pp. 631–32.
11. Thomas 1977, p. 87.
12. Ibid., p. 89.
13. Clark 1979, pp. 248–54.
14. Thomas 1977, p. 512.
15. Ibid., p. 513.
16. Larrañaga 1981, p. 24.
17. John Paul II "On Human Work" II. Work and Man, 4. In Genesis.
18. Gelderloos 1989, p.4.
19. Ormaechea 1986, pp. 13–14. Ormaechea, one of five founders of Mondragon's first cooperative, is now general manager of the Caja Laboral Popular.
20. Ibid., p. 23.
21. Oakeshott 1978, p. 172.
22. Quoted and translated in Johnson 1982, pp. 185–86.
23. Thomas and Logan 1982, pp. 17–18; Oakeshott 1978, pp. 168–170.
24. Thomas and Logan 1982, pp. 20–21; Oakeshott 1978, pp. 171–75; The Mondragon Experiment (Mondragon: Caja Laboral Popular, 1985), pp. 13–15.
25. Quoted in Thomas and Logan 1982, p. 20.
26. Oakeshott 1978, p. 175; Thomas and Logan 1982, pp. 21 and 31.
27. Quoted in Thomas and Logan 1982, p. 20.
28. Ellerman 1984, p. 5.
29. The statutes are detailed and explicit. For example, the 1981 edition of the *Social Statutes of the Caja Laboral Popular* is an eighty-page paperback book containing sixty articles printed in Spanish and in Euskara.
30. Gutiérrez-Johnson and Whyte 1977, p. 20.
31. Graham 1984, pp. 106–12.
32. Lévi-Strauss 1966, p. 34.
33. Gouldner 1980, p. 102.
34. Edelman 1988.
35. Pert 1988, pp. 109–112 (emphasis in original). Pert is chief of brain biochemistry, Clinical Neuro-Science Branch, National Institute of Mental Health, Bethesda, Maryland.
36. Harris 1980, p. 167.

3
Cooperation: The Basis of the Mondragon System

> It is no longer a choice between violence and nonviolence... the choice is nonviolence or nonexistence.
> —Martin Luther King

Mondragon is of particular interest for its vigor as a cooperative system. It uses cooperative entrepreneurship as the basis for building a dynamic, humane, and democratic social system in ways that go against the grain of both conventional and revisionist wisdom about cooperation. It transcends economicism and technique. If Mondragon has something to say to the postmodern world, its voice finds strength in the resonance of its understanding and application of cooperation.

Cooperation is a practical way for society to make new and rational choices that govern the conduct of industrialism. The rapidly growing importance of cooperative forms in the world essentially reflects a necessary antidote to the grave and interrelated crises of modern industrial civilization. But cooperation is more than simply a new grease for the gears of industrialism, more than a way to place limits upon its excesses; nor is it simply an artifact of abstract moral strength, or a political appeal. Cooperation as social practice is the active pursuit of equilibrio—of the social creation of unity in diversity.

Mainstream Views of Cooperation

Conventionally, cooperation is usually treated like a moral principle—respected, but observed largely in the breach. And as morality, cooperation can offer little in response to the ideology of domination that nurtures and sustains both the capitalist market and the labyrinthine hierarchies of bureaucratic socialism. Cooperation as morality shrivels in the heat of the market, is crushed under the weight of bureaucracy.

There is another view. Cooperation is increasingly seen as a way to improve efficiency and productivity. An expanding chorus of business, academic, and popular writers assert that cooperation, far from being a sentimental hindrance, is actually superior to conventional competition. Cooperation is offered in forms ranging from the so-called share economy to a model of international affairs as a non–zero sum game. Analysts point to Japan, the current capitalist archetype, and to the relatively more cooperative nature of relations beteween labor, management, and government there, as an essential ingredient in Japan's competitive superiority. Analyzing Mondragon's response to recession for the World Bank, Keith Bradley and Alan Gelb describe in detail the superiority and flexibility of the cooperative system when facing economic change.[1]

Industrial workers around the world now take part in management-initiated and controlled "quality circles," sometimes with the blessings of their unions. At a 1988 international autoworkers' conference in Germany, delegates from Japan, Mexico, the United States, Brazil, Spain, Britain, and Belgium reported with concern that management had instituted, or had attempted to institute, the team concept, which "involves workers learning several jobs and allowing management the flexibility to move them from job to job."[2]

Critics view quality circles and the team concept basically as management schemes to increase productivity without increasing wages and to undermine union contracts and work rules, not as ways to empower workers or to give them meaningful control of their companies beyond the shop floor.

This new interest in cooperation is decidedly not exclusively capitalist. If anything, socialists have adopted the ideology of industrialism with even more certitude, since it was a matter of faith that the abolition of

Cooperation: The Basis of the Mondragon System 63

private ownership would end the evils of capitalism. Under socialism, the ideology of scarcity, progress and technique was embraced with gusto as the means to right the wrongs of capitalist deprivation and, at the same time, to bring nationalist self-assertion in a world of great and hostile powers.

Following Mikhail Gorbachev's accession to power, *perestroika* brought the Soviets new cooperative enterprises that quickly amassed deposits of nearly $580 million in the state savings bank in 1987; in 1988 there was the promise of a cooperative bank. Basic assumptions of Soviet central planning were dramatically altered. According to Viktor Arkhipov, first deputy chairman of the Soviet Agro-Industrial Bank, "In starting *perestroika* we limited the monopoly of the state to foreign economic enterprises."[3]

The Chinese government, before the Tiananmen Square massacre and the supression of the democracy movement in 1989, was quite open to experimentation with cooperative enterprises. At present, the Chinese hierarchs are wary of worker initiatives that might potentiate resistance to the regime.

This new emphasis on cooperation and participation in both capitalist and socialist industrialism is more than just a conditional and transitory period of liberalization. The reemergence of cooperation as a respected principle of action is a result of common social and economic imperatives that have conflicting goals: the desire to end stagnation and decay and, at the same time, to limit change. Corporate and bureaucratic managers see cooperation as an effective response to the forces deforming the rigid structures of the modern industrial state, a way to let a little light and air into the system. They are willing to grant conditional freedom to encourage active participation within the context of the established social goals, to enlist people's creative energies to sustain and invigorate existing economic and political realms.

But the very freedom that is integral to cooperative vigor presents a grave danger to the hierarchies of power. Unchecked, the grant of freedom given by "cooperation" will sooner or later endanger the ideology of domination that is needed to maintain the essential elements of the status quo. Cooperation as practiced by the state and corporate bureaucracies is a manner of reform from above; it is not motivated by a sudden discovery of humane values, but by the profound global crises of modern industrialism. The question is not whether these reforms are "successful," but that they are necessary, since it is believed that maintaining present conditions poses a far greater risk to order. The situation in the Soviet Union is a clear example.

But the managers are struggling to sustain the unsustainable. Modern industrialism simply cannot continue to pursue ecological destruction and nuclear exterminism without catastrophe. Moreover, the managers face an ultimately futile task of balancing the people's need for freedom and their own need for power. It is futile not because they lack the requisite tools for co-optation, manipulation, and domination—on the contrary, the rapid development of computer and electronic technology greatly expands the armamentarium of deceit. But the paradox is that these very techniques in the long run exacerbate the crisis.

Looking back, we see that there was never a commitment more total (and more mad) to domestic fear and control than that of Stalin. But just as the design of Stalin (and of Hitler or even Robespierre) was not sustainable, neither will be that of high technology. Its application, even in the guise of a softer "friendly fascism," hastens the process of disintegration; it does not resolve the crises of the loss of belief that attend the ongoing processes of destruction.

Cooperation and the Development of Social Choices

In the broadest sense, cooperation is important because it reinvigorates social choices. Along with the pursuit of equilibrio, it can lead to a new social reality that will supplant the destructive ambitions of modernism with the human satisfactions of freedom and community, diversity and unity. Cooperation is a survival skill that will let us begin to limit the appetites of industrialism and to develop revivified cultures based upon human values.

Externally, the choices of cooperation appear to be a means to place social limits upon industrialism—limits only from the existing capitalist and socialist standpoint. For example, the abolition of wage labor by the Mondragon cooperatives and the equitable and democratic distribution of the social product is not merely an economic wrinkle. It challenges some of the basic assumptions and power relationships that have sustained industrialism and its underpinnings of scarcity and progress.

The concept of "limits" is, of course, not the general perception of the cooperators, but of those outside looking in. The cooperators' choices create the basis of the dynamic and enduring system; thus, in practice, cooperative policies that would be viewed as absolutely intolerable intrusions into the economic efficiency of capital have instead proven to be the basis of the co-ops' economic success in the capitalist market.

Over the long run, cooperation is antithetical to the sort of simple gains in efficiency and productivity sought by corporate and government managers. Cooperative praxis will lead to a restructuring; it will reflect the institution and reinstitution of a complex, interrelated group of social norms and forces that will place sane limits upon environmental and human destruction. Cooperation is more than simply an alternative—it is the antidote to the ideology of industrialism.

The predatory nature of modern industrialism is not any inherent feature of "economy" or "human nature." Modern industrialism at present is governed more by the complex transformation-disintegration driving the transition to postmodernism than by conflicts between capitalism and socialism. Cooperation, and the institution of new social choices, is not a call for a return to the past. It is instead the revivification of the concept of choice, choice that promises ecological survival, democracy, freedom, and community.

Clearly, cooperation is not the only solution to the tension in the modernist-postmodernist transition. It is possible, however, that by fits and starts power will be forced by circumstance to turn again to participatory and cooperative measures that will have an increasing presence as a basic social force. Cooperation, particularly when it rises from below as it has in Mondragon, will gradually begin to restrain the murderous forces of industrialism.

Mondragon and the Cooperative Transformation

The nature of Mondragon reflects its ability to prosper in a system that moves to the music of the industrial ideology. But it is easy to be absorbed in charts and graphs of output and economic importance and to miss the import of social choices. These choices have conditioned the development of the Mondragon system from the beginning and continue to evolve. They are elements of a social process, not simply a reform of the unsustainable, an effort to develop paths that lead in fundamentally different directions.

The ten Mondragon cooperative principles discussed in Chapter 1 are the basis for substituting the values of enduring community development and stability for the accumulation of wealth. The cooperators have begun to be more oriented toward production for use values than toward wealth. They have agreed to:

1. Abolish wage labor for owner-workers
2. Sharply limit the maximum differential between the highest- and lowest-paid workers
3. Base earnings on the average local wage
4. Have no claim on the earnings of future cooperators (Cooperators' earnings are based on their *anticipos* and a share of co-op surpluses for their own work. They do not sell their memberships in the co-op.)

5. Create more co-ops for the benefit of the expanding cooperative community and assist in this creation by limiting the accumulation of surpluses by individuals and co-ops
6. Institutionalize a 10 percent social contribution of profits as a basic principle of co-op functioning
7. Make the liquidity and mobility of capital subsidiary to the long-term health of the cooperative system (The co-ops are not sold or moved in search of higher profits. Instead, there is a commitment at all levels of the system to its continued durability.)
8. Develop appropriate mechanisms of cooperative democracy (These are consciously designed to democratize power, and they limit the influence of financial and business organizations and of economic technocrats within the cooperative system)

This list is suggestive, not exhaustive. The "freedom" purportedly brought by industrialism has been accompanied by the most profound imposition of bureaucratic and hierarchical structures, of stultifying limits upon human freedom and community. Thus it should be no surprise that industrialism's apologists are swift to dismiss the kind of choices made by Mondragon. And since the cooperatives have not obliged them by collapsing, even when the boom of the sixties turned to bust in the mid-seventies, they typically dispose of cooperation's gentle challenge by suggesting that the Mondragon model is uniquely Basque.

The co-ops have so far made only conditional changes in the ideology of industrialism, but they are well positioned for further steps in shaping the transformation to an ecological postmodern world, where the importance of cooperative entrepreneurship is not its ability to create wealth, but its ability to pursue equilibrio successfully and to encourage us to act dynamically and democratically in a manner conditioned by both human values and our experience.

Clearly, there is no lack of possible grim alternatives to the cooperative solution. But the forces at work are not at all likely to be quenched by managerial palliatives. As structures crumble, there is more space for freedom, and this is often freedom without history or community, expressed in hedonism, greed, desperation, violence. At the least, the Mondragon cooperatives can be seen as part of the emerging trajectory of practice accompanying the transition to ecological postmodernism. The rich Basque tradition provided the cultural basis for the emergence of the co-ops, but they are not focused on the past.

It is informative to review Basque traditions of peasant economy and community relatively unmediated by industrialism before examining some of the basic cooperative mechanisms of the Mondragon system.

Basque Cooperative Heritage—Basque Cultural Traditions as an Invitation and Not an Obstacle

The land itself, Basque history, and the dynamics of Iberian politics (as discussed in Chapter 2) combined to create a clear inclination toward independence and cooperative self-reliance, an extraordinary wariness of central authority, and a determination to preserve *fueros*, or traditional rights. These factors encouraged Basque mountain communities to maintain the vitality of traditional cooperative peasant practices long after they had vanished elsewhere in Spain. Writing in 1943, Gerald Brenan noted:

> All of this region has a simple type of rural economy that has come down more or less unchanged from early times and is not derived from the decay of feudal institutions. It is a country of small proprietors or tenant farmers, working on a family basis and possessing sufficient land to maintain themselves adequately. . . . [T]hey are not grouped in small towns or villages, but lie scattered in isolated farms and hamlets. As the rainfall is abundant and the soil adequate, they are fairly prosperous.[4]

That is the general cultural context. In many places, mountain life inclines people toward an ethos that combines self-reliance and cooperation—though it is very clear that such a heritage does not necessarily lead to the development of sophisticated cooperative systems.

Obviously, existing values and institutions helped the people of Mondragon develop their system, but the same cultural setting provided the impetus for the growth and development of a most vigorous and successful Basque capitalism. The Basques profited from certain values and institutions within their milieu, but community values and institutions of social unity exist almost everywhere and can form the basis for extraordinary examples of human transformation. (Poland's Solidarity movement is one compelling example.) The Mondragon model is of particular interest because it has proved effective, not because it is based on atavistic social forms.

For an organizer, it is possible to learn from the practice of the Mondragon cooperators and then draw upon the values and institutions that encourage social cooperation and solidarity anywhere. The task is not the obviously futile mission of re-creating the influence of rural Basque culture.

Basque Traditional Values and the Cooperative Setting

Dispersed settlement has meant that the center of traditional Basque rural life is the farmstead (*auzoa*) and the neighborhood (*vecinidad*). The farmsteads are unusually stable family units, in part because traditional Basque law and custom has required the entire farmstead to be passed to one chosen heir so the property remains a viable economic entity. As Steven Curtis Jackobs points out:

> Each farmstead has a name which it has kept since its founding, and the residents of the farmstead are known not by their surname, but by a combination of their first name and the farmstead's name. . . . [E]ach farmstead is linked to its neighbors in a complex system of ties of mutual aid and social interaction which remain intact regardless of change of occupants."[5]

Jackobs discusses a number of Basque cultural themes that are of particular interest in view of Mondragon practice. One is the ability to reach a consensus on new directions in times of change, directions based upon the spirit and intent of custom reinterpreted to fit new circumstances. For example, farmstead inheritance practices, which had long been maintained in spite of the Spanish law that explicitly dictates the divison of property among several heirs, have been modified. The interests of Basque minor heirs are now recognized, but in ways that alter, not destroy, the farmstead system.

The successful agricultural efforts of the Mondragon system are focused on processing and marketing co-ops such as Lana, dealing with milk products, and on the application of large-scale modern (i.e., industrial-type) methods to such tasks as animal breeding. Beyond reflecting the economics of modern agriculture, this emphasis is a recognition of the strength of traditional Basque farming patterns and of the lack of a consensus to apply new cooperative forms that moved beyond the traditional levels of communal cooperation. Jackobs notes that for the farmers, "[b]ecause their interests are essentially independent, their collective practices never test their solidarity, or seriously raise the question of mutual trust. They maintain collective practices to serve essentially particular ends."[6]

The persistence and strength of cultural values and practices centered on land as physical entity and as metaphor for community appear in the work of the Jewish philosopher Philo of Alexandria, writing two thousand years ago on the significance of the biblical verse "you shall not remove your neighbor's landmark, which they of old have set" (Deut. 19:14):

> Now this law, we may consider, applies not merely to allotments and boundaries of land in order to eliminate covetousness but also to the safeguarding of ancient customs. For customs are unwritten laws, the decisions approved by men of old, not inscribed on mountains nor on leaves of paper, which the moths destroy, but on the souls of those who are partners in the same citizenship. For children ought to inherit from

their parents, besides their property, ancient customs which they were reared in and have lived with even from the cradle, and not despise them because they have been handed down without written record. Praise cannot be duly given to one who obeys the written laws, since he acts under the admonition of restraint and the fear of punishment. But he who faithfully observes the unwritten laws deserves commendation, since the virtue which he displays is freely willed.[7]

The strength and endurance of underlying cultural practices are generally given little credence in the process of social change. Culture today is often presented as merchandise—a style we are intended to purchase and then discard. But humane postmodern freedoms must draw from the well of enduring cultural practice, modified to respond to new realities, not from the universe of commercial archetypes. Basque culture provided this resource for the development of the Mondragon system.

The stubborn persistence and durability of community-based social practices have been one of the factors that helped develop countervailing community power to resist the dictates of industrialism. In this sense, the failure of Marx's prophecy of proletarian revolution is due not so much to his misinterpretation of the logic of capitalism as (at least in part) to the inherent coherence of community culture that provided a basis for the great struggles from below of working people in unions and in the rise of social democracy.

A second Basque cultural theme involves a suspicion of differences which exists alongside a willingness to allow dramatic innovation. This process is not incompatible with innovation. The Basques appear to be less fearful of change than of stepping outside the social order. Jackobs reports that rural Basques had little interest in people who had left the region and found fame and fortune elsewhere. The acceptance of relevant change tends to be a social process based upon trial, discussion and proven practicality. Innovation tends to become community innovation.

In this the Basques bear some resemblance to the nineteenth-century Shakers, a communal religious group known both for their highly structured social order and for their creativity, inventiveness, and willingness to adopt new technologies and methods.

Jackobs notes, finally, that Basque leadership styles are unauthoritarian, involve consensual processes, and are aimed at harmonizing the group's feeling for collective ends with possible suspicion and lack of trust. A neighborhood's elected representative does not simply wield power, but builds consensus for group projects. This process often encounters problems of suspicion arising from individual and class differences. These are reflected in the relative difficulty of establishing agricultural cooperatives and point to the nonutopian nature of the Basque situation.

A major Mondragon achievement is to find means to harmonize individual and class differences in a highly industrial setting. Co-op leadership is most effective when it follows this consensual style, and least effective when it departs from it, as shown in the Ulgor strike of 1974 (see pp. 149-150).

The Urban and Industrial Environment

The Basque cooperative tradition, however, is not merely a case of surviving preindustrial practices. The growth of Basque capitalism, the rise of industrial towns and cities, and the development of such class-based responses to industrialization as unions and worker cooperatives were essential parts of the context in which cooperativism developed.

Life in Mondragon today is decidedly gregarious. After work, it is usual for people to socialize in bars and clubs, drinking small glasses of beer and eating *tapas* (appetizers; dinner is served late). There is strong community feeling: an assembly worker will sit and chat with the general manager, for there are no *señores* (bosses) here, the cooperators say. On weekends people walk from bar to bar, spending a few minutes chatting, eating and drinking lightly in each. A basic concept within this milieu is the notion, particularly for the young, of the *cuadrilla* (band or gang) of friends, which to a degree subordinates individual interest to group consensus.[8]

One reflection of this style of friendship is the existence of many small private eating clubs throughout the Basque country.

> Each society owns or rents a meeting place, which consists primarily of kitchen and dining room. Here the members eat and drink together at regular intervals. Beyond that, each member has a key and is free to come in at any time and eat and drink anything in the house.[9]

This contemporary urban scene exists over a substratum of traditional Basque rural values. One significant effect of this convivial atmosphere is the high degree of common knowledge shared by the people of Mondragon: there is sophisticated awareness of the dynamics and intricacies of Basque politics, of the government of Spain, and of the dynamics of cooperative functioning. Conversations on such matters are common and reasonably open to an outsider.

In comparison to the United States, where mobility and community disintegration are much more advanced, people in the Basque country forget much less of the past. Earlier Basque cooperative efforts (before the civil war) have had some impact on the Mondragon experience. The most noteworthy effort was in the town of Eibar, eleven miles north of Mondragon on the Deva River. Inspired by Toribio Echeverria, a local self-educated socialist, workers in Eibar converted a failing firearms factory into a cooperative that manufactured Singer sewing machines (without a license) for the Spanish market. At the outbreak of the war in 1936, Alfa had 201 workers and was producing twelve thousand sewing machines annually. (Eibar was the commercial center for the small village of Marquina, home of José María Arizmendiarrieta.)[10]

It is hard to judge whether the success of Alfa had any direct influence upon the origins and development of Mondragon. Toribio Echeverria, in exile from Franco in Caracas, had at least some clandestine correspondence with Arizmendiarrieta after the co-ops were established. In May 1967, Echeverria wrote:

> I am following with real interest the work you are carrying out in that locality [Mondragon], which has radiated so profitably throughout that region where industry flowers. I believe it is the best thing that has been done in suffering Spain in these 25 years.

And, some months later:

> I have received your magnificent book on the cooperative experiment in Mondragon in the Leniz Valley. . . . I believe your excellent work represents a true social revolution, having purged this word of its bloody reputation given it by certain literature and limiting it to its substantive meaning.[11]

While there is much in Basque history and circumstances that encouraged the Mondragon experiment, nothing made it particularly easy or predetermined, nor did the cooperative system spring full blown from the mind of Echeverria or Arizmendiarrieta. The Basques think a great deal about what they do and what it will mean. The physical and political constraints that have shaped the region's history have not left a people given easily to trivialities, and there is a characteristic thoughtful, almost stoic, reserve. Public displays of emotion are rare. Young Basques, even those dressed in punk styles, dance with a certain control. Such thoughtfulness emerges from a conservative culture, but in practice this conservatism often encourages strong and principled actions—not so much to preserve the status quo, but as a way to reclaim Basque culture, identity, and independence from the influence of the Spanish state. Mondragon cooperativism is an example of thoughtful and inspired collective risk taking.

Mondragon Cooperative Forms

The basic strength of the Mondragon cooperative system lies in the essentially consensus-seeking and cooperative spirit that informs the cooperators' behavior. True, the cooperators have created a number of unique structures and procedures crucial to the success of the system, but that success should be understood through the underlying relationships that encourage extensive dialogue crucial to a consensus seeking process.

The formal basis for co-op decisions is clear: most Mondragon institutions are based on one member, one vote, with either a simple or a two-thirds majority of the members required. But in practice, decision making tends toward discussion and the generation of consensus, not toward counting votes. If, after full discussion, the group is still clearly divided, the tendency is not to force the resolution of significant issues. Instead, a proposal will be dropped, changed, or set aside for future consideration and modifications that will bring the group together.

An example of this process in action came at the first meeting of the Mondragon Cooperative Congress in 1987. The 350 elected representatives approved, after discussion and some modification, detailed proposals prepared by working groups that dealt with a statement of the ten basic cooperative principles, rules governing the treatment of social capital, and regulations for FISO (the Intercooperative Solidarity Fund).

However, a proposal to increase the maximum wage differential between the lowest- and highest-paid cooperators from 4.5:1 to 6:1 resulted in substantial disagreement. Some argued that higher salaries were needed to attract key managers and technical personnel; others questioned whether the increase might not undermine the basic cooperative principle of solidarity. Those in favor responded that the change met a practical need and would no more upset the system than had an earlier increase from 3:1 to 4.5:1—"[the change is] not a panacea, but will be able to help with the recurring problem of high technology staff and managers." CLP general manager José María Ormaechea projected that the growing co-ops would need to hire 871 new highly trained managers and technical specialists over the next five years. The increase, in any case, is voluntary and up to each co-op.

Those opposing the increase made strong practical objections. "There are not a small number of examples of businesses that have failed with managers that are well paid; we can infer that there is no direct relationship between business efficiency and pay differentials." They also argued from principle, warning that increasing the pay differentials would create attitudes similar to those found in capitalist businesses and undermine the spirit of the cooperators.[12] After debate, the 6:1 differential was approved by a small majority. But then, the congress decided to defer action on the increase until detailed rules as to its application could be drafted and approved. Thus the cooperative solution was to respect both the concerns of the majority and of those who felt new pay scales might undermine co-op solidarity. The cooperators understand that it is central to the vitality of their system to respect differences and to continue to pursue what the Quakers call "a loving struggle to agreement."

Cooperation: The Basis of the Mondragon System 73

This was a contentious issue; such increases have always been highly controversial. When the maximum differential was raised from 3:1 to 4.5:1, the practice apparently was to continue to rank jobs on the 3:1 scale, with the option of adding another 50 percent (increasing 3 to 4.5) for jobs that required particularly long hours, travel, or special skills.[13]

Consensus in a political or business group is strongly conditioned by a need to make decisions in the short term. Quaker consensus arises from religious practice, and a change in doctrine may take decades. The cooperators must move in a timely way, while respecting the intertwined sinews of principle that animate the process of choice and community building: openness, shared information, and democratic rule; the independence of individual cooperators, cooperatives, and cooperative groups; and the solidarity of the group as a whole.

Thus, the pursuit of equilibrio is not a leisurely process for Mondragon. It involves determined action, dialogue, openness, and willingness to change—all within the bounds of explicit cooperative principles. When the consensus-seeking process is used well, it strengthens the decisions and the group's ongoing cohesion. The cooperators deal in values, not simply pesetas or legislative horse-trading.

"Consensus" does not imply that everyone agrees, or that there is no hierarchical organization or division of responsibility. Rather, in operation it means that after thorough discussion people will agree to support the group's decision. Consensus rests upon the belief that each person possesses some part of the truth, that each person's concerns will be heard and considered, and that a proposal can be modified. In this way, hard decisions can be made, and the bonds of community can be maintained and strengthened.

Consensus and Discipline

The consensus-seeking process is accompanied by a commitment to strict discipline and clear delegation of authority. The co-ops are not collectives, in which everyone becomes involved in every decision or all roles are routinely rotated. Co-op members have clear job titles and well defined formal responsibilities; management is "free to manage"—that is, to implement the plan agreed to by the cooperators. But co-op discipline is not the familiar assertion of power by management over the workers. Rather, all members share the responsibility to fulfill cooperative agreements and policies.

Trust within the co-ops rests upon the cooperators' common commitment, their past agreements, and the democratic process. All this discourages the exercise of arbitrary power and encourages dialogue. The framework of agreement is one in which the cooperators practice self-management. This entails more than just following orders. It means responsibility and self-discipline, a commitment to the reciprocal rights and obligations of other cooperators.

Cooperators are willing to change managers who cannot effectively fulfill co-op plans.

> On the cooperatives we have no pity. When a manager is not performing well the cooperateurs soon get rid of him. Cooperateurs believe that management must resolve problems and if they don't, they're changed. In a year often 12 cases occur when managers are dismissed. Managers are aware that they must succeed in order to maintain their jobs. Managers have often to justify their policies before the Direction Council and the collective.[14] Co-op managers, however, do not live in terror of losing their jobs. It is not a tragedy for a manager to fail; those who are replaced are reintegrated into the co-ops with another assignment.

Since the maximum-pay rule means that skilled managers receive only a fraction of what they might be offered in traditional firms, most come from within the co-ops or are young graduates attracted by their reputation. Few co-op managers choose to leave—a straightforward reflection of the freedom and community of the cooperatives in operation.

The clear codification (and application) of basic organizational and disciplinary requirements reflects the seriousness with which the cooperators approach their work—and an underlying agreement with Arizmendiarrieta that clear law, justly applied, is a protection for the poor and not merely an injunction to obey the rich. For example, the 1986 version of the *Estatutos Sociales*, or Social Statutes, put out by Co-op Group Ularco (now Fagor), an extremely clear and well-designed text, provides a graphic summary of all aspects of governance, control, discipline, and financial decisions affecting cooperators for the co-ops of the group.

The co-ops have established a workaday disciplinary code that includes three levels of offenses—"light," "serious," and "grave"—for various infractions involving punctuality, absence without notification, violation of co-op rules, and the like. Punishment ranges from small monetary penalties to suspension; expulsion, the ultimate (and extremely rare) penalty, can be imposed by the governing council with appeal to the general assembly. Grave offenses include disclosing co-op business secrets and systematically and publicly organizing against the co-op.

In a study comparing Mondragon cooperators with workers in similar neighboring capitalist enterprises, Bradley and Gelb report that nonmembers viewed co-op discipline as much stricter than in their own firms; the owner-workers considered co-op discipline to be about the same. Apparently, what some take to be discipline the cooperators see as self-management.

The Structure of Individual Cooperatives

Mondragon cooperators have created a number of structures that reflect the varied connections and relationships among themselves and their co-ops, as well as the co-ops' sizes and locations. Chart 3 is a general model of co-op organization. At first viewing the structure may be somewhat confusing; however, it reflects Mondragon's basic principles well. They include:

1. Grass roots empowerment and democracy. Ultimate power lies in the general assembly, which meets at least yearly (often twice yearly, in January and June). Each co-op member has one vote in the assembly.
2. Effective management. The elected governing council is responsible for the economic future of the co-op and can hire and replace management; the management council functions to provide effective working leadership and communication.
3. A voice for, and an open ear to, the concerns of co-op members. The social council plays a major role in matters of worker health and safety and in the setting of salary policies.
4. A healthy level of skepticism. The watchdog council monitors co-op operation and reports to the general assembly.
5. The sharing of information and power. Separating the roles of the elected governing council from the informal management council, the input of the social council, and the oversight of the watchdog council encourages broad dissemination of knowledge and discussion, and avoids a concentration of knowledge and power in any one body.

Chart 3. Mondragon Cooperative Organization

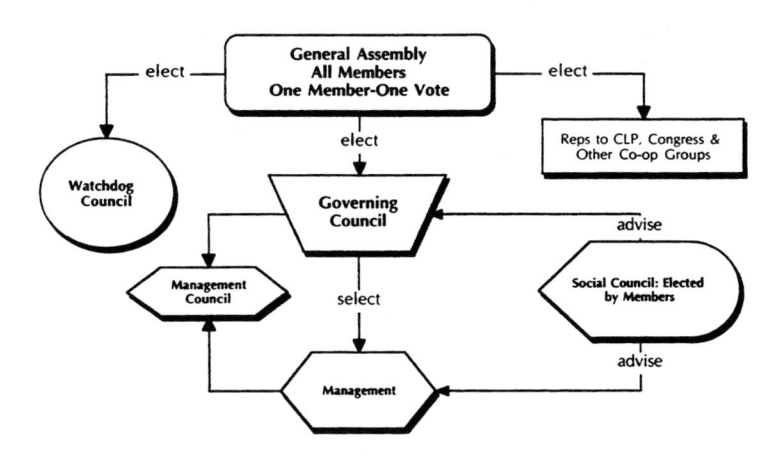

General Assembly

The general assembly has authority over all aspects of co-op management. The general assembly:

1. Reviews the conduct of co-op management
2. Distributes co-op earnings or losses
3. Approves co-op obligations
4. Decides co-op entry fees
5. Approves annual management plan
6. Decides issues of long-term development and issues affecting the Mondragon group
7. Elects and supervises governing council
8. Holds final authority on member admission and withdrawal, expulsion and readmission
9. Approves joining or withdrawing from second-degree co-ops (2/3 vote)
10. Decides co-op mergers, acquisitions, and dissolutions (2/3 vote)

The governing council sets the agenda for general assembly meetings; additional items can be added by the social council or by petition endorsed by 10 percent of the co-op members. Special or additional meetings may be called by 20 percent of the members. Decisions of the general assembly must be made with regard to Basque cooperative law and Spanish statutes.

Governing Council

The governing council is responsible for co-op governance and management following the instructions of the general assembly. It includes the president, vice-president, and secretary of the general assembly, and as many as nine others elected from the members of the general assembly. Council members serve four-year terms; half are chosen every two years. They receive no additional pay, and may be reelected. Auditors cannot serve on the governing council, which, under the authority of the general assembly, performs the following functions:

1. Appoints, supervises and removes managers and directors
2. Approves admission and removal of members
3. Determines job classifications
4. Presents annual reports and accounts
5. Proposes distribution of profits or losses to general assembly
6. Approves ongoing financial operations and obligations
7. Presents management plans to the general assembly

The governing council meets at least once a month, and reaches decisions by majority vote. Co-op managers may be present but have no vote.

Social Council

The social council is an elected advisory body chosen by co-op members on the basis of their work group or assignment. Ten or more members, depending on co-op size, elect a member of the social council, which is usually limited to no more than fifty members. The social council grew more important after the 1974 Ulgor strike (see p. 150). The social council:

1. Provides input on a broad range of personnel matters, including establishment of salary grades and amounts of salary advances
2. Deals with health and safety issues in the work place
3. Administers co-op social funds
4. Makes decisions delegated by the governing council

Members are elected for two- or three-year terms in staggered elections, and may be reelected. Meetings between individual representatives and members of their group are held periodically; the social council itself must meet at least once every three months. (Reports from individual co-ops show considerable variations in the terms of social council members, size of the council, and meeting frequency.)

The social council acts as the formal members' voice to the co-op's decision makers. This suggests that the social council operates as a kind of union or incipient union, particularly since there are no formal labor unions in the Mondragon cooperatives (it has also been suggested that the council is a denatured company union). However, its actual role is more ambiguous.

The social council plays an important part in the consensus-seeking process and the pursuit of equilibrio. It helps facilitate clear and quick feedback between owner-workers as a group and co-op decision makers. Effective communication obviously depends upon the nature of the cooperative milieu, of which the social council is a part, and on the distance between decision makers and owner-workers, rather than upon any organizational scheme. But communication alone is not enough for the healthy functioning of cooperative community: communication must rest upon a foundation of democratic control and the real practice of the basic cooperative principles.

To the extent that the cooperatives fulfill these principles, which include abolishing wage labor, creating internal and external solidarity, and recognizing the instrumental nature of capital, they command our attention as functioning cooperative communities. To the extent that they do not, their members will be moved to organize in order to assert their rights and affirm their dignity facing the power of management.

The social council thus exists in a state of dynamic tension between its intended role of facilitating members' communication and its sub-rosa existence as a union functioning to forcefully advance (or as a company union, to defuse) the demands of co-op members as workers. The social council is not a Mondragon union, but the nature of its work makes it a clear locus for members who seek to defend themselves if cooperative community breaks down. This is not to suggest that unions can play only a defensive role, or that the presence of a union indicates problems; quite the contrary, organized labor can be a vital part in the process of cooperative social transformation. It is very possible that at Mondragon or in Mondragon-inspired systems the work of a union could encompass that of the social council.

Unions and Mondragon

Mondragon was founded by working people acting in solidarity with other working people. It did not, however, grow out of the Basque labor movement. Under Franco, the Spanish government showed a particular antipathy toward Basque independence and union activity. It was only in 1956 (about the same time that the industrial co-ops were founded) that Basque unions were able to organize workers without the assistance and partial protection of the Basque Nationalist Party (PNV) and the Basque regional government.[15]

The co-ops operated independently from the renascent Basque union movement. During the ascendancy of Franco's corporatist state (1945–1950), Arizmendiarrieta wrote that "unions have the right to be autonomous" and that the autonomy of unions was "at least as significant as the autonomy of the companies."[16] This reflects his view that organizations of working people—unions and cooperatives—were agents of change and transformation, but not necessarily of revolution and his recognition, in principle, of the rights of business. (See Chapter 6.)

Arizmendiarrieta had little patience with ideas that divided working people. "The agricultural sector, industrial sector, service sector are members of one community, of the same economic process." Workers and the farmers unite in "mutual solidarity in order to strengthen the common fight for their interests."[17]

Mondragon cooperatives have tended to follow paths basically parallel to, but separate from, those of the Basque union movement. The unions' experience in capitalist firms did not provide clear definitions for those who participated in building the cooperative community, so cooperators maintained a respectful distance from them. In general, unions serve as a collective advocate for workers in relationship with management, whether it is the United Auto Workers' capitalist management in the United States and Canada, or Solidarity's bureaucratic socialist management in Poland. This role reflects the basic class and power differences unions are confronted with: in either the capitalist or the socialist system, their position is inherently adversarial, although unions' operating relationships with management may be cordial as well as acrimonious.

"Cooperation" is attractive to managerial elites who see that it can be used to weaken the power of unions, but union-busting is completely incompatible with cooperative community, and organized labor can play an important role in the processes of cooperative entrepreneurship and community building. It could be argued that unions are unnecessary within Mondragon or similar systems; since all members are also owners and elect the governing council, there is democratic control and accountability, and therefore no need for a countervailing worker organization. (A similar logic underlies arguments against free trade unions in socialist countries: since the people own and manage everything, how can the people want to organize against themselves?)

But this viewpoint is inadequate and simplistic. In reality, there are three reasons for union involvement in cooperative development:

1. Unions can be involved in founding and organizing new worker cooperatives. For circumstantial reasons this did not happen at Mondragon, but it remains a promising possibillity, for instance, in Massachusetts, where union workers plan to form their own contracting firms to build moderate-cost housing.
2. Unions can convert existing capitalist or socialist businesses to cooperatives. In Mondragon, existing capitalist firms have been converted for financial gain or to avert (the owner's) business failure, or by workers who want to save their jobs. In these cases, the firm's business difficulties must be overcome, and the new cooperators must be able to practice effective self-management and work harmoniously together. A few successful conversions have taken place.

    Typically, conversions of failing firms in the United States (e.g., Weirton Steel, Seymour Wire and Cable, Hyatt Industries) involve the unionized workers' hiring management personnel to supervise new employees. Such a situation places a heavy burden upon the new cooperative; waving the magic wand of cooperation does not resolve either the business problems of the firm or the relationships between management and labor.
3. Unions can organize existing worker co-ops. This may take the form of establishing solidarity with nonunionized workers and include sharing benefits and resources, such as union medical facilities and pension plans. Co-op members may also need a more formalized organization if they are to relate to, and, if necessary, negotiate with, co-op management. (This has not occurred at Mondragon.)

Mondragon Social Councils and Work Teams

The idea of production teams paced and managed by workers themselves is no doubt worthwhile, but when teams are controlled and manipulated by management there is a tendency to use "cooperation" to abolish hard-won worker rights on the shop floor, and to undermine the unions. An emerging paradigm behind "teamwork" is in fact management-by-stress, in which work teams must push and discipline themselves to meet increased production schedules.

The Mondragon social councils have had little hand in developing new work teams or forms for the organization of work. Programs involving "quality of work life" and "employee involvement" as the means to increase productivity (i.e., profits) are not a major part of the Mondragon system, where self-management provides both motivation and empowerment.

In fact, the new "team" job flexibility in the United States tends to mean the further deskilling of workers and the introduction of a new wave of Taylorist rationalization that minutely divides, and tightly structures, work that engineers the work of people as if they were machines. A prime goal is to have the workers, in effect, plan their own misery, with any labor-saving efficiency used to abolish jobs and increase profits. For example, in one General Motors plant, a 48-second soldering job is broken down to twenty-four steps, each with detailed instructions for hand positions.[18]

Of Mondragon, the Whytes remark, "We have been surprised by how little the social councils have been involved in the redesign of work, considering that some leaders and members of local unions have been actively involved in this area in the United States." Clearly, the social council plays a role quite different in intent and purpose from the quality circle.[19]

Conflict and Co-op Size

A Mondragon cooperative is not a utopia, and it is simply a fantasy to believe that there is no conflict or disagreement between membership and management in a cooperative community, or that the social council can rectify all problems.

The cooperators have discovered that even given the best of intentions and the most dedicated applications of cooperative principles, the consensus-seeking process can only function properly if the size of the co-ops is kept on a human scale. By this is meant that there are few levels of bureaucracy intervening between co-op members and decision makers, decision makers are well known and accessible, and the cooperators can usually deal with each other as individuals and human beings. This is the efficiency secret behind the Mondragon organizational success.

Thus, at Mondragon, co-ops are limited if at all possible to no more than 500 members. Larger co-ops usually have been able to spin off divisions or divide as they grow. For example, a 300-member co-op with a twelve-member governing council and three top managers would have a 20:1 ratio between key decision makers and members. Ulgor, at its height, had 3,500 members, a ratio of 233:1—and it was at Ulgor that serious problems developed between membership and management.

As noted above, individual cooperatives maintain their essential independence but are not isolated entities; most also belong to cooperative groups based on geographical location or type of activity. The groups vary in many ways. In Fagor, with its very strong orientation toward export and its need to deal with competition from transnational corporations in foreign and domestic markets, there exists a growing tendency toward a greater integration of operations and planning.

The Watchdog Council

The watchdog council is elected by the general assembly to monitor co-op operations and accounts, and ensure that all co-op business is conducted in an open, honest manner, and is accessible to the review of members. Typically, three members are elected to four-year terms, but there may be five or seven in the larger co-ops. The watchdog council is a straightforward expression of the collective responsibility of the membership and the general assembly for the operations of the co-op. The council is independent of management.

The watchdog council:

1. Reviews all co-op accounts, operations of the governing and management councils, and examines all materials submitted for approval of the general assembly
2. Requests assistance when needed from the staff of the Caja Laboral Popular and other experts
3. Calls for special meetings of the general assembly to consider problems

As part of its support work, the Empresarial Division of the CLP regularly receives detailed, current computer information on co-op operations. In this way, the CLP helps the watchdog council gather data, but at the same time it markedly increases the amount of information generated, thus complicating the council's task. (In the CLP itself, the watchdog council plays a very detailed and formal auditing role.)

The Management Council

The management council's focus is the co-op's ongoing performance and operations. It is an advisory body whose members are drawn from the governing council and from senior co-op managers. Although the composition and precise role of the management council vary, it always includes the president of the governing council and the co-op manager. The management council provides a dynamic and flexible forum in which to discuss co-op decisions and make appropriate recommendations to the governing council, the co-op manager, and the general assembly. In a sense it represents a kind of co-op cabinet, without formal power but with considerable influence and importance. It is clearly designed to encourage detailed and open consideration of problems, challenges, and opportunities facing the co-op.

The Broader Cooperative Framework

Each Mondragon co-op is nested in a broad framework of supporting and interacting cooperative structures and organizations. These follow the basic organizational principles and design of the individual cooperatives, modified as appropriate. All of them attempt to follow the spirit that informs the conduct of cooperation in action; the cooperative social system rests upon the generalized and reciprocal practice of freedom and responsibility that is the reality of self-management.

The Mondragon system certainly is not a monolithic collection of rigid and fixed entities, nor does its retinue of cooperative structures follow a fixed blueprint. It would not be possible to take Mondragon at any given point in time and transfer it whole to a new setting, like casually constructing a generic shopping center pulled from a plan book. Mondragon is constantly changing as the world changes and as its cooperators learn, so the forms that have grown upon the foundation of the individual cooperatives have evolved into an elaborate and complex community system. The success of this system, however, rests not upon organizational acumen or technical fixes—although there are plenty of them at Mondragon—but upon the reality of cooperative principles in action. These principles, these values, are the basis for an ethics that helps guide and inform the behavior of the cooperators and of their system.

A Question of Value

The Mondragon cooperative structures reflect the moral, political, and organizational insights of Arizmendiarrieta and the Mondragon cooperators. In practice, they work to reconcile what often seem to be irreconcilable desires for freedom and community. The forms and structures are impressive, sometimes intimidating, but our task need not be to build another Mondragon. The first lesson, the point of departure for our own cooperative journey, is simpler.

The Mondragon discovery is the discovery of new choices. Its cooperators have learned to see the world with new eyes and to take action, and in those acts new worlds are built. This is the plain drama of social transformation, rising from below as a product of tension, dissonance, aspiration, and hope within the social landscape.

Although we are in the process of making the fateful choices that will lead either to calamity or renaissance, the subject of value somehow only intrudes episodically into our consciousness. There are small flashes of dread when we hear the evening news, drink our perhaps tainted water, eat our additive-filled food; there are also sparks of joy at the selfless love of children, the seamless mystery of the wild, tangled woods, and the transforming affirmation of our choices as builders, lovers, peacemakers. Our task is much closer to home than the construction of new world systems. The imperative, individually and collectively, is to act and to act cooperatively and nonviolently.

Cooperation is the common discovery of new choices in working toward freedom and community. Ultimately, we are dealing with people, not objects; with value. Value is a rather uncomfortable term for modernists: it raises the spectre of prescriptive morality and worse, sentimentality, for those of us dizzy with the wonders of science. We have little difficulty accepting the idea of technical wisdom as social prime mover, and somehow find it easier to place our faith in vague beliefs rooted in Marx's or Milton Freidman's economic determinism than in people. Our economicism, our scientism, our industrialism are, after all, supported by equations.

Our moral struggles are relegated to the private realm, with public life and community ceded to the invisible operations of the market, the party, the computer, the omnipresent bureaucracy. This abnegation of personal agency, and therefore of responsibility, is not just a matter of deferring to higher, presumably wiser, authority. As Jacques Ellul writes, "The rules obeyed by a technical organization are no longer rules of justice and injustice. They are 'laws' in a purely technical sense."[20]

But by rejecting the efficacy of value and ethics, we have rejected freedom. We can appreciate the facts—the equations—that guide nuclear missiles and create extermination camps, but not the facts—the ethics—that embody the practice of freedom and community and the creation of unity in diversity.

The modern utopia is no longer that of the party, the transnational corporation, or the shopping center, but of the smart machine, the Skinner box, and the robocop: the ecclesiastical transcendence of the information age. Daniel Berrigan writes of the 1980s, "Perhaps no one was in charge: perhaps the machinery, the atoms, the nukes, the computers, had themselves taken control, frictionless, mad malevolent, whirring along on their own momentum. . . . Thus the president had available a genie, a mechanical guru, a perfect uncontrollable machine, greased with self-interest, violence, blindness. It did his work and called the work his own."[21]

Dazed by modernity, we come at our idealism from the back side, as given to us by the "laws" of technique; how strange and how sad this is. Cooperation represents a divergent choice using humane values as a guide to practice, and challenges us to reclaim faith in ourselves and in each other. The practice of freedom and community represents an affirmation from below, from the grass roots, of humanity, and a challenge to power.

The practice of the Mondragon cooperatives refers largely to the practice of freedom and the building of community: freedom expressed formally, as democratic control, voluntary association; and the support of humane community on all levels.

Arizmendiarrieta encountered enough of the desolation and sadness of war and of Franco's state to search not simply for a technique and a means to accumulate power, but for a way to connect theory with practice, to join means with ends. That way, at bottom, is not an organizational chart or technique. It is participation in the adventure of freedom and community.

Even a bank, the Caja Laboral Popular, can be a key outcome of that adventure of discovery, as we shall see.

Notes

1. Bradley and Gelb 1985.
2. Slaughter 1988, p. 7.
3. Washington Post 1988, p. 9.
4. Brenan 1960, p. 95.
5. Jackobs 1979, p. 21.
6. Ibid., p. 39.
7. Quoted in Urbach 1987, pp. 291–92.
8. Jackobs 1979, pp. 40–41.
9. Gutiérrez-Johnson and Whyte 1977, p. 22.
10. Thomas and Logan 1982, pp. 17–18.
11. Letters dated Caracas, May 2 and October 2, 1967, cited in Thomas and Logan 1982, p. 39. Echeverria died in exile in Caracas in 1968.
12. See "El Congreso Cooperativo Fortalece el Sentido de Grupo," *Trabajo y Unión* no. 307 (October 1987), pp. 5–7.
13. This information from "Proyecto De Estatutos Sociales Cooperativos Grupo Ularco, 1986."
14. Interview with head of Empresarial Division (July 1979), reported in Bradley and Gelb 1983, p. 62.
15. Clark 1979, p. 247.
16. Azurmendi 1984, p. 122.
17. Ibid., p. 288.
18. Parker and Slaughter 1988.
19. Whyte and Whyte 1988, pp. 215–16.
20. Ellul 1964, p. 133.
21. Berrigan 1987, pp. 331–32.

4
Caja Laboral Popular: The Creation and Use of Social Capital

> Caja Laboral Popular has a vocation characterized by promoting community.
> —Alfonso Gorroñogoitia

If Mondragon has succeeded in beginning to tame and limit the abuses of the market, the cage within which the beast has been controlled is the Caja Laboral Popular, the Working People's Bank (in Euskara, Lankide Aurrezkia). This is no mean feat. But to make this assertion is not to suggest that Mondragon offers simply a modest reform, motivated by high-minded and eleemosynary impulses of the sort that gave rise to the paternalism of welfare capitalism in the United States in the 1920s and that largely vanished with the Great Depression. Nor is the bank's mission to impose reform and cooperation from above so as to improve efficiency and productivity. The Caja Laboral Popular is at the heart of the economic life of the Mondragon cooperatives, but it is an expression of the Mondragon system, not its master.

Overview

With the CLP, the cooperators have been able to create enduring community, or social, capital based upon voluntary association in a market economy. Its performance as an enterprise founded by owner-workers is extraordinary: with $2.9 billion in total assets at the beginning of 1988, CLP is the thirteenth-largest savings bank in Spain.[1] It has a staff of more than twelve hundred, and 180 branch offices; 178 in the Basque country, as well as a branch in Madrid and another in Barcelona. Its operations are divided between the Banking Division, which includes basic financial and banking operations, and the Empresarial Division (discussed in detail in Chapter 6), which is responsible for promotion and support of the cooperatives of the Mondragon system.

Through the CLP, the cooperators have entered the domain of commercial and investment banking. And they have done so in a manner that refutes the conventional wisdom of what is economically feasible and prudent. The CLP has taken a giant step toward demythologizing the primacy of banks and private capital in a market economy. It is a cooperative financial entity whose resources are based upon the labor and savings of the co-ops, the cooperators and community members; its success assures the Mondragon cooperatives and their communities that they cannot be starved by a capital strike, destroyed by disinvestment, or constrained by a redlining-type practice.

In operation, the CLP embodies the basic Mondragon cooperative principles, asserting that working people have sovereignty over their lives and jobs and that capital is accumulated labor. In short, the CLP effectively places the power of finance in the service of cooperative values and of freedom and community. The Caja Laboral Popular completes the circle of power begun by the work of the industrial cooperatives. Profits (surpluses) created by the co-ops become part of the collective capital to be reinvested for the benefit of the cooperators and the community. In practice, this means that the CLP helps found and promote new co-ops and works to keep them economically viable.

Discussing community capital and banks is all well and good, but the mention of billions of dollars or financial maneuverings tends to make our eyes glaze over. For most of us, paying next month's bills is challenge enough; the idea of banks calls up only mystery and foreboding. But the grave demeanor of the bankers, the majesty of the marble halls, and the enormous complexity of the balance sheet conceal a simple fact: banks grow wealthy essentially because they are able to create "new money" from the funds that strangers have deposited. This is done by loaning out those funds, which are, in turn, deposited, and can be loaned out again, and so on. Banks continue to exist on the basis of the shared illusion that deposits are backed by real money reposing in an impressive chrome steel vault. As John Kenneth Galbraith points out, "The process by which banks create money is so simple that the mind is repelled. When something so important is involved, a deeper mystery seems only decent."[2] With the Caja Laboral Popular, the cooperators have transcended the normal limits on the participation of working people in the operations of this magic money machine.

Accomplishments of the CLP

The Caja Laboral Popular is first of all a success as a bank— the bottom line is impeccable—but it has produced much more than money. Over thirty years, the CLP has decisively demonstrated its ability as a unique cooperative institution to:

1. Meet the financial needs of its member cooperatives
2. Attract a consistently growing number of depositors and financial assets
3. Possess financial resources and knowledge to provide the Mondragon cooperatives with special financial assistance and expert advice on almost all aspects of co-op operations, from birth to mature restructuring
4. Provide financial and social services to the cooperators and their families (Social services are coordinated by Lagun-Aro, first a division of the CLP and now an independent superstructure cooperative whose financial resources are in the CLP.)
5. Maintain its nature as a cooperative with a fundamental commitment to the ongoing development and health of the Mondragon system as a social and as a business entity

The Banking Division

Headquarters of the Caja Laboral Popular is a spectacular modern building dug into a hillside, part of the complex of cooperative institutions on the edge of the town of Mondragon. The cooperators built the Eskola Politeknikoa and Lagun-Aro social insurance headquarters here, as well as the small foreign-language-teaching co-op CIM; then, moving up the hillside, come the Ikerlan research co-op, the CLP headquarters, the computer-data-processing building, and the new Empresarial Division building.

Organizationally, the CLP is a hybrid, as its members are both other Mondragon co-ops and its own owner-workers. This has enormous significance for the dynamics of CLP operations. More than 90 percent of the CLP owner-workers are in the Banking Division, which consists of the following units:

1. Risk Department: administers, studies, and backs banking operations and policies; actively involved with financing of and investment in the associated cooperatives
2. Planning Department: assists all departments in planning and policy development
3. Marketing Department: helps implement savings and investment decisions and does public-relations work
4. Foreign Department: Is concerned with import-export transactions, which are a major part of the business of the associated cooperatives
5. Internal Auditing: the watchdog council, consists of three special auditors who monitor all operations

The Banking Division has a regional manager and headquarters for each of the four Spanish Basque provinces. These offices stay in touch with local savers, soliciting their input and concern.[3]

Financial Resources and Performance

There has been a spectacular growth in the CLP's financial resources from approximately $7.25 million in 1965 to $1.771 billion in 1986 (see Table 4-1).

Table 4-1. Growth of CLP Net Financial Resources*

Year	Million Pesetas	Dollars
1965	435	7.25 million (at 60Ptas/$)
1970	3,745	
1975	17,001	
1979	46,110	
1986	203,652	1.771 billion (at 115Ptas/$)

*Net financial resources are total balance-sheet assets, minus the value of such fixed assets as buildings and property; they do not include "below the line" special memorandum accounts.

The enormous average annual rate of growth in CLP assets of 28.5 percent from 1970, when the bank was already well established, to 1986 is exaggerated by inflation. However, when adjusted to constant 1985 pesetas, the real rate of growth in those years still amounts to an annual increase of 12 percent.[4]

Analyzing the balance sheet and financial performance of the Caja Laboral Popular, which operates under the regulations and accounting conventions of Spanish and Basque law, is a daunting task. Fortunately, a thorough anaylsis of the bank's performance through 1979, conducted with the CLP's cooperation by Henk Thomas and Chris Logan, provides a point of departure for some observations on the present state of the CLP.[5]

Growth of Financial Assets

The resources of the CLP have continued to expand rapidly in the 1980s, despite the severe economic downturn affecting the Spanish and the Basque economies. Chart 4-2 indicates that CLP net financial resources grew at a faster pace than total co-op sales. In 1979 co-op sales were equal to 124% of CLP resources; by the end of 1986, although co-op sales had increased 279% (an annual rate of 16%), they were just 74% of total CLP resources—which had increased 440% (an annual rate of 24%). When inflation is taken into account, the average annual rate of increase for CLP resources for 1979 to 1986 is still estimated at 11% (just below the 12% average for 1970 to 1986) and at 4% for total co-op sales (compared to the average 6% real growth for the period).

The remarkable growth of the CLP, even during the prolonged Spanish economic downturn that ended in 1987, goes counter to traditional expectations that would have predicted contraction of CLP resources, and perhaps collapse. During this time, the associated cooperatives made increased demands on the CLP for investment and financial assistance. But the bank showed it was not the sort of marginal entity that could prosper only in good times. In fact, to judge by the behavior of its Basque depositors, the CLP inspired confidence with its prudent management and came to be seen as an institution whose investments were more likely to be in their interest and in the interest of the Basque country than those of other competing banks.

Expansion of the Scope of CLP Investments

The growth in CLP assets has transformed its relationship with the associated cooperatives. As late as 1982, Thomas and Logan, after noting that the increase in co-op assets had overcome early capital-shortage

Chart 4-2. CLP Resources and Total Mondragon Sales (In millions of dollars)*

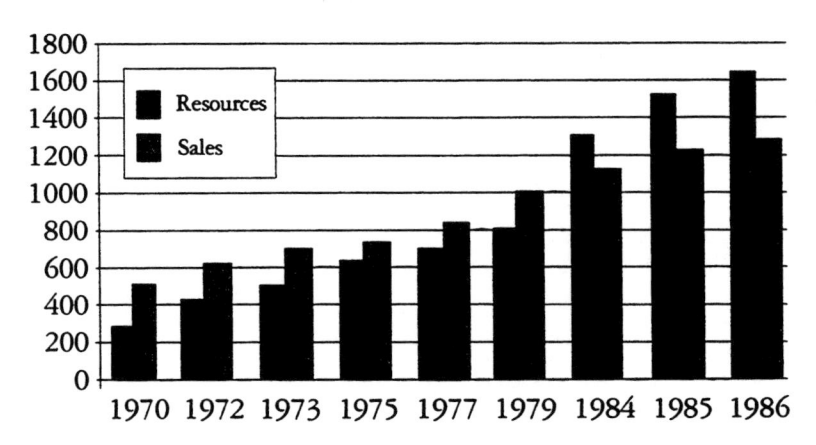

[Bar chart showing Resources and Sales for years 1970, 1972, 1973, 1975, 1977, 1979, 1984, 1985, 1986]

---

*To adjust for inflation and to provide a comparative sense of the value in dollars, actual co-op sales and CLP assets in pesetas were first adjusted for inflation to 1985 constant pesetas and then converted to dollars at the exchange rate of 115Ptas/$. The chart provides a basis for the comparison of the growth of CLP assets and coop sales. The dollar figures in the chart, since they are based upon a 1987 exchange rate, should not be used as a reliable measure of the actual dollar value.

Original peseta data from Thomas and Logan (1982) for 1970 to 1979 and from CLP annual reports for 1984 to 1986. Inflation adjustment was based upon data from United Nations (1985) for 1970 to 1982; from *Boletín de Estadística*, September–October 1985 and *Anuario Estadístico, 1984* for 1983 to 1984 and provided by Embassy of Spain; CLP annual report for 1985; 1986 was estimated based upon journalistic sources. CLP asset figures are net financial resources and do not include CLP property and fixed assets and certain special financial memoranda accounts.

problems, saw that "the objective is to obtain equilibrium between aggregate cooperative sales and CLP's financial resources."[6] Today, CLP resources have expanded to such an extent that the percentage of its funds invested in the associated cooperatives has been reduced.

Under the original regulations set by Spanish co-op law, the bank could only invest funds in, or make loans to, member cooperatives and depositors. As CLP resources grew, this made it difficult sometimes to find enough productive investments to allow the bank to maintain the 8 percent ratio between its own funds and total assets required, by law, to assure the bank's financial stability (see p. 92). Over time, these regulations were liberalized to allow loans to individual cooperators and to customer-members of the large Eroski consumer co-op and, more

Caja Laboral Popular: The Creation and Use of Social Capital   91

recently, to permit investments in nonco-op firms and in Basque government projects. In 1986 the CLP reported that investments in the co-ops equaled approximately 25% of resources.[7]

A comparison between the distribution of CLP assets in 1979, 1984, and 1986 (Table 4-3) reveals a considerable evolution. Total assets increased 71 percent from 1979 to 1986, adjusted for inflation. While the percentage of resources in middle- and long-term investments stayed about equal, the CLP's cash position has markedly increased, and the percentage of investment held in commercial bills discounted has dropped. This change suggests that some CLP assets are being invested very conservatively while some CLP co-op investments entail considerable risk. The strength of the cash position means that a large amount of secure funds is available to provide for a very broad range of needs for the associated cooperatives.

Table 4-3. Distribution of CLP's Assets (By Percentage)

	Cash	Bond	Discounted Bills	Medium- and Long-Term Credits	Fixed Assets	Miscellaneous Accounts
1979	12	20	28	32	8	—
1984	25	22	13	30	6	4
1986	32	15	12	34	5	2
1987	32	12	10	38	5	3

"Cash" includes demand deposits and other liquid assets to meet needs of depositors and co-ops.
"Bonds" are obligatory investments in state bonds and certain stocks.
"Discounted bills" are short-term commercial credits for co-ops and other firms.
"Medium- and long-term credits" are investments in the associated co-ops and other firms.
"Fixed assets" are offices and property of the bank.
Data are from Thomas and Logan (1982) for 1979 and from CLP annual reports for 1984–87.

Economic Performance

A basic measure of Caja Laboral Popular's financial fitness is its ability to generate surpluses sufficient to keep the bank's own resources (that is, those owned by the CLP and the owner-workers) equal to at least 8 percent of total financial resources. This ratio is significant, given the

Chart 4-4. CLP's Own Funds as a Percentage of Total Resources*

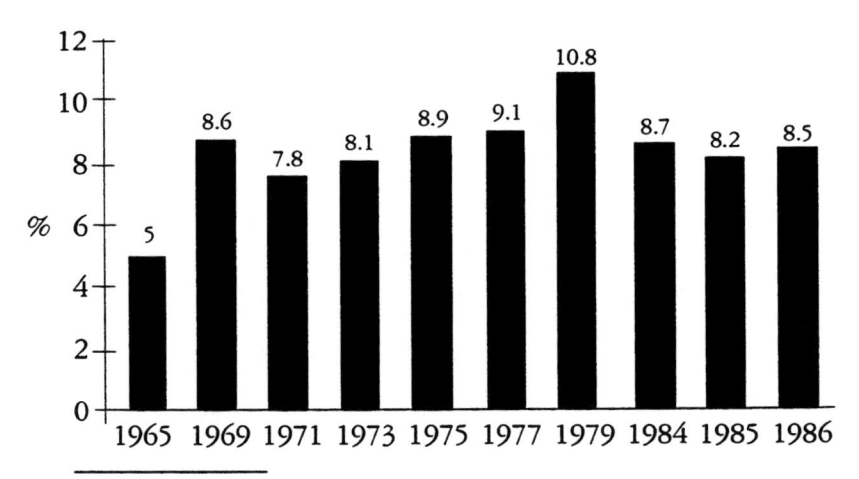

Year	%
1965	5
1969	8.6
1971	7.8
1973	8.1
1975	8.9
1977	9.1
1979	10.8
1984	8.7
1985	8.2
1986	8.5

*"Own funds" includes the CLP's collective reserves plus the capital accounts of the owner-workers.
"Total resources" includes all financial assets except CLP fixed assets in facilities, land, and equipment and special memoranda accounts and nominal deposits that are, in financial parlance, "below the line."
Data are from Thomas and Logan (1982) for 1965–1979 and from CLP annual reports for 1984–86.

arcana of Spanish bank finance, as an indication of the CLP's ability to meet its financial demands.[8]

Chart 4-4 indicates that CLP maintained the 8 percent ratio in the 1980s—evidence of the bank's continuing financial soundness, especially as it also continued the basic 10 percent social contribution of profits made by all Mondragon cooperatives.

Table 4-5 details the distribution of the $32.1 million Caja Laboral Popular surplus in 1986. It was a good year for the bank's owner-workers: they each received an average of about $4,300 in interest payments on internal capital accounts and new funds credited to their accounts from the surpluses. This payment is divided about equally between the obligatory interest payments and a 10 percent share of the net surplus voted by the cooperators. Ellerman reports that the CLP surpluses are not distributed on the basis of the economic fortunes of the bank itself, as in other co-ops, but on the average level of profits or losses of the associated cooperatives.[9]

This egalitarian measure not only emphasizes the solidarity of the bank with the cooperative group, but also motivates CLP staff to work in support of the associated cooperatives.

Table 4-5. Distribution of CLP's Surpluses, 1986

	Amount (In millions of dollars)	Percentage of Total
Gross Surplus	32.1	100.0
Required deductions		
Interest paid on members' internal capital accounts	(2.7)	(8.4)
Corporation tax	(3.3)	(10.3)
Net Surplus	26.1	100.0
Distribution		
Social fund contribution	2.6	10.0
Credited to individual capital accounts	2.6	10.0
CP reserve funds	17.0	65.0
Special reserves for losses (required by law for co-ops)	3.9	15.0

From CLP annual report, 1986; exchange rate of 115 Ptas/$.

However, the overwhelming proportion of the net surplus—80 percent—went into CLP common reserves, not individual capital accounts. This continues a trend: more and more, CLP's own resources are made up of retained earnings rather than internal capital accounts. This has advantages for the CLP and for the whole Mondragon group, as such funds cannot be withdrawn by cooperators who leave or retire, thus shielding the system from possible decapitalization problems. This trend toward the increasing proportion of CLP common reserves is shown in Chart 4-6.

Chart 4-6. Individual Capital Accounts as a Percentage of CLP's Own Funds

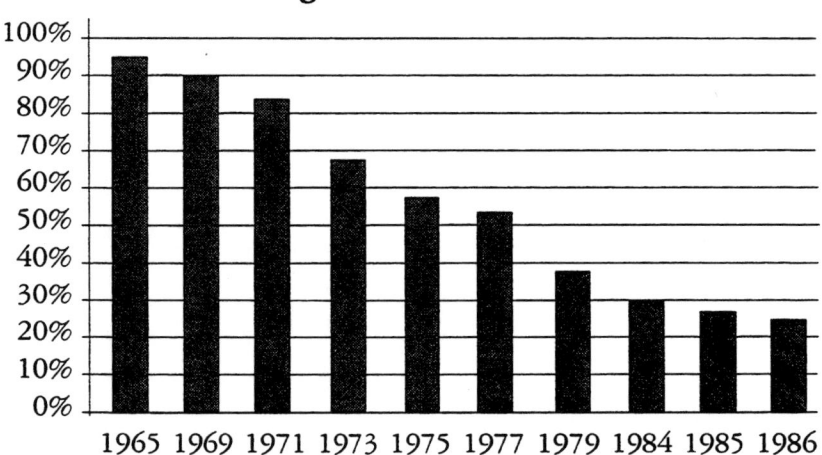

Year	Percentage
1965	~94%
1969	~90%
1971	~83%
1973	~67%
1975	~57%
1977	~53%
1979	~37%
1984	~30%
1985	~26%
1986	~24%

Data are from Thomas and Logan (1982) for 1965–1979 and from CLP annual reports for 1984–86.

CLP and the Associated Cooperatives

In short, the Caja Laboral Popular strengthened its resources and financial stability during a prolonged period of economic hard times in Spain and in the Basque country. The CLP has also had the requisite financial (and technical) resources to assist the associated cooperatives during the downturn and to help them face the increased competition from transnational corporations that has accompanied Spain's entry into the European Common Market.

The ability to supplement advice with loan funds at very favorable terms, while preserving the CLP's financial integrity, is crucial to the co-ops' success and stability under even severe economic pressure. In 1986, CLP planned $135 million in loans that carried reduced (or no) interest to provide special assistance to cooperatives. These included: for co-op startups and restructuring ("reconversion"), interest-free loans equal to 4 percent of credit resources, or $60 million; and, for co-ops in financial distress, reduced-rate loans at 8 percent that are equal to 5 percent of credit resources, or $75 million dollars.[10] (This support has been supplemented by financial assistance for job creation from the Basque government.) As the Spanish economic situation has improved (in 1987 Spain had real economic growth of 4 percent, the highest in the Common Market), the CLP's resources and expertise have provided an excellent basis to complete the restructuring of the Mondragon co-ops that is now under way and for the next round of Mondragon growth, aimed particularly at helping relieve the 20 percent Basque unemployment rate.

Governance of the CLP

We must understand the nature of the Caja Laboral Popular if we are to understand why and how the cooperators have avoided economic collapse or succumbing to the lure of maximizing profit and why they instead continue to direct their experiment along the paths of basic cooperative principles. This success is not a secret of the organizational chart, although there is clearly an organization, or the triumph of technique, although there are definite techniques (tools) employed.

The dynamics of the CLP as a superstructure cooperative is a classic Mondragon formulation. The input of owner-workers helps deal with the problem raised by economists who object that a bank run by its customers would soon face irreconcilable conflicts between its fiscal survival and the needs of the firms to which it had loaned money.

But the concept of a decision-making membership was just the beginning. Out of a mixture of economic and legal necessity, shrewdness, serendipity, and experience, the cooperators have created a balance of the needs and interests of the owner-members, the Caja Laboral Popular itself, individual co-op members, the whole co-op system, and the broader community.

As with other Mondragon institutions, the bank is not a bureaucratic hierarchy. Nor can its functioning be described as a system of checks and balances: Mondragon's democratic pursuit of equilibrio stands in sharp contrast to a constitutional system, such as that of the United States, which eventually enhances the power of the central authority and perpetuates the status quo by institutionalizing divisive class and factional interests so as to force stabilizing compromise.

The spectacular physical setting and sumptuous interior of its headquarters suggests the importance, perhaps the dominance, of the Caja Laboral Popular in the Mondragon system. But while the CLP has been central to the development of the cooperatives, it is a hallmark of their dynamism, durability, and commitment to democratic values that the developing Mondragon structure has diffused power and removed it from concentration in the CLP. The new Cooperative Congress and council of groups, and the increasing autonomy of the CLP's Empresarial Division (although it is still legally a part of the bank) have worked to resist the tendency to concentrate technocratic power over the cooperatives in the CLP.[11]

The Caja Laboral Popular itself is governed by representatives of the associated cooperatives and by its owner-workers, but the broad and basic policy decisions that control the work of the bank and the entire co-op system are now made by these new representative bodies.

Structure

The internal structure of the CLP is basically the same as the other Mondragon co-ops, but it is governed by a combination of the votes of its owner-workers and the votes of the cooperatives that have signed the contract of association with the bank. Thus, its general assembly consists of owner-workers and a proportional representation from the associated co-ops; assembly members elect a twelve-member governing council, which has eight representatives from the co-ops and four CLP owner-workers. Half the members of the governing council are elected every two years. Typically, five or six of the co-op members come from the major industrial and agricultural co-ops, one is from Eroski, the consumer co-op, and one or two come from the superstructure co-ops.[12]

In the early years, community savers were represented in the general assembly, but this course was ultimately rejected on the grounds that "making shareholders out of all savers would have hindered the administration of the credit institution."[13] Clearly, there is a potential for conflict between the interests of community savers and the CLP's basic commitment; this entails, at times, considerable risk and employing strategies (such as reducing interest rates or forgiving loans to co-ops in distress) that a conventional financial institution would not undertake. The CLP does hold a series of annual regional meetings for depositors in which the bank's management outlines its policies and discusses the ideas and concerns of depositors.

As with other co-ops, the CLP structure includes a social council (with one representative for every twenty CLP workers), a watchdog council (three internal bank auditors), a management council, and other committees that deal with various aspects of the bank's operations.

Contract of Association

The detailed contract of association between the Caja Laboral Popular and the individual co-ops establishes the basic requirements of internal organization and functioning of the cooperatives and their relationship with the CLP. The contract is the first, but not the last, word on these issues. While it serves as a framework, it permits the co-ops' own democratic decision-making bodies to institute needed changes, both in

Caja Laboral Popular: The Creation and Use of Social Capital 97

formal terms and in operational practice, in response to altered circumstances.

Examples of formal changes are the amplified and expanded principles for the treatment of social capital agreed to in 1987 by the cooperative congress to be ratified by the general assemblies of the associated cooperatives (see Chapter 3), the co-op's establishment of the FISO (Fund for Intercooperative Solidarity) to provide a self-financed level of protection for the co-ops beyond that afforded by the CLP, and the adoption of the ten basic principles of the Mondragon Cooperatives. As for changes in operational practice, during the prolonged economic recession the monitoring and oversight role of the CLP's Empresarial Division was greatly expanded, in order to detect or to predict economic difficulties at the earliest stage.

The provisions of the basic contract of association include the following points:[14]

1. Co-ops agree to the basic tenets of the group, including open admission, democratic control, membership principles, wage solidarity, and fixed interest on capital contributions
2. The co-op is a voting member of the Caja Laboral Popular and must invest capital in it
3. The co-op will deposit all surplus cash and liquid assets with the CLP
4. Surpluses (or losses) of the co-op will be distributed according to a basic formula, which also affects the long-term handling of this social capital (not less than 20 percent is to be retained by the co-op for reserves and reinvestment; 10 percent or more is contributed to a social fund; and the remaining 70 percent or less is distributed to co-op members, but remains with the co-op and is deposited in the CLP until the owner-worker leaves.)
5. The co-op provides the CLP with an annual balance sheet, monthly financial data, and a plan for the next year's operation
6. The CLP will audit co-op accounts at least once every four years

The Caja Laboral Popular in Context

The operations of the CLP are crucial to the Mondragon process of cooperative entrepreneurship. Together, the Banking and Empresarial divisions have facilitated the co-ops' ability to operate successfully as a democratic and humane system, both in boom times and in deep recessions, and to respond to structural economic changes.

A Broader View

In a broad, idealized sense, the activities of the Banking Division represent the community-building and integrative work of the Mondragon co-ops, while the Empresarial Division manifests and symbolizes the expansive, embracing freedom that is their life's energy. This view is of course schematic; the two themes meld, blend, and interpenetrate in all the Mondragon institutions. The Banking Division's accumulated financial resources, which the cooperators understand as accumulated labor or human resources, are focused and released in the transformative work of the Empresarial Division.

The capital of the Mondragon system is essentially community or social capital, not capital simply owned or controlled by government, the cooperatives, or the CLP itself. The various accounts and resources of the co-ops, the cooperators, and other community savers is social capital in the sense of its social commitment: it is the working capital of the co-ops (retained earnings, personal internal-capital accounts, personal savings accounts, buildings, machinery, land), much of it voluntarily committed by individuals or by groups of cooperators.

The Caja Laboral Popular is the organizational form which ensures that this dynamic social capital is employed democratically for the benefit of the Mondragon social system. The CLP's durability and success reflect the strength of the Mondragon principle of voluntary association. This is voluntarism conditioned by the pursuit of equilibrio and inspired by a combination of idealism and enlightened self-interest. Its success is manifested not only in economic gains but in the unquantifiable, though palpable, social benefits of the operation of the bank and the cooperatives.

In fact, Mondragon does not rely upon any arcane structures. The CLP makes hard decisions, characterized by the pursuit of equilibrio, a process that fully airs the ramifications of particular choices to the cooperatives' system and to the community on all levels. Indeed, the Mondragon system appears to deliberately cultivate the tension between the interest of the whole and the interests of various individuals and co-ops. Conventionally, this may seem to be less efficient than simply considering how to maximize profit: success in response to change is measured by gain in the market, and questions of liberty, democracy, and solidarity do not enter into the equation. The market is a level playing field on which inexorable and neutral economic forces determine the future; it is the mechanism that somehow decrees our communities will be deindustrialized and redlined, family farms foreclosed and absorbed by agribusiness, forests clear cut and abandoned, water, air, and food poisoned.

But on a closer look the dichotomy between economic efficiency and humanity proves false. Mondragon makes it clear that market or planning decisions are value decisions. Basic choices are made that distinguish between long- and short-term benefits. Exalting short-term maximization of profit leads to the creation of a sterile, unproductive world of electronic risk arbitrageurs who can move billions of dollars in microseconds. In contrast, it is often argued that the ascendancy of Japanese capitalists is predicated upon their willingness to make long-term investments.

Mondragon is efficient. It does respond to market signals—to the needs of its customers—but these responses are conditioned by a decided belief in the long-term existence and healthy growth of the cooperative system that informs the pursuit of equilibrio. Collective values allow the cooperators and the Caja Laboral Popular to make extraordinary efforts to sustain cooperative firms and to expand cooperative jobs, while preserving the economic integrity of the entire system. The genius of the Mondragon cooperators has been their ability to understand and to respond to these challenges in a manner conditioned by humane values. In this sense, the global meets the local.

The process is one of unleashing human creativity. The CLP operation is not a programmed mechanism; rather, the Mondragon system is animated by the wind of freedom, whose fundamental rule is change. Throughout its history, Mondragon has developed creative solutions to "insoluble" technical and organizational problems. The cooperators do not question the reality of the market, but they have tampered with the existing formula of power. Their success in responding to changing circumstances is not so much a reflection of unusual talent as of the social conditions created by cooperative evolution. Their ability to insulate themselves from bad fortune and to make democratic decisions guided by values of freedom and community is an invitation for us to do likewise.

A developing concern involves the long-term impact of the very success of the Caja Laboral Popular and its transformation into an institution that has only about 25 percent of its funds invested directly in the industrial cooperatives. The CLP's financial resources and cooperative management have been crucial to the system's ability to respond to cyclical and structural economic changes. Has the CLP, and by implication Mondragon, been "sentenced to success"? Must it now follow a trajectory that will divert it from its mission into existence as a conventional bank?

Choices made by the CLP, controlled by the votes of its owner-workers and the associated cooperatives, will ultimately reflect the decision of whether to continue the Mondragon experiment. The cooperators understand this. In fall 1987, just before the first cooperative congress, José María Ormaechea, CLP general manager and president of the new General Council of the cooperative group, was unequivocal in his assessment of future needs: "If the group stops developing and promoting new jobs, the cooperative experience will have begun to die."[15]

Growth for Mondragon is not the pursuit of profit but the elaboration of cooperative community. The choice that Ormaechea sees, I believe, is between a commitment to the development of community and social involvement, or a turning inward that will lead to a static bureaucraticizing of the co-op. In the long run it is a dynamic cooperative system that can make the community-based choices to condition, in broad terms, the nature of growth.

In the short run, clearly what is at stake here is the question of whether the Mondragon group will continue as a vital social system. The cooperators do not raise the flag of ideology when discussing their accomplishments. This is not merely a result of circumspection cultivated during the Franco years, but reflects their commitment to the democratic pursuit of equilibrio and its underlying cooperative principles: the creative dynamism of a community in motion. For example, in September 1986 Iaki Gorroño of the CLP told Kenneth Clarke, minister of employment for the conservative Thatcher government, that "Mondragon has never tried to create a 'third system,' which could overcome the extremes of capitalism or socialism." But he added immediately, "It is simply considered to be an 'experiment,' a dynamic process, open to the future, but without renouncing the principles of liberty, democracy and solidarity."[16] They pursue not a "third way," but their own way.

In sum, by nature the CLP is not simply a cooperatively run bank. As its president Alfonso Gorroñogoitia points out, it serves as the mechanism to place people's "savings at the disposal of the cooperatives and as the paper promoter of the Empresarial Division in the creation of new businesses, new jobs and the application of new technologies." But it is also "the channel for disseminating the cooperative business culture . . . day by day."[17]

Ground Level

In the Mondragon system, essentially all the surpluses created can remain with the cooperators and their communities. The economic and social practice of the Caja Laboral Popular arose in part from the basic, and shared, social assumptions that labor creates all wealth and that capital is accumulated labor. And while the cooperators had little capital at first, they had a considerable supply of skilled and willing labor.[18]

In practice, the Mondragon cooperatives have collapsed the roles of worker, capitalist, and entrepreneur into the same group of people. At that point, it does not especially matter if economists decide that wealth is accumulated partially through the use (exploitation) of technological forces and material resources as well as the use (exploitation) of labor, or through the special role of the entrepreneur in the labor process. Historically, the labor theory of value has been employed to exalt the role of the capitalist or entrepreneur in the creation of wealth and to disparage or even deny the role of the wage earner.[19]

The Caja Laboral Popular has helped the Mondragon cooperatives succeed in the particularly difficult task of actualizing the often hollow freedoms promised by economic and political liberalism. The elaboration of the cooperative system leads to a convergence between the practice of democracy and the building of community. Freedom in this context includes the right to make agreements, but becomes much more than a narrow economic or political abstraction, or the largely theoretical (and often violated) rights of isolated and powerless individuals.

The Mondragon experience provides a refreshing contrast to the enormous disparity between theoretical liberty under capitalist or socialist industrialism and the reality of working life. Canadian writer and poet Tom Wayman articulates the frustration and confusion of our common experience:

> You cross that factory gate or office door and it is like time-travel— back to when people like you and I did not have the vote, and had to shut up and obey orders and so on. As soon as you cross back outside you are expected to be this free responsible adult citizen, in whose hands the destiny of nations lie.[20]

The Caja Laboral Popular, as the organizational basis for cooperative entrepreneurship, has facilitated the ability of the cooperators to experience democracy and power within the context of dynamic economic and community development. The point of departure is not any high-minded utopian projection of the world as it should be— quite the contrary. The Caja Laboral Popular, like the rest of the Mondragon system, arose from a very sober reflection upon the world as it was and could be by Arizmendiarrieta and the Mondragon cooperators.

Notes

1. ICA newsletter Fall, 1989.
2. Galbraith 1975, p. 19.
3. The distribution of the 180 local branches (1987) is as follows: Alava 24, Guipúzcoa 62 (plus central office in Mondragon), Navarra 33, Vizcaya 59, Barcelona 1, Madrid 1.
4. In 1985 pesetas, this is an increase from 30,443 million pesetas in 1970 to 187,378 million pesetas in 1986 (616 percent), an impressive performance. [Sources for these figures are given in Appendix 1-2.]
5. Thomas and Logan 1982.
6. Ibid., p. 86.
7. Irastorza 1986, p. 3.

8. This law was liberalized in 1985 (CLP annual report, 1986, p. 13), when it was redefined as the ratio of "own resources" to "creditors' resources," not "total resources"— a change that may reflect financial difficulties experienced by banks during the recession. The analysis here continues to use the original standard.

9. Ellerman 1984a, p. 18.

10. Irastorza 1986, p. 4.

11. Whyte and Whyte 1988, pp. 183–87.

12. Ellerman 1984a, p. 17.

13. Irastorza 1986, p. 2

14. The Mondragon Experiment (Mondragon: Caja Laboral Popular) 1984, pp. 7–8.

15. Ginto 1987b, p. 11.

16. Gorroño 1986.

17. Ginto 1984, p. 6.

18. I am indebted to Terry Mollner for his observations on the available labor power of the people of Mondragon.

19. For an examination of the labor theory of value and its precursors, see Wolf 1984 and Burkitt 1984, pp. 19–35.

20. Quoted in "The Work Taboo," *In These Times* 12, no. 9 (January 20–26, 1988): p. 24.

5
An Encounter With *Homo Oikonomia*

At this point, we should examine the sources of our identity as abstract economic beings so that we may begin to make sane choices toward recovering our humanity. We will glance briefly at the ghost that animates the machine of the market before examining cooperative entrepreneurship in detail.

From Adam Smith to Milton Friedman, the mechanistic operation of the laws of economics has been raised to an article of faith. Economic behavior, and therefore human behavior, is believed to follow the mathematically verifiable principles that govern the operation of markets, such as the law of supply and demand. These equations purportedly predict, not the behavior of atomic particles or chemical reactions, but the behavior of people.

In fact, economic "science" rests as much, or more, upon fanciful supposition as it does upon mathematical certainties. Classical and neoclassical economics (and Marxist economics in reaction) arise from root assumptions about human nature that have, in fact, developed along with the growth of capitalist markets and industrialism. These assumptions amount, in their crassest form, to self-serving rationalizations endowing a drive for profit maximization with morality.

Thus the logic of economists is tautological: they write equations that claim to predict human behavior, but the equations are based upon suppositions that humans act in accord with the principles that underlie the equations. They are then caught in circular reasoning, sustained by what they see as the weight of evidence of human behavior.

If we put economic science to a basic test held to apply to physical science, economics fails. The doctrine of falsifiability holds that scientific knowledge is limited to hypotheses capable of being proven false by experiment: if one cannot hope to prove something false, then it is not accessible to scientific proof. By this principle, scientists point out that such questions as the existence of ghosts or reincarnation appear to be beyond the reach of scientific method.

When the theories of economics are regularly violated by events, there are no headlines even remotely like those that would greet the news that Einstein's theory of relativity has proven to be true on Mondays and Wednesdays, but false on Thursdays. Such momentous events in physics could lead to questioning—and ultimately rejecting—the ordering paradigm of current science,[1] but in economics flat contradictions cause hardly a ripple. Economics is essentially not a science, but a philosophy. It does have mathematical and quantitative components: a good poker player knows and considers the odds, but also considers the history and habits of the opposition. Poker is an art, a matter of human judgement informed by knowledge and catalyzed by luck.

Economics, as practiced, is a philosophy of social navigation. Those who watch the progress of the journey, and suffer its consequences, are told the sky is dark, that no stars guide our course, when in fact it proceeds by following the constellations of sex, race, and class. We are supposed to be in the power only of invisible and disinterested precepts of mathematics and "human nature."

It may be argued that predictions about the future behavior of complex human social and economic systems are handicapped, not by deficient science, but by a lack of data and by the very complexity of the system. With enough data, enough equations, enough computers, we could predict the future. But the amount of data needed to forecast even the behavior of a stock market would tend to approach the knowledge (quantifiable or not) of all the participants in that market. For example, how people "feel" about the future, their confidence as investors, may be conditioned by the reported money supply, the recent victory of their favorite basketball team, the quality of their love life, the nature of their infant toilet training, and so on.

Even if we could collect and quantify the necessary data, we would still run into the human analog of the Heisenberg uncertainty principle. Physicists cannot measure the position and the momentum of a subatomic particle accurately at the same time, as the very act of measuring to determine one characteristic alters the other. Indeed, the more precisely the one is measured, the less that can be known about the other. An economist fully knowledgeable about the system would find that the very act of probing the collective consciousness skews the results. The questions themselves would affect what is being measured.

The ideology of capitalism, then of proto-industrialism, crystallized around the arguments of Adam Smith (a philosopher, not a scientist). He divined that the primacy and morality of the self-interested pursuit of profit and its consequent social utility arose from two general human attributes.

First, the principle of sympathy conditions our desire to trade and channels it toward the conduct of mutually effective persuasion. "It is chiefly from this regard to the sentiments of mankind, that we pursue riches and avoid poverty."[2] Wealth, according to Smith, also has a magnetic appeal: it delights and casts a spell upon all who bask in its reflected glory.

Smith was not preaching the survival of the fittest. He was a moralist who found in the pursuit of self-interest a means to regulate the harmonious conduct of human affairs. In his view, "[a]ll members of human society stand in need of each other's assistance, and are likewise exposed to mutual injuries. Where the necessary assistance is reciprocally offered from love, from gratitude, from friendship and esteem, the society flourishes and is happy." Discussing the actions of the rich, Smith noted that, "they are led by an invisible hand to make nearly the same distribution of the necessaries of life which would have been made had the earth been divided into equal portions among all its inhabitants; and thus without intending it, without knowing it, advance the interest of the society, and afford means to the multiplication of the species."[3] Self-interest was thus a means to serve both the individual and collective good.

In this sense capitalism's initial sympathies lay with those who shared a rather positive and optimistic view of human nature, in contrast to Thomas Hobbes, who viewed life in its natural state as "nasty, brutish and short" and called for the absolute power of the state to regulate relations between people. Capitalism advanced with the philosophy that found an inborn human propensity for personal harmony that went hand in hand with social cooperation.[4]

Second, and more ominously, Smith agreed that there was an innate human drive for order and design. Wealth is not attractive in itself, but for the elaborate social systems the accumulation of wealth permits and requires. This celebration of hierarchy reflects his view of an integrated universe whose constituents were subject to scientific investigation, explanation—and exploitation. This was a universe whose constituent parts behaved according to laws of cause and effect, but not simply mechanistically: they were connected and ordered in a hierarchy of design that was reflected in the nature of things and filled the entire universe.[5]

Much current criticism of classical thought speaks of an atomized, materialist, and soulless universe, the philosophical concomitant of industrialism. But classical science itself (or, more broadly, technique shorn of social context) is not the chief villain. Central to the problems inherent in the world view of industrialism is the resolute secular faith that equates a belief in the unity of all things with a sense of order and hierarchy. People chose order as a governing principle of industrialism instead of an interactive and ecological concept of unity in diversity. Hierarchy with its dualisms, in a universe animated by principles of cause and effect, follows the trajectory of progress and growth, not of renewal and balance. Order and hierarchy are at the core of the capitalist project. It subsists upon inequality and domination; order is a product of the power wielded to maintain the concentration of wealth, though it is mystified and elaborated by the attribution of moral and spiritual qualities. The benefits that flow from capitalist wealth and social justice rest upon this root injustice. The foundation is utilitarian: see what riches have been created by progress.

From the beginning, the accumulation of capitalist wealth, catalyzed by the exaltation of individual and personal greed, was a call for the investiture of the new merchant princes of money. The establishment of dynastic fortunes and the social trappings that accompanied them motivated the entrepreneurial activity that Joseph Schumpeter considered central to capitalism's success. The attempt to separate the drive for wealth and a human propensity for order is, in fact, largely a self-serving sleight of hand. The two amount essentially to the same thing. Obviously, accumulating great wealth does not—contrary to Smith's sentimentality—confer grace either upon those who witness it or upon the social order that permits and maintains it.

It is possible to offer a psychological, as opposed to a social, explanation for the development of capitalist ideology. That is, in choosing order and hierarchy over independence and flux, Adam Smith made a fundamental epistemological error based on the idea that people tend to project onto the world the order they find in their minds. Freud saw this process as explaining of the origins of both magic and animism in "primitive" cultures, phenomena that would evolve into the more mature and "civilized" forms of religious and then scientific thought.[6] Freud quotes James George Frazer: people "mistook the order of their ideas for the order of nature, and imagined that the control they had, or seemed to have, over their thoughts, permitted them to exercise a corresponding control over things."

Such an explanation is ahistorical, basically an inverted attempt to explain away the social formulations and deep structures informing the creations and ideology of industrialism. It suggests these are errors made by the "primitive" mind, but in reality order and hierarchy are more the creation and refinement of the "civilized" mind than the product of traditional cultures—cultures in which daily life and the world view were rooted in an ecological and integrated consciousness. In fact, two of the three apparent solutions to the problems of industrial modernism call for the further elaboration of order and hierarchy. First is the continuing expansion of social command and bureaucratization that leads to an elaboration of technocratic systems in a sort of transnational capitalism (which the United States and the Soviet Union are both approaching from different starting points). Second is the further mystification of power and order, which holds within it the seeds of a fascist denouement.

A third solution involves the growth of systems based upon cooperative entrepreneurship that can harmonize individual and collective action, manifested through the democratic pursuit of equilibrio. This is what Mondragon cooperative entrepreneurship is about.

Bodies in Motion

Economics, as a patriarchal philosophy operating in accord with the prevailing social dualisms, collided with a problem: economists established a quantitative system to explain economic behavior, but it did not provide reliable explanations for human agency or for economic fluctuation, growth, and change. This failure is understandable; given the real complexity of the issues, it could hardly be otherwise. But capitalist economists continue to offer apologias for human misery and new predictions, while Marxists continue to speak about the approaching final crisis of capitalism and the glories expected to flow from the next planning cycle.

Joseph Schumpeter injected the dynamic human element into his analysis of economic systems with what he called the process of "creative destruction." The market destroys the unproductive, uncompetitive, and unresponsive and raises up the more efficient and productive for the betterment of society. The agent, according to Schumpeter, is not lumbering bureaucracy or the mechanical action of markets, but individuals; heroic entrepreneurs who translate the opportunities of the marketplace into productive reality.

> The opening up of new markets, foreign or domestic, and the organizational development from the craft shop and factory to such concerns as U.S. Steel (now U.S.X.) illustrate the same process of industrial mutation . . . that incessantly revolutionizes the economic structure from within, incessantly destroying the old one, incessantly creating a new one. This process of Creative Destruction is the essential fact about capitalism. It is what capitalism consists in and what every capitalist concern has got to live in.[7]

The entrepreneur, then, is not just a profit maximizer or an accountant, but a risk taker, a builder, a creator. Schumpeter and the economists who have followed him postulate that the rhythms of the business cycle are influenced by the action of entrepreneurs responding to opportunities created by economic change. He viewed individuals, not anonymous market forces, as the agents and prime movers of economic growth and bemoaned what he saw as the destruction (a fruit of capitalism's very success) of the conditions that encouraged the individual entrepreneur.[8]

The mystified and heroic vision of the economic leadership of entrepreneurs unavoidably connects to the notion of transcendent leadership that animates fascism. It is simply not possible to maintain a social order inspired solely by greed without resort to ceremony and magic. Magic permits the atomized and alienated to become an ecstatic crowd of coparticipants and worshippers. We have retail ceremonies and the rituals of the shopping mall to replace the cathedral. On a higher level there is the final recourse of capitalism to fascism.

Schumpeter also shared the fascists' antagonism toward the critical spirit of intellectuals, which, he found, undermined the glories of capitalist accomplishment and the motivation of the entrepreneur: "the mass of people never develops definite opinions on its own initiative . . . unlike any other type of society, capitalism inevitably and by virtue of the very logic of its civilization creates, educates and subsidizes a vested interest in social unrest."[9]

The economist feared that the entrepreneur was an endangered species, threatened by the social order and the growth of giant bureaucracies. The values of bureaucracy—aversion to risk, maintenance of the status quo—are antithetical to the raison d'être of the entrepreneur. Thus, the interlocking bureaucracies of corporations and governments could choke economic initiative and destroy the atmosphere for entrepreneurial opportunity:

> Faced by the increasing hostility of the [social] environment and by the legislative, administrative and judicial practice born of that hostility, entrepreneurs and capitalists—in fact the whole stratum that accepts the bourgeois scheme of life—will eventually cease to function. Their standard aims are rapidly becoming unobtainable, their efforts futile.[10]

Schumpeter was more correct than is generally acknowledged. The capitalism of heroic effort that he memorialized is fading into the heavy dance of the transnational corporations. On the ground level in the United States, we experience the preoccupation of business with financial manipulation and with short-term profits through mergers, takeovers, and corporate raids, accompanied by what appears to be a systematic dismantling of much of the country's industrial capacity. Factories are moved to cheap-labor havens overseas, or the corporation becomes merely a marketing and distribution network for goods manufactured by foreign-owned firms. Even *Business Week* is horrified by the "hollow corporation."[11] The alternative is supposed to be a service and information economy.

While there are styles of classical entrepreneurship reflected in the dominant social paradigm for capitalism—first British, then American, and now Japanese—the essential motivation is individual greed and heroism. Cooperative entrepreneurship turns the motivation on its head. Individual aspirations find full satisfaction, not in pursuit of profit, but through a cooperative, harmonized personal and social striving. Arizmendiarrieta wrote that the co-ops' "fundamental character is an affirmation" that is "fully capable of satisfying the human spirit."[12] But it is not an abstract process: in response to critiques of the co-ops' ideological position he observed that "[w]e will make our choices by deeds more than by words."[13]

Cooperative entrepreneurship and the democratic pursuit of *equilibrio* can allow us to regain control over our lives and the future of our communities. The Mondragon cooperators offer a lesson that can serve as inspiration for us to create and follow our own roads to economic and social self-determination. We have the power to choose.

Notes

1. Kuhn 1978.
2. Quoted in Meyers 1983, pp. 113–14.
3. Quoted in Lutz and Lux 1979, p. 28.
4. Meyers 1983, pp. 50–57.
5. Lovejoy 1960.
6. Freud 1950, pp. 75–99.
7. Schumpeter 1950, p. 83.

8. Ibid., pp. 131–73.
9. Ibid., p. 145.
10. Ibid., p. 156.
11. Business Week 1986.
12. Quoted in Azurmendi 1984, p. 480.
13. Ibid., p. 619.

6

Cooperative Entrepreneurship: A Key Social Innovation

> A company cannot and must not lose any of its efficiency just because human values are considered more important than purely economic or material resources within that company; on the contrary such a consideration should help increase efficiency and quality.
> —José María Arizmendiarrieta

Cooperative Entrepreneurship

Cooperative entrepreneurship is the means used by the people of Mondragon to change their lives. It is at the core of the model, the essential prime mover through which the cooperators focus and channel their energies and create their businesses, schools, and houses—a complete cooperative social fabric, woven with their labor.

The conventional definition of entrepreneur is a person who organizes, operates, and assumes the risks of business ventures, a role often considered central to the functioning and dynamics of market economies. David Ellerman of the Industrial Cooperative Association in Somerville, Massachusetts, a leading U.S. source of technical assistance and financial resources for developing cooperatives, has described the Mondragon accomplishment as the institutionalization and socialization of entrepreneurship,[1] making it accessible to ordinary working people and supported by a structure of cooperative institutions democratically controlled by their owner-workers.

Mondragon cooperative entrepreneurship is not simply a matter of business ventures begun by groups instead of individuals, the transmutation of private power into a social or collective instrument. Rather it is, at heart, the pursuit of equilibrio conditioned by the shared values and ethics of community, democracy, and justice.

William Foote Whyte called cooperative entrepreneurship a "social invention," conferring on social change the importance conventionally attributed to such mechanical marvels as the steam engine.[2] It is more accurate to consider cooperative entrepreneurship as the applied practice of a fundamental social innovation. But to speak of invention and innovation is to speak of technique, not of liberation. Mondragon is not a convenient technical fix for capitalism.

Cooperative entrepreneurship can have the same revolutionary resonance for cooperative social systems as the advent of the printing press had for book production. It holds momentous promise for the larger world: it can transform the way we organize our labors and create wealth, a transformation nearly as significant as the development of the division of labor was for industrial mass production.

The most important results of cooperative entrepreneurship are moral and spiritual: justice, solidarity and other social and moral "goods" are part of Mondragon's bottom line; ethics and human value are inseparable from its production. Through the individual and collective application of energy and love, the system has created a humane and durable social order, enriching the lives of an expanding number of people.

Mondragon's success represents much more than simple quantitative change, the erection of buildings and the accumulation of bank balances. Its expansion has proceeded in a manner that is largely consonant with ecological models of life within a harmonious and self-regulating biosphere. At Mondragon the elements of an integrated social system appeared, developed and were elaborated in harmony with a humane social ecology. As a human institution, however, Mondragon is subject to human failings.

The cooperators aspire to make successful cooperative business practices a concomitant of cooperative social success. This is not acceptance of Adam Smith's invisible hand that transmutes private self-interest into public good, but the application of social choices. From the start, economic growth was moved and guided by basic cooperative principles and values and by the pursuit of equilibrio. Mondragon has demonstrated that cooperatives can adapt to a changing environment at all stages of development and solve problems in a manner consistent with cooperative principles. A passing specialist in organizational behavior would say the co-op's attitude is entrepreneurial. It is certainly the antithesis of static bureaucracy, but cooperative entrepreneurship has a soul.

The Empresarial Division of the CLP

The Empresarial Division of the Caja Laboral Popular substitutes creative renewal for Schumpeter's creative destruction. Its staff of approximately 115 provides a broad range of information and technical assistance for cooperatives.[3] Although it is supposed to become an independent cooperative, legal and tax considerations have made it desirable for it to remain a division of the CLP at least until 1991.[4] The new official name of the Empresarial Division is Lan Kide Suzraketa (L.K.S.), but it is generally known as the Empresarial Division and that term will be used here. The word *empresarial* can be translated as "management," but as Ellerman points out its real meaning and nature transcend management or entrepreneurial functions, so it seems best to use "its uniquely proper name."[5]

The Empresarial Division is organized into seven departments: Advice and Consultation; Studies; Agricultural and Food Promotion; Industrial Promotion; Intervention; Auditing and Information; and Urban Planning and Building.[6] This gives Mondragon the ability to foster new cooperatives (from the initial interest of a group of prospective cooperators, through a detailed process of planning and training that lasts from eighteen months to two years, to the break-even point where a viable cooperative has emerged) and to provide needed advice and, if necessary, intervention.

This extraordinary degree of collective support and assistance, combined with the financial resources of the CLP, is the primary reason for Mondragon's business success.[7] Over thirty years, fewer than 3 percent of the co-ops have failed. These failures have been willful: in each case, the cooperators involved and the CLP decided that it was in the interest of the Mondragon system to dissolve the cooperative. The general success of the co-ops does not mean that they did not experience difficulty, but that the system was able to respond humanely and effectively. This sense of collective managerial panache is one startling quality of the Mondragon cooperatives: they are dynamic, not static, institutions.

A cooperative in difficulty may decide to develop a new product line, retool, or replace management. The CLP can support such moves by interest reduction or moratorium, or by write-offs: during the severe Spanish recession of the early 1980s, the CLP wrote off more than one million dollars in co-op loans and declared an interest moratorium on about 40 percent of the rest.[8] This action was accompanied by an aggressive redevelopment plan and the strengthening of the Empresarial Division's intervention abilities. The cooperatives retrenched, survived, and have continued to prosper.

Inefficiency and failure are not exclusively artifacts of capitalism, the product of market-driven forces. Under either a planned or a market-organized economy, inefficient or unproductive producers must eventually be supported or disappear. A parallel can be drawn between a hypothetical Soviet car factory and the Chrysler Corporation. In their darker days, both Chrysler and the Soviet auto industry manufactured cars that people did not want, cost too much to produce, and were expensive to operate. Yet both continued to operate, and their workers went on receiving wages (and Chrysler's investors continued to receive interest payments and dividends). This meant that, in some fashion, the failure had been socialized. Under capitalism, politicians decided that it was desirable not to allow Chrysler to go bankrupt, so the government offered to guarantee its debts; under socialism, inputs continued despite the fact that they were less than outputs—again, a portion of the social product was shifted to maintain the troubled enterprise.

The issue is not whether capitalist markets are more efficient or cruel than the efforts of socialist planning. Instead, we need to develop a means to decide about investment and enterprise based upon democratic choices of the people directly involved, in the context of humane social values focused upon the well-being of the owner-workers and their communities. Mondragon's decisions are conditioned by market signals, some of which are reasonably legitimate. Market socialists, for example, while they favor planning and public ownership of, most often, utilities, some basic industries, and capital markets, also appreciate that

> It just does not make sense for a central planning board to make decisions about the relative quantities of salami and garlic sausage that its citizens need; nor would such issues enhance the tone of debate in the democratic assemblies arising in a socialist society. One of the virtues of markets is that, by transferring these decisions to a small group of sausage makers, it clears the decks for more important discussions.[9]

Cooperative Entrepreneurship   115

But Mondragon is neither worker capitalism nor socialism in capitalist clothing—it is a cooperative system that operates within capitalism. The strength of cooperative entrepreneurship is its ability to allocate parts of the collective social product in a manner that is in accord with cooperative goals. The coordinated efforts of the CLP and the Empresarial Division emphatically do not mean a simple socialization of risk combined with bureaucratic planning, with the CLP calling the shots and sometimes stepping in to bail out failing enterprises. Rather, there is sufficient flexibility, expertise, resources—and collective commitment—to make successful investment decisions that allocate human, material, and financial resources in ways that help restore economic viability to co-ops under stress while maintaining their jobs and community ties.

Organization of the Empresarial Division

The seven departments of the Empresarial Division are designed to provide a full range of integrated services and assistance to every phase of co-op development.[10] The Management Council of the Empresarial Division is composed of the division's director and the heads of the seven departments.

1. Advice and Consultation—
   Export Department (develops and coordinates export policy; direct sales of some products; technical export information)
   Marketing Department (research; market studies; product development; training sales personnel)
   Production-Engineering Department (development and modernization of production technology)
   Personnel Department (full personnel-services assistance, including recruitment, training, and organization)
   Administrative Financial Department (accounting and financial-control systems; management of economic and financial resources)
   Legal Department (assists in all legal matters, including internal organization and business transactions)
2. Studies—undertakes in-depth economic studies and forecasts for co-ops, Basque provinces, and Spain, as well as tracking international economic developments; maintains library for the Empresarial Division and the co-ops
3. Agricultural and Food Promotion—assists existing agricultural cooperatives and aids in further cooperative development; provides socioeconomic studies of agricultural-development strategies

4. Industrial Promotion—
   Product Department (finds and researches new products and activities for industrial co-ops)
   Promotion Department—"Form, study, and help in the promotion and launching of new industrial cooperatives supported by the Caja Laboral Popular. Through successive stages in the formation of a new cooperative, this department gives guidance and assistance to any promoting group, especially in topics like feasibility studies and marketing. In addition, the Department performs studies and selects new products and marketing policies to introduce in cooperatives with economic problems or on the way to conversion."[11]
5. Intervention—consults in co-op planning and management, intervenes in problem co-ops to provide instruction or assistance
6. Auditing and Information—
   Auditing Department establishes accounting procedures and monitors implementation
   Information Department—studies long-, medium-, and short-term prospects for cooperatives based upon their plans and their performance
7. Urban Planning and Building—
   Urban Planning Department (urban planning and public-works development for new co-ops; new town planning and development)
   Industrial Building Department (civil-engineering activities for new plants; renovation of existing plants)
   Housing Department (promotion and technical services for the organization and construction of housing cooperatives)

The Empresarial Division and the Reasons for Cooperative Formation

The Empresarial Division can facilitate the formation of new cooperatives, but it does not recruit new members for specific ideas. The division explores different product lines and opportunities, but specific co-op development awaits a suggestion by an appropriate group of people. In a sense, the division is like a hospital emergency room: while it tries to be prepared for all logical contingencies, it is never sure what will come in the door.

Cooperative formation follows a number of different paths, as the Mondragon system has carefully nurtured the means to make entrepreneurship accessible to groups of ordinary people with various talents and motivations to help them create a dynamic cooperative enterprise.

Classically, the initiative for a new co-op may come from a group motivated by the challenge and excitement of beginning a new enterprise or by the need for jobs and community development in their region. Somewhat less glamorously, members of an existing co-op might approach the Empresarial Division with an idea for a new cooperative that is part of the group's long-term development plan to increase employment. Co-op groups, though they superficially resemble conglomerates, do not expand by buying other companies through leveraged paper transactions or by funding startups; instead, they work with the Empresarial Division.

Another possibility involves converting an existing noncooperative business to a cooperative either at the initiative of the owner or the workers. Such initiatives usually do not prove satisfactory for a variety of reasons (see p. 174). There have been some successful conversions, but most such overtures from conventional firms are not consummated.

At other times, the growth of an existing cooperative makes it desirable to form a new co-op from one of its divisions. Thus Ulgor, the appliance manufacturer, begat Fagor from its electronics division, and Fagor begat Aurki to make numerical controls for machine tools. By the mid 1970s, Ulgor had already led to the formation of a half-dozen cooperatives. Another factor that encourages investment in new co-ops is the legal requirement that Caja Laboral Popular maintain satisfactory financial ratios, and so find productive long-term investments within the cooperatives. This provides a degree of supply-side push (pp. 90-91).

The Life Cycle of a Mondragon Cooperative

In broad outline, the life cycle of a Mondragon cooperative can be depicted as a seven-step, self-renewing process:[12]

1. Founding cooperators
2. Feasibility study
3. Funding
4. From start-up to break-even
5. Final correction
6. Fission (hiving off new co-ops)
7. Future innovation and adjustment

Mondragon co-ops are planned carefully, struggle toward economic durability, and expand—but then, instead of following the familiar paths of continued growth and bureaucratization, or failure and dissolution, cooperative entrepreneurship relies on mechanisms of hiving off new cooperatives and intensive capital reinvestment, when needed, to renew older co-ops' vigor. These steps facilitate processes of creative renewal that benefit both the individual cooperative and the whole system.

Use of the term "life cycle" indicates that an individual cooperative is a dynamic and complex human system within the Mondragon cooperative community. The co-op is not a thing, a simple economic unit, but a structure animated and sustained by human values. Its humanity allows it to violate the supposedly "rational" calculus of self-interest and social agony. The cooperative is planned with impeccable concern for the efficient and productive use of its resources, but what it maximizes is community.

Ellerman calls the Empresarial Division a "factory for factories,"[13] but cooperative entrepreneurship transcends this: it is not simply another way to organize the founding of new businesses in response to market forces. The Mondragon co-ops have grown stronger because their actions have been conditioned and guided by cooperative and humane ethics and values.

The process of cooperative foundation and promotion involves the use of a series of screens, so that only those groups considered able to succeed go on to the next step. The Empresarial Division's hard-headed analysis eliminates many groups for a variety of reasons: for example, an inability to work together cooperatively; failure to choose a suitable product or to develop an effective business plan that is likely to provide at least forty jobs within five years; failure to obtain needed self-financing or collateral.[14] This filtering process is a major reason why failure is so very rare for Mondragon cooperatives, while it is the general rule for both ordinary companies and cooperatives.

Ellerman contrasts a "survival of the fittest" process with Mondragon's management of investment resources.[15] It is clear that the entrepreneurial impulse to launch new co-ops and new products even in poor economic times is balanced by a firm desire not to take foolish risks that will endanger the entire system and the workers in a co-op that is unlikely to succeed.

Mondragon business planning employs the notion of labor as a fixed cost: layoffs are the last, not the first, recourse in the event of an economic downturn. Such a position tends to increase the need for realism in developing business plans and the need to be somewhat conservative in assessing risks. A conventional entrepreneur might plan to reduce staff sharply if lagging seasonal sales create a cash-flow problem, but that is not the way Mondragon cooperatives are planned.

Founding Cooperators

In Mondragon, a cooperative is more than a business plan, a factory building, or a collection of tools; it is, above all, a group of people committed to working together. Thus the Empresarial Division's first and most important task is to assist prospective cooperators from the time they walk in the door until the new cooperative is self-sustaining. While such assistance is technical and financial, it is also a matter of spirit, education, and solidarity.

In the first phase, the potential cooperators meet with the Promotion Department of the Industrial (or the Agricultural and Food) area. The group must:

1. have a positive orientation toward working cooperatively and as entrepreneurs;
2. choose one of their number as a promoter/manager who will be paid a salary and work on developing the detailed business plan with the assistance of the Empresarial Division;
3. make sure the promoter/manager has the ability to work cooperatively;
4. have a reasonable concept for a product or service based upon their own ideas or the prefeasibility studies product bank of the Empresarial Division; and
5. be able to provide a guarantee or collateral for the loan made by the CLP to cover the cost of the promoter/manager's salary for the planning period.

At the start of the promotion period the group and its proposed manager work with an advisor sometimes called *padrino* or godfather (as yet there seem to be no godmothers), who will stay with the group, if the cooperative is launched, for several years, until after the break-even point. The advisors are experienced co-op managers, most with a strong technological backgrounds.

The group can take advantage of a "product bank" of numerous prefeasibility studies developed by the Product Department of the Industrial Promotion area. These are highly detailed investigations of a range of products (for example, computer software and peripherals) that consider projected demand and prices, as well as production costs and requirements. The department notes when some markets are almost or entirely saturated (in recent years, machine tools, forge and foundry products, and appliances) or relatively flat (recently, shipbuilding, truck production, and printing), as well as identifying potential new markets for a range of high- and low-tech products, from parts for the European Space Agency to toilet-paper holders. Other studies available in the late

1980s included analyses of industrial robots and numerically controlled devices, piping, material transport (forklifts and robotic stackers), public-works machinery (small dumpers and excavators), wood construction, plastics, and agricultural machinery.[16] As we will see, one of the responses to the prolonged recession of the mid 1970s to the mid 1980s was to deemphasize the use of broad prefeasibility studies and to concentrate more on specific product development.

If the group of cooperators prove to have the right stuff, the CLP will provide a no-interest loan to pay for the new co-op manager's salary during the eighteen- to twenty-four-month promotion period. The loan must be backed either by the guarantee of an existing co-op or by other individuals, or collateralized by the cooperators' assets. Thus cooperative entrepreneurship requires the participants to be at some risk from the first and to commit not just time but their own resources or reputations. The new co-op is then incorporated under Spanish law. The Basque regional legislature, given broad authority by Madrid, has also passed laws in the 1980s governing co-ops within the Basque provinces. These govern legal structures and set particular financial requirements for the CLP and the co-ops.

Feasibility Study

The manager of the nascent cooperative is given an office in the Empresarial Division and begins to work with the advisor on the detailed feasibility study and business plan that must be completed and approved before the new co-op is actually launched. The study refines, focuses, and polishes the information in the prefeasibility study or in the cooperators' initial suggestion. With the advisor's assistance, the group must be prepared to reject their original product ideas if they cannot meet basic economic tests.

The completed feasibility study is detailed and sophisticated. Volume one contains product, marketing, and supply information; volume two details the structure and plan for the co-op, including engineering, economic, and organizational aspects; volume three considers the economic feasibility of the plan. In David Ellerman's description:

> For details of the marketing part of the study the promoter can consult the Marketing Department. To explore export possibilities there is the Export Department, to plan out the production process there is the Production Department, and to design an appropriate factory for the manufacturing process, there is the Industrial Building Department. For information about the personnel system and member payment arrangements, there is the Personnel Department. The Legal Department handles the incorporation procedure, obtaining the necessary licenses and patents and drafting the necessary contracts. The Auditing

Department and the Information and Control Department help to set up the accounting and management control systems so that the progress of the cooperative can be monitored by the manager and the CLP.[17]

Planning with Labor as a Fixed Cost

Mondragon business planning is based upon the notion of labor as a relatively fixed cost. In conventional firms, production goals—and therefore the amount spent on "direct labor"—are based on projected sales plus desired levels of inventory. Labor is a variable cost, and workers are hired or fired as demand changes. Rent, costs of the facility, capital costs, and the wages of supervisors and other "indirect labor" are generally looked upon as fixed costs for planning, at least for one year.[18]

In short, in conventional, nonunionized firms, the lives of workers are subject to the day-to-day vagaries of the market. Indeed, the accepted gospel holds that not only employment but wages vary according to the demand of the market: as demand drops, workers will lose their jobs; in time, some will offer to work for less and then, supposedly, be rehired. Long-term unemployment, in this fairy-tale view, should not exist.

In Mondragon business planning, however, labor is a semifixed cost. Membership (after a brief probationary period) is taken as a constant for workers; permanent members are not laid off with impunity, nor are new permanent members hired to meet seasonal increases in demand. In the planning process, production reflects the output of the members working productively and full-time, and sales must meet these goals.

Flexibility is achieved through a skillful combination of marketing and some price cutting to maintain sales if demand falls and, if necessary, not replacing those who quit; other approaches involve reduced work time, temporary reduction in profit advances (wages), or temporary transfers to other co-ops. Temporary layoffs are the last resort. On the other hand, if demand increases, the co-op may initiate overtime work, engage in subcontracting, or hire some temporary workers.

The use of subcontracting and of temporary workers provides a very good fit with the nature of both the cooperative groups and the entire system. A co-op's business plan can include the use of other co-ops for subcontracting during periods of peak demand and as a source of temporary workers when business in other co-ops falls below planned levels. This is a major strength of the cooperative entrepreneurial system and "one of the many risk-pooling advantages of federating cooperatives together."[19]

David Ellerman notes of Mondragon's marketing efforts:

> Instead of treating sales as an outside-determined variable given by the market, [co-op] management should maximize the cooperative's control over the volume of sales to offset the fixity of labor. There is reason to believe that the worker-members' identification with their products

would lead not only to higher quality products but to more dignified and accurate product advertising . . . cooperative production should lead management to put more emphasis on the sales effort, not less.[20]

Marketing and advertising in this sense have a place in co-op planning.

The constraints of planning with labor as a fixed cost encourage new co-ops to begin with a relatively small number of workers (consistent with required economies of scale) and, in some cases, to test-market subcontracted products before making major capital commitments. It also pushes them to be concerned about the market share they are seeking in order to avoid predatory competitive responses from larger firms.

A Mondragon co-op can reduce profit advances to maintain profitability (economic surpluses) under severe economic stress, but this has a very different effect from wage cuts (or wage cuts exchanged for profit sharing) in conventional firms. By reducing advances in the short term, its owner-workers allow the co-op to maintain surpluses, 70 percent of which are distributed to their individual accounts. An instructive contrast is offered by a recent General Motors–United Auto Workers contract that required the company to pay out 10 percent of before-tax profits to workers only if those profits exceed 10 percent of GM's net worth and 5 percent of its assets. Even if the company is swimming in profits (as the auto industry was then) management argues that profit sharing should be based on anticipated future profits (and a supposed, but not agreed upon, program for capital reinvestment), not upon the money in the bank. Management claims the company will soon face fierce competition and profits will fall, so current surpluses are needed if they are to reinvest and maintain competitiveness.[21]

Conventional corporate management fiercely defends its "right to manage" surpluses, that is, to control investment decisions. Profits can be, and in reality are, paid out as increased dividends to stockholders and as higher wages and bonuses to executives, used to acquire other companies, spent to construct new plants in states or foreign countries with low wages, or earmarked to install new technologies that eliminate jobs without any benefit to the workers. Too often, corporate schemes that reduce workers' wages in return for a share in the profits are part of a strategy to increase profits and reduce both labor costs and the power of unions.[22]

We might also contrast the Mondragon system with the heralded lifetime-employment guarantee of major Japanese firms (which is, in fact, based upon the heavy use of subcontracting, and of temporary and seasonal workers who bear the brunt of the fluctuations of demand). These companies have externalized unemployment. Satoshi Kamata describes the life of a seasonal worker for Toyota whose job automatically ends after six months on the assembly line:

> The Toyota method of production appears to the outside world as the systematization of the 'relationship of a community bound together by a common fate' (Ohno, Toyota Method of Production). But truthfully, it's nothing more than the absolute determination to make all movements of goods and people in and out of these plants subordinate to Toyota's will.[23]

On his third day as a seasonal worker, Kamata is given:

> Conditions for Discharge
> 1. If the employee is no longer needed
> 2. If the employee has physical problems
> 3. If the employee is absent for more than twenty days because of an accident outside his work
> 4. If the employee is absent more than fifteen days for personal reasons
> 5. If the employee is absent for more than four days without reporting[24]

Kamata concludes:

> While management journalism may applaud Toyota's high profit and the 'kanban' method which they see as supporting it, the human costs of Toyota methods—suicides, injuries, job fatalities, and occupational disease—increase at a horrifying rate.[25]

For example, Kamata notes 267 cases of injury and death at Toyota between January and September 1979. This is the reality that conditions and supports Japanese "lifetime employment" for a select portion of the Japanese workforce.

The Mondragon cooperatives' use of a planning process based upon labor as a fixed or semifixed cost is not merely a way of externalizing unemployment. In essence, the co-ops have shown the ability to reduce advances ("wages") under severe stress in a way that is far more flexible than the practice in conventional firms. Since co-op advances are deliberately targeted to equal the prevailing wage in the area, does this mean the co-ops are breaking solidarity with other workers for their own economic benefit? Does it mean economic survival is only achieved through self-impoverishment? These issues will be explored later.

Funding

When the new co-op's feasibility study is completed, it is reviewed by the Operations Committee of the CLP's Banking Division, which makes a final decision on providing the necessary loan for start-up capital. At this point, the loan is very rarely denied. Under a job-creation program, the Spanish government provides 20 percent of co-op start-up costs through a low-interest loan.[26] The remainder comes from the CLP and the normal cooperative membership contribution.

The increasing capital intensity of the technological workplace has meant that investment per job continues to grow and requires substantial funding by the CLP through loans, in addition to increased cooperator membership contributions. The availability of Spanish government loans for job creation does not appear to lead to undertakings of greater risk by the CLP or to a reduction in membership contributions. Rather, it enhances the ability of the CLP to use its resources to support all aspects of co-op operations.

Originally, the cooperative membership contribution was about 20 percent of initial capital, but as the amount of capital invested per job has increased the percentage of initial capital required from workers has decreased to 15 percent or less. In dollar terms, the membership contribution has risen from around $5,000 payable over two years to about $10,000 payable over four years.[27]

This substantial investment is in accord with the basic entrepreneurial philosophy of the owner-workers being at personal, as well as collective, financial risk.

The increasingly technological nature of new efforts reflects the co-ops' response to the Spanish recession and to growing international competition. In the long run, the technological imperative is part of fundamental changes in the global economy that flow from the adoption of computerized automation and integrated flexible production techniques. Capital investment in new plants now tends to produce fewer jobs per dollar, and reinvestment in existing plants tends to eliminate jobs if ordinary levels of production are maintained. Developing responses to this phenomenon (e.g., job sharing, hour reduction without pay reduction, etc.) is one of the challenges the co-ops must face in the future.

For example, in 1986 the Mondragon co-ops created 338 new jobs, with an average capital investment of approximately $83,000 per job—a 75 percent increase over 1985.[28] A $5,000 membership investment is only 6 percent of the per-job total; $10,000 is 12 percent. To some extent, increased technological intensity is reflected by increases in productivity in 1986 of 6.7 percent (13.2 percent in the capital-goods sector of the industrial cooperatives). The 338 added jobs is a net figure: it includes a reduction of 105 jobs, presumably by attrition and transfers, in the consumer-goods sector as a result of the reconversion modernization process.[29]

Despite the high level of unemployment in the Basque region, the co-ops have not taken a low-tech approach. Possibly they have decided that labor-intensive, low-technology production would not be economical in view of low-wage international competition and that they are not well-equipped to enter new low-tech service sectors where wages are already depressed and competition intense at a time when demand for services is weak. The co-ops have an industrial orientation, weighted toward high-value-added technological production that their research indicates can be supported in current domestic and international markets. They have not taken steps toward developing a Gandhian type of indigenous, low-technology economy that requires little investment per job. But the greatest increase in jobs in 1986 did come in the service and commercial sectors through the expansion of the existing cooperatives.

Clearly, the job-eliminating effect of new capital investment will have profound long-term impact upon the nature of work throughout the world, not just upon the Mondragon cooperatives. Despite full-employment planning, in the long run a substantial change in the nature and organization of work seems inevitable (see Chapter 7).

From Start-Up to Break-even

A typical business plan will anticipate losses (or negative net income) for three years following start-up. Start-up is the point where a plan becomes a living cooperative organization, interacting with the other cooperatives and the rest of the world. The advisor, backed by all the resources of the Empresarial Division and the CLP, is a key figure during this period. The initial loan from the CLP is usually scheduled to be repaid over seven years, with no interest charged for the first two years, 8 percent interest for years three and four, and 14 to 15 percent interest for the last three years.[30]

Losses and the Founders' Equity

Since 70 percent of all net losses are subtracted from the members' personal equity accounts, three years of losses would probably wipe out their contribution; as the co-op becomes profitable, then expands and hires new members, the new owner-workers would share only in profits and bear none of the losses. This would be a strong economic disincentive for workers to start a new co-op. For this reason, co-ops have developed an accounting method in which start-up costs and the anticipated losses do not simply wipe out the founders' initial investment.

Here again, Mondragon cooperative entrepreneurship has been able to provide a solution consistent with its basic principles and humane intent. Seventy percent of the start-up losses are capitalized, instead of being charged against workers' accounts: this means these expenses are treated as if they were an asset on the co-op's books, like investment in machinery or buildings, and depreciated over seven years. Therefore, instead of 70 percent of the loss simply being absorbed as it occurs, a depreciation charge is taken against the co-op's income dividend over seven years from the date of each loss. This means that both the founders and the new owner-workers share in the start-up costs and the profits over a nine- to ten-year period. The other 30 percent of start-up losses is charged as a normal business expense in the year it occurs.[31] Additional support and risk-sharing for the emerging co-op is provided by the cooperative groups, which also pool varying percentages of profits and losses to be shared by the whole group.

Final Correction

The new co-op is not simply allowed to sink or swim in the marketplace. The advisor continues to work closely with it, and the Auditing Department carefully monitors its performance. During the start-up period, the co-op must not only function as planned, but be able to change its plan in response to positive and negative developments.

At the first sign of trouble, the Empresarial Division and the CLP institute an integrated series of measures. Since the new co-op does not have the financial resources to weather major losses, necessary interventions often require not just adjusting the business plan but focusing on the need for additional capital, especially if the proposed modifications include new equipment and a new product. At this point, the CLP and the Empresarial Division may decide to reduce or suspend interest payments, call for new investment by the members, or make an additional loan, depending on both the co-op's financial needs and its ability to modify its plans and activities.

The CLP is unwilling to subsidize co-ops indefinitely. This is not simply a response to the law of survival of the capitalist jungle, but a recognition that it is not desirable to use scarce social resources and energy to maintain an unproductive enterprise. The decision to terminate assistance to a co-op has been made in only three cases—Copesca (1973), a fishing cooperative; Labeko (1983), a chocolate factory; and Scoiner (1983), a furniture-veneering-machine manufacturer.[32] Two of these failures were departures from the Mondragon model. In the case of Copesca, a substantial loan from the Spanish government diminished the owner-members' commitment; Labeko was a conversion of a small conventional company (see Chapter 8). Even with these failures, deciding to dissolve the cooperatives was not simply a matter of bottom-line economics. Rather, the owner-workers and the CLP agreed that they no longer wished to attempt to go forward together.

Fission—Hiving Off New Cooperatives

Cooperative entrepreneurship has led cooperators in a different direction in terms of size and scale than that of conventional firms or other cooperatives. It became clear that while certain economies of scale encourage the growth of large organizations, there are decided social and organizational diseconomies of scale that can help undermine the cooperative spirit through the growth of administrative apparatus in large organizations.

The cooperators have learned that as the number of owner-workers passes two hundred, face-to-face intimacy and trust begins to fade; by the time there are four hundred to five hundred members, bureaucratization inevitably sets in. At that point, if possible, parts of cooperatives can be hived off to start new independent co-ops. Not all the co-ops involve fewer than five hundred workers; Ulgor, the first and by far the largest industrial co-op, has a few thousand workers, which reflects the scale of its operations in the consumer-appliance industry. But where possible Ulgor has shed its subsidiary divisions to form new cooperatives.

It might be possible to have large, centrally administered co-ops with satellite divisions, but the evolving model has been to create large numbers of independent co-ops associated in groups, but maintaining a high degree of independence and initiative. When possible, new cooperatives are created rather than building one large firm in each category. This allows a large number of people to use their energies and creativity, rather than having them smothered beneath a blanket of bureaucracy. For example, there are 15 co-ops besides Ulgor in the Industrial Consumer Goods area, and 30 co-ops manufacture intermediate goods that often serve some of the needs of the Consumer Goods and Capital Equipment co-ops. The Mondragon system today consists of more than 170 cooperatives of widely varying size divided into eleven areas or subareas (see p. 14).

Cooperative entrepreneurial growth, then, is much more than simply a matter of expanding the system. For an individual cooperative, the target is to reach a size that optimizes the balance of social and economic efficiency, a balance that in the long run is vital to the economic as well as the social durability of a co-op. This is not sentimentality. As E. F. Schumacher notes,

> any organization has to strive continuously for the orderliness of order and the disorderliness of creative freedom. And the specific danger inherent in large-scale organization is that the natural bias and tendency favour order, at the expense of creative freedom.... The larger the organization, the more obvious and inescapable is the need for order. But if this need is looked after with such efficiency and perfection that no scope remains for... [people] to exercise... creative intuition,

for entrepreneurial disorder, the organization becomes moribund and a desert of frustration.[33]

Schumacher's solution to the problem of the large organization was the establishment of what he called "quasi-firms,"[34] each with conditional independence within the larger body, which would foster a degree of risk-taking, creativity, and entrepreneurial spirit. Schumacher set down basic principles for large organizations that want to maintain their flexibility and freedom of action in the face of the tendency toward bureaucratization and inertia. In a sense he was attempting to graft onto such firms some of the characteristics that the Mondragon cooperators have found to be integral to organizations of up to five hundred members.[35] Mondragon's avowedly entrepreneurial cooperatives by their nature accomplish all Schumacher's goals within the context of the social fabric of their communities.[36]

Future Innovation and Adjustment

Each cooperative and group remains an entrepreneurial organization. Thus, mature cooperatives are vital community organizations, but they are not allowed to stagnate or to be deliberately exploited like older, established divisions of large corporations that are milked for profits that may be used for new acquisitions or for new plant construction in other regions or in countries with lower wages and less environmental regulation.

Rather, capital reinvestment and modernization are an integral part of the ongoing functioning of mature co-ops under cooperative entrepreneurship. Sometimes dramatic changes are made: the Spanish recession that began in 1972 and Spain's entry into the Common Market led the CLP, the Empresarial Division, and the associated cooperatives to develop a comprehensive reconversion plan for modernization and technical innovation, including a complete retooling and redesign of Ulgor's main production facilities (see Chapter 8).

To recapitulate, the co-ops' response to hard times involved retooling and capital improvements, self-help financial measures (including a reduction in advance payments, additional contributions of capital by the owner-workers, transfer of staff between cooperatives, and emergency unemployment benefits) financial assistance from the CLP, management help (including more sophisticated services from Empresarial Division), and improved training for co-op managers.[37]

Historically, the co-ops appear to have moved through one complete cycle on the classic S curve of growth. Their performance over thirty years has been largely congruent with the broader economic climate. They began to grow slowly in the mid 1950s, when the Spanish economy was first opened to expansion, then shared in the worldwide industrial boom of the 1960s. As this dissolved into recession and depression in the 1970s, co-op growth continued, but gradually slowed (at the top of the S curve). At this point, the co-ops began their successful reconsolidation, and they appear to be entering a new phase as growth again begins to increase. (This topic is explored further in Chapter 8.)

The Mondragon co-ops have not banished all evils of the market system, but they have demonstrated the possibility and durability of the system of cooperative entrepreneurship.

Intervention Area

The recession made the Empresarial Division recognize the need for an expanded and systematized response to economic downturns for both new and mature cooperatives. The co-ops, while vigorous, were not necessarily able to survive the vagaries of general cyclical economic disruptions or structural changes affecting entire sectors of the economy. The Empresarial Division had developed with the boom, and it originally intervened mostly in response to occasional mistakes or inadequate planning. Good times encouraged rather straightforward solutions, combining technical assistance coordinated by an advisor assigned to troubled co-ops with the financial resources of the Caja Laboral Popular.

But hard times needed creative and prompt responses, so the Intervention Department was established in 1983 as a separate area within the Empresarial Division, and a new three-stage assistance and intervention process, based upon a hierarchy of risk and response, was established. This depends upon careful monitoring by the Auditing and Information area to learn of possible problems early and to develop response plans before a problem becomes a crisis.

The three levels of intervention are

- Low risk (warning or alert from Empresarial Division)
- Medium risk (the Empresarial Division intervener may work with the co-op one day a week)
- High risk (all aspects of the co-op's functioning are closely supervised by the Intervention Department)

Ellerman notes that certain "alarm bells" alert the Auditing and Information area. For example, the cooperative might ask the CLP to reschedule loan payments, or CLP auditors might require the bank to add a bad-debt reserve for the co-op. As for action, interest payments might be reduced at the second level or suspended at the third level.[38]

The Empresarial Division usually executes a contract of intervention with a co-op in difficulty, detailing the responsibilities of the division, co-op management, co-op governing council, and the CLP. This helps assure that the process is a cooperative one and helps keep co-op management from trying to sweeten the true picture so as to win further loans or credits. Intervention measures may involve changes in marketing techniques, product modification, installing new production equipment and retooling, new management planning (and, if necessary, new management or a new board of directors), additional loans from the CLP (or additional capital contributions from the owner-workers) transfer of cooperators to other co-ops, reduction in advance payments, and, as required, temporary layoffs. The final step if intervention fails is to dissolve the co-op.[39]

David Ellerman reports that thirty-four interventions in 1983, during an intense period of cooperative reconversion and consolidation, resulted in the replacement of two general managers, eight other managers, and three members of boards of directors. Two cooperatives were closed.[40]

This performance can be compared with that of the typical "work-out" team sent by banks and creditors when conventional firms are in serious trouble. The Mondragon system is designed to monitor and respond to problems at the earliest level, with the expertise and resources of the Empresarial Division and the CLP—not just to step in at the last moment to safeguard loans over the objections of managers.

The work-out team's goal is to save the investment of its banks or investors; the fate of the company's workers is decidedly secondary. At Mondragon, the Intervention Department wants to save the jobs of the owner-workers (and to save the co-op as a community resource) as well as the investment.

The work-out team wants to make sure the debt can be repaid; beyond this, the company can be sold, milked, or abandoned, choices left largely to management and stockholders. In contrast, the Intervention area is not focused on short-term financial salvage but works within the context of the long-term health of the co-op and the co-op system.

The Intervention area operates within the context of detailed projections of long-term trends in the local and world economies. Studies of business conditions and of structural economic changes are an important part of the work of the Empresarial Division, and not just simply as a way of gathering expertise to maximize profit or even to grant or deny credit. The information is democratized: the popular co-op magazine, *Trabajo y Unión* publishes detailed yet accessible articles, for example on the machine-tool industry and the phenomena of computerization and overcapacity forcing structural economic changes.

The Mondragon system places its faith in the collective knowledge and wisdom of all its members. Solutions to its problems are developed from within, in accord with basic cooperative principles. This is why the system of cooperative entrepreneurship has endured and succeeded. As Arizmendiarrieta understood, the co-ops have been the means through which the strength and power of the people is used for their benefit.

Conclusion

There is cause for optimism. The Mondragon system of cooperative entrepreneurship is a model for the social renewal and humanization of both business enterprise and technology. Cooperative entrepreneurship takes the essentially limitless creative human resources possessed by any group of people and combines them with material resources to re-create a self-renewing and dynamic community. This allows the cooperatives to form and reform themselves, to transfer information, and to share their spiritual and material resources.

Cooperative entrepreneurship arises from the consciousness or soul of the community. It is not a separate artifact. Its root, as Arizmendiarrieta noted, is the individual drawn together with other individuals within the social context of community. The bonds are not visible, but the mode of operation is specified and concrete.

The particular genius of the Mondragon cooperators is not that they have found a mechanism to make money or create wealth—something done all the time—or that they have discovered a way to institutionalize the establishment of new business. Those are only part of the means to the end of creating and strengthening the bonds of chosen and discovered community.

Cooperative entrepreneurship and the pursuit of equilibrio provide a way to begin to reintegrate the corrosive dualisms that have torn apart the inhabitants of industrial society. The cooperators act primarily from the heart, from insights conditioned by collective experience, not merely according to legalisms and precepts. Their method unleashes soaring human energies; their legacy is a reminder that cooperation works—with documentation for the skeptic.

Socially, cooperative entrepreneurship, mediated by the pursuit of equilibrio, allows us to become conscious of our membership in a universe of life and mystery unfolding, from the realm of possibility. Cooperative entrepreneurship is then a tool for social transformation and social development that can exert a healing power. Arizmendiarrieta concluded, "In short, this Cooperative Experiment has demonstrated that workers are mature enough to be entrusted with broad social influence."[41]

The experience of the Mondragon cooperatives is emphatically neither religious nor utopian, but at its core are elements that fly from materialist superstitions, connecting it with a domain of the spirit that transcends the structures of hierarchy and power. It is in this domain that the cooperators find for themselves, in the words of Mircea Eliade, "the very heart of the real." This is for Mondragon a consciousness of participating in a community that is creating a humane social order. Through the practice of cooperative entrepreneurship and the pursuit of equilibrio the ends and means become one. As Mircea Eliade noted:

> Religion 'begins' when and where there is a total revelation of reality; a revelation which is at once that of the sacred—of that which supremely is, of what is neither illusory nor evanescent—and of man's [and woman's] relationship to the sacred, a relationship which is multiple, changing, sometimes ambivalent, but which always places man [and woman] at the very heart of the real.[42]

A visit to the Basque region will quickly confirm the humanity of the cooperators and the bond between them and other members of industrial society. They go to work in the morning in factories, offices, and schools; they worry about rising prices and think about vacations, children, their homes; they are concerned about birth control, abortion rights, independence from the Spanish state, and the place of political violence; the kids listen to rock and roll and ride motorcycles. That is the point. They are ordinary, yet somehow they have become different. The development of community, the pursuit of equilibrio and democracy are means for change accessible to people who share membership in industrial society. At the center is the human experience that brings individuals into the social fabric of democratic community. We can rely upon our integral and common humanity.

Notes

1. Ellerman 1984c.
2. Gutiérrez-Johnson and Whyte 1977.
3. The Mondragon Experiment 1985b.
4. Personal communication from Terry Mollner, July 1987.
5. Ellerman 1984c, p. 281.
6. The Mondragon Experiment 1984a, pp. 22–25.
7. In the period between the founding of ULGOR and the founding of the CLP, Ormaechea and his colleagues had exhibited extraordinary entrepreneurial ability in the formation of the cooperative Ulgor, Arrasate, Funcor, and the operations which eventually became Ederlan, Copreci and Eroski. When the bank was formed, Ormaechea generalized and institutionalized this entrepreneurial experience in the Empresarial Division of the CLP. Ellerman 1984a, p. 2.
8. Ellerman 1984c, p. 287.
9. Miller and Estrin 1987, pp. 359–60.
10. Experiment 1984a, pp. 22–25.
11. Ibid., p. 24.
12. This description of cooperative foundation is based in large part upon Ellerman 1984a and 1984c.
13. Ellerman 1984c, p. 274.

14. Kaswan and Kaswan 1986, p. 18.
15. Ellerman 1984c, p. 289.
16. Ellerman 1984c, p. 283; Ellerman 1984a, p. 25.
17. Ellerman 1984c, p. 285.
18. Ellerman 1984b, pp. 6–8.
19. Ibid., p. 26.
20. Ibid., p. 8.
21. "The Realities of Profit Sharing" in *Economic Notes*, vol. 55, nos. 7–8, July–Aug. 1987, pp. 6–7.
22. Ibid.
23. Kamata 1982, p. 200.
24. Ibid., p. 49.
25. Ibid., pp. 210–11.
26. Ellerman 1984a, pp. 28–29.
27. Ibid., p. 29.
28. Annual Report 1986, p. 65.
29. Ibid., p. 64.
30. Ellerman 1984c, p. 286.
31. Ibid.
32. Ibid., p. 288.
33. Schumacher 1973, p. 229.
34. Ibid., p. 231.

35. Schumacher's five principles are subsidiarity (lower levels maintain their highest function and greatest practical amount of freedom); vindication (profitability is the measure of efficient functioning, with appropriate adjustments for particular conditions); identification (a separate balance and profit-and-loss sheet for each division); motivation (people work for more than just money); and middle axiom (management by instructions that are less than inspirational speeches and more than simple orders). Ibid., pp. 230–37.

36. The U.S. antinuclear action group Clamshell Alliance reached conclusions similar to those of the Mondragon cooperatives about the optimum size of groups. Clamshell occupations and blockades of the construction site of the Seabrook nuclear project in New Hampshire involved as many as six thousand people in the 1970s and continued on a somewhat smaller scale into the late 1980s; they are based affinity groups of ten to twenty people organized into "clusters" of two hundred to six hundred people. Each cluster is able to make its own decisions about its conduct during an action, in accordance with nonviolence guidelines and other existing collective agreements.

The cluster, through support people drawn from its affinity groups, also has its own logistical capability. To the extent feasible, these support people work cooperatively with other clusters and the central support organization. The clusters can come together, if they wish, to make joint political decisions. Clamshell found a remarkable difference in collective and individual strength, flexibility, and community between an activity organized around five thousand individuals and one that had fifteen clusters of three hundred to four hundred people, each cluster being composed of twenty to thirty intimate affinity groups.

The affinity group is roughly analogous to the Mondragon work teams: small, voluntary associations of people who have come together as neighbors, friends or coworkers. They function as a group and provide assistance and mutual support to each other and to other affinity groups. Such groups originated in the organizing practice of the Spanish anarchists in the first third of the twentieth century, serving as basic units of self-management in a wide range of activities. Murray Bookchin observes that affinity groups were informed by a commitment of individuals to be "free to take all you want of things, destiny, and daily life" (Bookchin 1977, p. 197). In Clamshell, affinity groups and clusters make decisions by consensus following the Quaker model; this does not require a unanimity of view, but rather agreement on a common course of action.

37. Experiment 1984b, pp. 55–57.
38. Ellerman 1984c, p. 287.
39. Ibid., pp. 287–88.
40. Ibid., p. 288.
41. Experiment 1985b, p. 5.
42. Eliade 1957, p. 18.

7
Social Structures: The Elaboration of the Mondragon Experiment

"Cooperation is a seed."
—José María Arizmendiarrieta

The goal of cooperative entrepreneurship is not simply economic success, but social success. While the former can be measured, the latter is rather like happiness and beauty: it exists, but cannot simply be counted, stored, or hoarded; it is an expression of the quality of daily experience. At Mondragon, social success is the result of a living, dynamic, and renewing process, a reflection of the reality constructed by the cooperators through their ongoing pursuit of equilibrio.[1]

Building cooperative social reality is a formidable social challenge. It must be voluntary, as liberty is the catalyst for the creation of community. But the mere exercise of freedom by individuals does not of itself bring the formation of community. As Arizmendiarrieta notes, it is difficult to establish a harmonious [equilibrado] social balance in some communities where the individuals are unmoved by the sociological injunctions of the importance of education, town planning, public health, and, nevertheless, with very sharp eyes are conscious of the splits that weaken our social being, finding cause for their present longings for consumption, selfishness and greed.[2]

The Mondragon cooperatives did not begin with a blank slate. The cooperators were heir to the strengths and weaknesses of Basque culture and were as afflicted as most people by the ills of industrialism, including inequality, hierarchical structures, sexism, acquisitiveness, disregard for the environment, and the exaltation of technology and instrumental science in service to the machine.

The Mondragon accomplishment must be considered as an evolutionary process. This does not mean that we should overlook, for example, the persistence of sexist patterns, but it does allow us to examine the nature and trajectory of the cooperative response to change in the Basque context. We must avoid, at one extreme, masking co-op failures under a curtain of weasel words and a blanket of cultural relativism or, at the other, dismissing Mondragon because it fails to live up to the highest standards of political "correctness."

The evolution of the Mondragon system is reflected in the growing diversity and unity of new co-ops and new structures, which now tend to encompass many of the spheres of life formerly considered the province of private firms or of the state. These new institutions represent the creation of independent, convivial, and cooperative organs of civil society. The world of ecological postmodernism rises from below, in response to perceived needs; it is not conditioned by dreams of conquest, but by the expansive, creative impulses that animate a healthy community in motion.

Counting: The Measure of Happiness?

The consideration of social success, of the nature and attributes of the good life, is enormously complex. While it is not difficult to reject such bald materialist measurements as number of automobiles per household, such popular nonmaterial standards such as the utilitarian belief in the pursuit of happiness (for groups) or Freud's pleasure principle (for individuals) are also unsatisfactory and must be seen as part of the ideology of industrial modernism.

Any number of statistical measures can be employed to provide evidence of material robustness, particularly in comparison to a previously aggrieved condition. Thus, houses for the homeless, a decline in the suicide rate among adolescents, and employment of women in new types of positions reflect change, and probably change for the better. But these are not sufficient measures of social success—housing can be prisons, suicide avoided through sedation, and new employment found as executioners.

We need to be suspicious about counting, which has much to do with the conduct of the megamachine of industrial modernism. It is a function that tends to identify the limitless, geometric expansion of compound interest with the economic imperatives for growth and expansion and to ignore the reality of a living, finite, and fragile world community. Ignoring ecological reality in favor of the psychosis of perpetual growth is an error central to the practice of industrial modernism and to its ideology. It is an artifact of the philosophies of growth and of conquest (with which growth shares psychic space).

Counting, which feeds the growth mania, is in part the creature of a complex of deep social structures that shape the identity and nature of the megamachine. Counting, below the surface, becomes a quintessential patriarchal preoccupation. Founded upon difference and separateness, it helps provide the ground upon which the objectified "other" is created. Counting, driven by psychological anality and compulsion, is a basis for order and therefore for the exercise of power and the formation of hierarchy.

Counting is the rhythm of the clockwork universe. Its regularity defines, limits, and encapsulates people and objects in time. Counting confers identity by providing a number that is not only a label, a scalar quantity, or a representation of an acknowledged physical relationship and form, but is, in effect, the attribute of a quality that is defined within the domain of the machine. As the philosopher Ludwig Wittgenstein notes, "[i]f calculating looks to us like the action of a machine, it is the human being doing the calculation that is the machine."[3] Counting has become an expressive act of definition and self-definition, of power, order, lust, and fear. This is the lava ground state of our scientific "objectivity."

The compromised complexities of the deep social structures supporting industrial modernism inform even what seem to be such fundamental and value-free activities as writing and mathematics. Writing itself appears to have been invented by accountants in the service of the ancient despotic empires of Sumer and Elam, the originators, in the view of Lewis Mumford, of the prototypical social megamachine. Mathematics, the "purest" of the sciences, is no more external to the social framework than are the other sciences that in the name of "progress" are held to open up neutral and inevitable pathways to new technologies. Yet a considered skepticism about the value of counting in analyzing society does not mean that measured data are necessarily unimportant. For example, if the daily per-person intake of calories and protein in a society drops below a certain level, there will be starvation, malnutrition, disease, retardation, and, as a consequence, social deformation and collapse. But above the level necessary for health and active living, daily food intake is useful largely as a matter of comparison and may reflect a number of diverse cultural and climatic factors.

Counting clearly can help us interpret and describe—indeed, the economic chapters of this book contain charts, graphs, tables, lists of percentage returns and annual increases, and logistic curves. We civilized humans are a numerical troop. Still, we can ask, does good just mean more?

In practice, the conduct of the industrial megamachine (capitalist or socialist) is justified with arguments that the need to satisfy basic wants translates into an endless and endlessly escalating desire for more. This justification attempts to reconcile the exaltation of the material cornucopia of the machine—the ultimate manna and goodness—with the protection of individual rights by the state, particularly the rights to pursue and keep wealth and power. Producing commodities and counting them is, of course, what the industrial megamachine does best; it is, in fact, what the industrial megamachine does. This is the traditional interpretation. It is a straightforward argument not only for capitalists but for some socialists. Ivan Illich points out that

> Stalinism makes it possible to interpret as revolutionary whatever increases the amount of schooling, expands the road systems, or increases the productivity of extraction and manufacture. To be revolutionary has come to mean either to champion the nation that lags in production and to make its members keenly aware of the lag, or to inflame the frantic and frustrated attempts of underconsuming minorities in rich countries to catch up.[4] But the desire for more is continuously redefined as the productive power and geographic reach of the machine expands. It has gone beyond the desire for objects and services to become the pursuit of ephemeral, commercialized archetypes that are held to represent our identity.

Freudianism is the psychology of industrialism: it exalts unconscious drives as the motivation for human behavior, including competitive lusts for limitless satisfaction of individuals that are a perfect analog to the drives inculcated to create the limitless demand for products required by industrial megamachine. Behaviorism outdoes Freud: it removes the unconscious drives and construes the human being as programmable mechanism.

The capitalist system has rather surprised itself, and such pessimistic ideologues as Joseph Schumpeter, by its staying power. It has been able to "reform" without breaking and has relied on the technical efficiency of its market mechanisms to be able to produce more, when more is what matters, than the centrally planned economies.

Ideologically, both the capitalist pursuit of freedom and the socialist search for harmony and equity now must rest upon a corruption of the Benthamite appeal for the greatest good for the greatest number—and more and more of it, as Jeremy Bentham's search has become a vulgar justification of capitalist and socialist materialism and consumerism that also undermines his firm support for effective democratic control of society.

Communist thought smoothly embraced dictatorship to guard against the danger of capitalist backsliding and revanchism. Similarly, the founding ideologues of capitalist freedom provided a justification for capitalist democracy to protect itself from the "tyranny" of the majority. In 1838, as worker resistance to the industrial revolution increased, John Stuart Mill was quick to warn of the dangers of democracy:

> The numerical majority of any society whatever must consist of persons all standing in the same social position and having, in the main, the same pursuits, namely, unskilled manual laborers.... Surely, when any power has been made the strongest power, enough has been done for it; care is thenceforth wanted, rather, to prevent that strongest power from swallowing up all others.[5]

Today, the debate between capitalists and socialists has sadly become a matter of which band of technocrats manages industrialism more "efficiently"—that is, who produces more products with fewer inputs, including human labor (our life energy) and irreplaceable resources (the totality of the natural world). Outputs include the effluvia of poisons and wastes and human wreckage, as well as the rain of objects and services.

The New Creation of the Organs of Civil Society

The heart of the Mondragon experiment exists outside the domain of counting and input-output analysis. Counting is the record of the frozen and finite; equilibrio is dynamic and expansive, essentially alive. At Mondragon, economic success is not the chief purpose and accomplishment of cooperative activity but, rather, part of a social process that results from the cooperators' democratic social choices and that leads to unfolding social benefits.

Freedom for the cooperators is not liberty to purchase, to spend, to hire, to establish individual life-styles. Freedom for Mondragon is the concomitant of community. It is suffused with the basic cooperative principle of solidarity and with a social-ecological consciousness supporting diversity and unity. All this is manifested in the evolutionary process by which the cooperative social institutions are created as independent organs of civil society removed from the power and bureaucracies of both government and corporations. Thus Mondragon is not just factories, or factories plus the Caja Laboral, or factories plus CLP plus schools, but an evolving and dynamic social system whose search for equilibrio naturally leads to the elaboration of the experiment.

The creation of the independent organs of civil society is a popular theme in the social transformation under way in central and eastern Europe, where citizen action from below is counteracting the pervasive grasp of the state in a largely nonviolent process. The basic theme of creating such organs is, however, not limited to such countries: it is applicable to nation-states everywhere and to the global reach of corporate power and bureaucracy. The nominal distinctions between public or private bureaucratic structures that manage industrial modernism have become increasingly meaningless: there is little to choose from, for example, between Soviet "public" design bureaus and institutes that produce weapons and "private" U.S. military contractors, or between corporate and state-owned transnational oil giants. Huge telephone companies, public or private, are rather indistinguishable.[6]

This is not an attempt to extinguish all differences between public and private organizations, or between market and planned economies, but rather to suggest that the power and pervasiveness of bureaucratic structures is increasing, as is their effect upon people and communities. Industrial managers are now largely immune to the concerns of individuals, as well as of communities, nations, and even global regions; they are the incarnation of industrial modernism, the propagators of its ideology and values. In both the capitalist and socialist worlds, they identify themselves, more or less successfully, with "freedom" and "prosperity."

Education and Theory

The Mondragon system began with the small school for industrial apprentices established by Arizmendiarrieta in the 1940s; it became the League for Education and Culture and is now called Hezibide Elkartea. In important ways, the schools set the stage for the development of the whole system. While this book focuses mostly on the industrial cooperatives, their supporting institutions, and the process of cooperative entrepreneurship, the nature and success of Mondragon is integrally related to its growth and development as an educational system.

José María Arizmendiarrieta was essentially a teacher, not a businessman. But he was an educator with a fundamental commitment to social change and with an entrepreneurial spirit that led him to create, together with the people of Mondragon, a liberatory social system. Education was to be technical, moral, political, and social, in the classical Greek spirit of *paideia*, for the development of the good society. Arizmendiarrieta called education "the best service to humanity."[7]

Arizmendiarrieta understood education not merely as what happened inside classrooms, not only for the young, but as a fundamental means for social change. As Joxe Azurmendi points out, for Arizmendiarrieta education was an active process that joined study and work, extended to all parts of society, and continued throughout life. Thus, connections in the cooperative system were not limited to those between schools and industrial firms but were part of a fundamental process of revivification for the Basque country.[8] As Arizmendiarrieta wrote: "One is born man or woman, but not a lathe operator or a modeller, and much less a doctor or engineer. . . . One is not born a cooperator, because to be a cooperator requires social maturity, a training in social coexistence [*convivencia*]. . . . One becomes a cooperator through education and the practice of virtue."[9]

Arizmendiarrieta focused on progressive and secular education in the face of the resolute determination of Franco's government and the local corporations to deny such opportunities to the Basques, and despite the very conservative and limited nature of most available Catholic education. His effort was not without local historical antecedents. Azurmendi notes that at the turn of the century the socialist union UGT in the Basque province of Vizcaya had a stong focus on education. Its "houses of the people" (Las Casas del Pueblo) became "schools of moral, intellectual and political education."[10]

And in nearby Barcelona, the "Modern School Movement" (La Escuela Moderna), originating at the beginning of the twentieth century in the work and writings of Francisco Ferrer, had a global impact on progressive education. Ferrer became an international cause célèbre when he was unjustly imprisoned and subsequently executed by the Spanish government following an anarchist revolt in Barcelona in 1909—an action in which he was, at most, peripherally involved. His last words as he faced the firing squad were "Look well my children! I am innocent. Long live the Escuela Moderna."[11]

Ferrer's thinking prefigures some of Arizmendiarrieta's ideas, as in the following passage:

> The word "education" should not be accompanied by any qualification. It means simply the need and duty of the generation which is in full development of its powers to prepare the rising generation. . . . In a word our business is to imprint upon the mind of the children the idea that their condition in the social order will improve in proportion to their knowledge and to the strength they are able to develop.[12]

Ferrer's strong antipathy to all religion (in the anarchist tradition) was combined with hostility to what he called political education and government inculcation of patriotism. In opposition, Ferrer emphasized the virtues of science and the liberation of the individual. For Arizmendiarrieta, liberation is more an integrative social and moral process of education, choice and action. For Mondragon, the instrumentalities of science and of individual initiative are conditioned by the search for equilibrio within the context of cooperative principles.

Arizmendiarrieta and Mondragon cooperativism stand outside (or, perhaps more precisely, have moved beyond) the tradition of anarchist thought that focuses upon the "free" individual. For example, in the nineteenth-century classic *The Ego and His Own*, Max Stirner writes:

> If your efforts are ever to make "freedom" the issue, then exhaust freedom's demands. Who is it that is to become free? You, I, we. Free from what? From everything that is not you, not I, not we. I, therefore, am the kernel that is to be delivered from all wrappings and—freed from all cramping shells. What is left when I have been freed from everything that is not I? Only I; nothing but I. But freedom has nothing to offer to this I himself. As to what is now to happen further after I have become free, freedom is silent—as our governments, when the prisoner's time is up, merely to let him go, thrusting him out into abandonment.[13]

This credo at times appears consistent with the conduct of capitalist industrialism and the pronouncements of such of its ideologues as Milton Friedman, who tell us we are "free to choose." Ferrer and Stirner seem to treat education as if it were an instrument to unleash the potential of individuals upon a world in which, freed from constraints, their choices would tend to create the best of all possible worlds. But Mondragon cooperativism marks a departure from the tradition of self-management and education that found liberty, as did Pierre Joseph Proudhon, in "[t]he government of each man by himself, that is, *Anarchy* or *Self-Government*."[14] Mondragon cooperativism is based on the recognition of a much more social, interactive, and educative process.

For Arizmendiarrieta, education was a process that reflected the social maturity of a group of free persons, and not only the freedom from indoctrination to a life of obedience to power. Social maturity for Mondragon reflects individual empowerment, the ability to make new social choices to exercise freedom and to build community. It is a secular education—not because Arizmendiarrieta repudiated religion or moral values, but because the social choices were to be made by free people, outside the authoritarian structure of the church. He emphasizes morality and virtue as a recognition of human freedom and the consequent importance of moral choices in the active pursuit of social re-creation.

Arizmendiarrieta's thinking is reflected in his appreciation of the writings of Jacques Maritain and Emmanuel Mounier, who insisted upon a moral as well as a material education and upon "the necessity for a new education for the establishment of a new order."[15] Azurmendi notes that

Arizmendiarrieta read carefully the work of Paulo Freire and saw the parallel between the education of the oppressed and the education of the worker—underlining the passage stating that education for the oppressed "must be worked out *with* him and not *for* him."[16]

It is often remarked that Arizmendiarrieta eschewed any position in the industrial cooperatives or in the Caja Laboral Popular. His "only" official role was as director of the League for Education and Culture, but Arizmendiarrieta saw this as a central position. Education for Mondragon is an active practice, the foundation of the life of the cooperative system; it helps provide the basis for the social choices that shape its nature and development.

Education and Practice

The variety and depth of the cooperative educational system, ranging from day care to continuing education for people of all ages and all interests, is striking. For adults, it goes beyond practical connections between vocational training and the well-being of the cooperatives to, for example, a major effort at customer education by the Eroski consumer co-op. Three examples illustrate the system's operation.

The continuing education of cooperators is a major part of the co-ops' response to economic change. In 1987, Fagor, the largest of the cooperative groups, reported that 2,010 (or 30%) of its 6,602 cooperators were involved in technical or professional training courses. These lasted an average of almost 57 hours per person, for a total of 116,000 hours at a cost of $2 million. This is in addition to $730,000 spent by Fagor on more general social-education programs for its members.[17]

The Iranukor organization, through Eskola Politeknikoa in Mondragon and ETEO (Escuela Universitaria de Estudios Empresariales) in Oñati, offers about one hundred continuing-education courses in a number of fields. There is considerable emphasis on computer- and microelectronics-related subjects.[18] Although Iranukor is oriented to the needs of the Mondragon system, its services are available to other interested individuals and companies. Iranukor also offers scholarships and fee reductions to unemployed workers. Its general courses are supplemented by specific programs developed for in-company training to meet particular needs at various levels. For example, a 320-hour course was developed for the Ikerlan research cooperative to help plant engineers accelerate technology transfer in microelectronic areas, and a 160-hour course on general business practices was designed for Eroski managers.[19]

The Eroski retail co-op, with 1987 sales of $363 million in 271 stores and more than 130,000 consumer members, offers a wide range of educational programs. In 1987, it provided 1,150 consumer and nutrition-training sessions for 57,000 people. These featured:

- Detailed courses offered at Hondarribia Consumer School and the Centers for Promotion of Women and the Cultural Centers in San Sebastian
- First Young Navarrese consumer sessions and food program in Bilbao
- Cooperation and collaboration with other consumer-oriented organizations
- Discussion of issues in the broadly circulated co-op magazines *Eroski* and *Eroskide*

Women and the Mondragon System

The role and status of women in the Mondragon cooperative system is of particular interest as a matter of education and of social practice. The industrial co-ops were conceived and founded by men during the Franco dictatorship, when politically, legally, and socially, sexism was dominant. The victory of Franco and of fascism marked the triumph of state and corporate power over working people and of the patriarchy over women.

General Climate

Of course, sexism did not begin with the rise of the Falange. There is a long record of the imposition of patriarchal patterns and power in the Basque country, including the repression of women as "witches" and their resistance during the Inquisition.[20] But the position of women in the co-ops must be examined in light of Franco's vengeful efforts to crush Basque political liberty.

Women had a strong role as leaders and as participants in the Republican struggle. This is clear in the extraordinary pictures taken at the time. I am looking at a July 1936 photograph of Barcelona workers of the CNT union who had taken up arms to oppose the attempt at a Right-wing coup that began the Civil War. The photograph is taken from above. About twenty people, women and men, young and old, are crowded, standing, in the back of a pickup truck. The letters CNT are painted on the windshield. The workers are wearing street clothes: some are talking to others crowded around the truck, some are staring with great attention at something in the distance. There is an air of revolutionary excitement, of inspired ad hoc action, of risk and commitment. Only two rifles are clearly visible, both apparently held by men; an artillery piece sits in the street nearby. It is a picture of women and men in struggle prepared to risk their lives.[21] A second photo is of a lone militiawoman, dressed in black with a military hat, standing against a background of clear sky. She is smiling broadly. In one hand she is holding aloft in a victorious gesture a plain red flag on a wooden pole. Her other hand clasps the top part of her rifle.[22]

The women's movement, the end of Francoism, the surprising resurgence and durability of Spanish liberal democracy, and the increasing integration of Spain into the European community have all led to a dramatic change in the position of women. The overt —at times almost semifeudal—air of repression I observed in 1965 and 1969 had changed dramatically by the late 1980s. There are abundant political graffiti, posters, and wall paintings in the Basque country, including clear signs of feminist agitation—¡Aborto Sí! ("Abortion Yes!") was popular on walls, and can accompany ¡OTAN Afuera! ("Nato Get Out!"—together with startling color posters promoting a *korrika* (race) to benefit Basque nationalist efforts. In Mondragon in 1985 it was reported that local women, after town officials remained adamant in refusing to accede to their demand for easy availability of contraceptive devices, threw chairs through the windows of the room as they left a meeting.

Another symbol of the reentry of women into the mainstream of Spanish life was the return, after a long exile in Moscow, of La Pasionaria, Dolores Ibárruri, a Basque woman from an impoverished Vizcaya mining family who became a Communist leader and famous orator during the Spanish civil war.[23] In her eighties, La Pasionaria, who came to represent the spirit and courage of the fight against Spanish fascism, was elected to the newly democratic Spanish Cortes in 1977, just months after her return.

A focus on women as revolutionaries should be undertaken with some caution. Activism, politics, and revolution are not men's work, nor are they the sole measure of value. It is, in part, a product of history written by men to identify women's worth with their participation in violence. In patriarchal doctrine women tend to be rendered invisible unless endowed at least with some of the virtues of men. Taking a different tack, Robert Clark associates the patient and persistent nonviolence of the Basque Nationalist Party (PNV) with

> the dominant role of women in Basque society generally and the mother in a Basque family in particular. . . . There seems little doubt that this dominance of the female in Basque culture has worked to soften a resort to violence that might otherwise have become much stronger given the provocative and suppressive environment within which Basques have lived for several generations.[24]

Again, to see women as the moderating and civilizing influence on brutish men is to look through a patriarchal lens. In a postpatriarchal world, women must be understood and valued as actors and agents of history, not merely as those who condition the work of the real actors, men.

To understand accurately the shape of a postpatriarchal Basque culture, where women will be empowered and no longer invisible, is as difficult as it would have been to predict the 1990 condition of the Mondragon cooperative system in 1955, before its founding. Such a culture must be struggled for and built, not simply theorized. But it can be realized through the pursuit of an *equilibrio* that admits the concerns of women, making it fuller and more genuine, and hence stronger, more durable, and more creative.

Origins of the Co-op Experience

The fascist dictatorship's campaign against Basque self-assertion was very much in line with the inclinations of those who believed a woman's place was in the home. Certainly, such sentiments were quite generally held: in 1951, Arizmendiarrieta wrote that "[w]omen's destiny is in the home"—and for "home," he used the Spanish word *hogar*, which literally means "hearth," rather than the more neutral *casa*, thus underlining the message. He proposed establishing a Feminine Vocational School for "future wives and mothers" to learn about "preparation for the home."[25]

It is reasonable to assume that such attitudes were typical among Arizmendiarrieta's students and cohorts. Women were not seen as equals, capable of independent action, and were therefore considered unable to undertake nontraditional activity within the patriarchal structure. Such fetters of patriarchal culture are forged and maintained not simply by men's overt physical violence—witch burning, rape, battering and murder, and the like—and the complementary economic and social violence of discrimination, but by a pervasive, basic, and internalized sexism that arises from deep social structures, infuses the language and thought of both women and men, and immobilizes and isolates women.[26] Women are confined, in the words of Adrienne Rich, to "having to tell our truths in an alien language."[27]

Formation and Development of the Industrial Cooperatives

By 1955, as the first industrial cooperatives were being formed, Arizmendiarrieta's view was changing—a process Azurmendi suggests parallels that of broader Mondragon society. Women were now to be incorporated into social life. Arizmendiarrieta's practical side asserted itself: "A woman has to think in her own defense of appropriate work."[28] Still, the early co-ops were essentially male institutions, founded by male engineers with a strong technical orientation. Women were not only denied equality by co-op rules—single women could work, but married women could not be cooperators until 1971—but had even less opportunity to obtain advanced technical education than Basque men, for whom an engineering degree at the time often involved a valiant struggle.

Not surprisingly, women in the co-ops were effectively ghettoized into low-paid office support and blue-collar jobs or into such management areas traditionally open to them as personnel, effectively excluding them from line management. In the 1970s, however, more women joined the co-ops, and by 1978 4,760 of the 17,020 cooperators (about 28%) were women. At the beginning of the 1980s, Christine Clamp noted that the Association of Women's Commissions (organized by women in the cooperatives) in Ularco (now Fagor) found that women were underrepresented in the group's decision-making bodies: they account for only 6 percent of supervisory board members, 20 percent of social council representatives, and 3 percent of supervisors. Clamp argued that "women have yet to overcome the social and educational barriers which keep them in the nonprofessional positions and underrepresented in decision making bodies."[29]

But that is not the end of the story. The participation of women in the co-ops is a process of change marked by such accomplishments as the recent appointment of a woman as manager of one of the three divisions of the Fagor group—a group that is of great economic and symbolic importance at the geographical and historical heart of the Mondragon system. The appointment of one woman does not a feminist revolution make, but it suggests movement toward the full participation of women in Mondragon. Two events reflect this development: the founding and development of the women's co-op Auzo-Lagun, and the role of women in the Ulgor co-op strike of 1974 and its aftermath.

Auzo-Lagun

By the late 1960s the world, the co-ops, and the thought of Arizmendiarrieta were moving away from the resolute and reflexive sexism of the early 1950s. Arizmendiarrieta was now not only openly critical of masculine "superiority" but called stongly for equal rights for women in the cooperative movement. He wrote that "half of the adult population does not have the right to rule the destinies of the other half." He believed that work—for both women and men—was not only a means for economic gain but a pathway toward individual and community self-realization. "Work is before all a service to the community and a form of personal development."[30]

But his specific interest at the time was in how married women in the cooperatives combined the roles of mother and wife. Auzo-Lagun was begun as a service cooperative by twenty women with the active assistance of Arizmendiarrieta in 1965. It allowed married women, especially those with children, to work either morning or afternoon shifts. By 1985, the co-op had 340 members with an average age of 45 (younger women now tend to join other co-ops as full-time workers). Many used a day-care center, established for all Mondragon workers in 1981, and now independent.[31] Auzo-Lagun is now open to men but remains overwhelmingly a women's co-op. Managers for five areas (food, kitchen, sales, administration, and personnel) and a general manager are elected by the general assembly.

Despite economic and organizational problems over the years, by 1985 Auzo-Lagun provided commercial food services (which produced more than four thousand hot and cold meals daily), institutional cleaning services, and subcontract assembly work for other co-ops. Its new headquarters was built in 1979 with a loan from the Spanish government, which has now been paid off.

In 1985 the average pay grade in Auzo-Lagun, according to González, was 1.4, compared to 1.6 in the other cooperatives and to 1.7 in Caja Laboral Popular—13.5 percent less than the average Mondragon cooperator (including women). This is an improvement over the United States, where women's wages average 31 percent below that of men, but it still reflects an undervaluing of "women's work" in the service co-op. Auzo-Lagun clearly represents a transitional stage in the participation of women in the cooperative system. Twenty-five years after its founding, the opportunities for women within the co-ops are far more varied than the pursuit of traditional areas of cooking and cleaning that are the loci for women's self-management.

The Ulgor Strike of 1974

A strike in Ulgor and Fagor Electrotécnica in July 1974 had important implications for the development of the Mondragon system. This must be seen in perspective: the years 1973 to 1975 marked a tumultuous period in the Basque country and in Spain, a time of fundamental and sometimes violent political and social upheaval, the end of the Franco regime, and a great expansion of Basque nationalist activity. There were also disputes within the cooperatives, many of them centered on Ulgor, which had grown swiftly to become a very large and rather bureaucratic organization of thirty-five hundred members. The troubles in Ulgor were not simply a creature of the broader political climate, but the times encouraged the questioning of authority and existing patterns of power.

Background: The Tumultuous Years 1973–1975

In December 1973 Franco's prime minister, Admiral Carrero Blanco, was assassinated in a spectacular Madrid car bombing, the action of the revolutionary Basque separatist organization ETA. The regime retaliated fiercely, moving to repress ETA and Basque nationalists with a special Decree on Military Rebellion, Banditry, and Terrorism.

In 1974, there was a successful Portuguese revolution in April, along with many small acts of resistance by ETA's military branch, including, in December, "a series of shootings and robberies in Mondragon and Urdaliz [that] resulted in one ETA member killed, two Guardia Civil killed."[32]

Then, in November 1975, Francisco Franco died after a prolonged illness. People throughout Spain were awaiting, and sometimes helping to foster, the end of the Franco regime, as the dictator lost his health and his political grip. This was nowhere more true than in the Basque country. In 1975, the Whytes found:

> Unofficial political mobilization was especially evident in the Basque provinces, although the Basques were by no means unified. Marked divisions existed along class lines, political ideology, and commitments to Basque nationalism. Resentment against the tight control of Madrid was generally shared, but Basques were divided between those who hoped for greater regional autonomy and those who pursued the ideal of an independent Basque state.[33]

The Strike for Equality in Ulgor

The dynamics of the Ulgor strike of 1974 are still not entirely clear. Following a long-running dispute over a two-year job-reevaluation program, more than 400 cooperators (most in Ulgor, but others in Fagor Electrotécnica), finding they could not convince co-op management and governing councils to abandon plans for systematizing and adjusting cooperator pay grades, struck for eight days in July 1974. Management and line workers found themselves locked in a confrontation that led to a struggle for power—definitely not a widened pursuit of equilibrio. The strike failed. The governing councils of the two co-ops expelled 24 cooperators as strike leaders, 18 of them women (in Ulgor 14 women and 3 men were dismissed; in Fagor, 4 women and 3 men), and disciplined 397 other cooperators.[34] The councils acted on the grounds that the strikers had ignored the available democratic procedures for resolving their grievances and endangered the basis for co-op democracy; this position was supported by votes of the general assembly.

It was not until 1978 that the general assembly of Ulgor voted to readmit the expelled members, and more than half of those expelled were readmitted; Fagor Electrotécnica took similar action. One of the strikers' demands was for greater equality of *anticipos*. The system being put into place established a number of fine distinctions and included a "merit factor" based on an immediate supervisor's judgement. This amounted to a 15 percent pay differential for the lowest-paid cooperator and a 5 percent differential for the highest-paid. These matters particularly concerned to women, who had experienced substantial discrimination within the co-op system.[35]

Despite extensive analysis of the strike by outside observers and a month-long Ularco study in 1985 by a group working with Professor Davydd Greenwood of Cornell University, little has been written on the role of women and of feminist issues in the strike. The strike transcended the question about wage discrimination and the assertion of management prerogative. The strike was an attempt to challenge in the name of equity and fairness the growth of bureaucratic hierarchy. While the strike was lost, in the long run the strike was a catalyst to the further democratization of the co-ops.

There is general agreement that the strike represented the most traumatic event in the co-ops' history. It led to substantial changes, including:

1. Greater attention to participation and dialogue and to the search for equilibrio. [This is reflected in Ulgor's response to deep recession in the late 1970s (see Chapter 9), with substantial individual and collective sacrifices by the cooperators.]
2. Comprehensive steps throughout the Mondragon system to limit individual co-op size wherever feasible to fewer than 500 members and to reduce bureaucracy
3. Successful redesign of the compensation system in 1978–79 under recessionary stress. This demonstrates what Gutiérrez-Johnson calls "the conditions under which collective 'rational' decision-making is possible."[36]
4. Development of new co-op norms to regulate work stoppages in 1976–77 that recognized the political strike in solidarity with other workers outside the co-op
5. Organizational strengthening of the social councils

Unfortunately, the role and importance of women on a policy level in these matters remains minor. It is clear, however, that their participation in Ulgor increased substantially after 1974. Women have organized formally as the Association of Women's Commissions and have begun to move into line-managerial posts. The declining numbers of women who leave the co-op due to marriage indicates another shift. This presumably reflects changing attitudes and the availability of child care and parental leave. Resignations due to marriage dropped from 93 in 1973 to 7 in

1978. In 1977, 36 percent of the 1,500 women cooperators in Ulgor were married.[37]

Conclusion and Perspective for the Future

The future of women in the Mondragon cooperatives remains uncertain, but change is a basic characteristic of the system, and the co-ops' leadership generation is retiring. Some of the young women I was privileged to meet in Mondragon in 1985 were actively pursuing education and independent careers. They had grown up in Mondragon, but their ambitions and training did not seem to be leading them toward the cooperatives. It is crucial for the future development of Mondragon that it attracts such intelligent, spirited, and energetic young women. Historical circumstances meant that the first generation of cooperators was largely without feminist leadership; it will be an enormous handicap for their successors to repeat this experience.

Co-ops and Revolution

The various strains of Marxism have viewed the idea of cooperatives as agents for social change with skepticism. The anarchist movement, particularly in Spain, and libertarians and "council-communists" had a more nuanced and favorable view of "autogestion" and the potential revolutionary valence of cooperative forms. But Marxist groups—which have become, at least in the public imagination, largely synonymous with the revolutionary aspirations of the Left—simply assert, whatever the complexities of their analyses, that co-ops, within the framework of capitalism, are not effective means for social change.

Since Marx's scathing critique of the cooperative mutualism of Proudhon, co-ops have been denounced as betraying the class struggle that is at the core of Marxist doctrine; as ahistorical (and therefore doomed) utopian efforts that ignore, even delay, the inevitable progress toward proletarian revolution; and dismissed as isolated organizations reflecting a pinched "enterprise consciousness" that betrays (for the sake of success and survival in the capitalist market) not only other workers, but the very humanistic and cooperative values they were formed to advance.

Marxists seem indiscriminately hostile to co-ops, regardless of the enormous variety of conditions to be found in Spain under Franco or under liberal democracy; in the late capitalism of the United States; in such newly industrialized states such as South Korea; or in a mixed economy such as that of Nicaragua.

An example that gives the flavor of the Marxist critique of cooperatives appears in an article in the U.S. socialist journal *Monthly Review* by sociologist Jerry Lembcke that views cooperatives as doomed attempts to counter the workings of the capitalist market, attempts that ignore the central reality of class struggle:

> Desperate and confused, the unemployed workers embrace the co-op alternative, not for its socialist potential but for its appeal to the individualism and self-sufficiency they have internalized through years of capitalist socialization. The victimized workers busy themselves with a self-rescue effort that is destined to fail because it must operate in an arena where monopoly capital sets the rules. . . .
>
> [Co-ops] were "utopian" in Marx's view because they assume the harmonious cooperative relations of production can be achieved immediately without the intervening stages of organization building, the development of class consciousness among workers, and the struggle for economic reforms. Marx's criticism is important, because many of the current economic democracy movements embrace the rhetoric of reform and go-slow evolutionary socialism.[38]

Or consider this critical analysis of the Mondragon co-ops by one of the "tendencies" within ETA, included in a four-page handout circulated during the July 1974 strike:

> In order to break with capitalism, we must place ourselves in the land of reality (the class struggle) and not that of wishful thinking. These errors start from one basic point: denying to the working class the role of agent for destruction of capitalism and of its bourgeois state; this means the cooperative project remains trapped in its own laws (the laws of the capitalists) against which they should naturally want to fight. We must not forget the role of the state as supervisor and engine of capitalism and that of the working class as the only agent capable of destroying it. . . . [T]he cooperative bureaucracy is set up to guarantee the bourgeois order in the Léniz Valley, in committed defense of capitalist property facing the combined efforts of the working class.[39]

On a less ambitious but similar note, people argue that co-ops can undermine worker solidarity, encourage "givebacks" in wages and working conditions, facilitate union-busting, and ease the departure from master contracts that set patterns for entire industries. For example, U.S. trade unionist Lance Compa observes:

> From the standpoint of the labor movement, adopting the objective of greater worker control is bad policy because it emphasizes "enterprise consciousness" rather than class consciousness. When workers control a firm, their interests are identical with management's. They no longer struggle for the betterment of workers in general or for the betterment of those in a particular trade or industrial sector; they think in terms of making their own workplace more profitable. In effect, workers become capitalists with capitalists' problems.[40]

Edward S. Greenberg administers what seems to be the coup de grace to cooperative pretensions:

> With respect to the outside world, the producer cooperatives seem to nurture outlooks characterized not by community, mutuality, equality, and confidence in others, but outlooks more congruent with the tenets of classical liberalism: those of individualism, competition, limited government, equality of opportunity and inequality of condition, and so on.[41]

Thus we have come nearly full circle. Not only are co-ops vain and counterproductive attempts to usurp the historic revolutionary role of the working class, but they, in effect, reproduce the attitudes and social relationships they were organized to transcend.

Critique of Critique

Co-ops can indeed be co-opted by management and undermine the struggle for human dignity and efforts for social transformation. But it is historically and empirically myopic to view the efforts of cooperative systems as essentially futile and counterproductive, if not counterrevolutionary. A fundamental premise of this book is that co-ops—in particular, such systems as Mondragon—can play a crucial role in the transformation from late industrial modernism toward an ecological postmodernism. This assertion is based on the social and economic performance of the Mondragon system. Its ten basic principles are not merely palliatives to weaken the resolve of working people. Open admission, democratic organization, sovereignty of labor, and the rest are clearly understood by the cooperators as the building blocks for a new social order. The Mondragon system is rooted in the democratic search for equilibrio, which includes a fundamental and multilayered support for solidarity within the co-ops, with Basque working people, and with broader international movements for social change (see Chapter 10).

The Mondragon cooperative system, for Arizmendiarrieta, represented the potential for a gradual and truly profound revolution to be created day by day. The desire for "instantaneous revolution" may involve revolutionary means but fail to achieve truly revolutionary human ends—these can only be created step by step through liberty and cooperation, with maximum participation by all concerned. As Arizmendiarrietta wrote, "There is nothing more prejudicial for a revolution than illusions, and nothing that is more useful than the clear and naked truth"; in practice, "a daily revolution consists in transformations effectively consolidated in new structures." But such a revolution is not simply a bureaucratic exercise: "Doubtlessly our cooperativism is going to hurl into the fray valuable answers for an incorruptible people with an age-old love of their liberty."[42] This is not a call to the barricades, but a call for direct action and participatory social change in the creation of a new social order.

In the debate following the 1974 strike, Arizmendiarrieta did not criticize the ideals of co-op critics, many of which he shared. Indeed, the dialogue included a surprisingly radical critique of industrial cooperatives (particularly of their denial of the right to strike) in a pastoral letter by the social secretariat of the diocese read in all local churches. The structural and operational changes made by the co-ops after 1974 indicate that some elements of the critique were indeed accurate, despite the vigorous defense co-op management mounted against the New Leftists of ETA, dissident co-op members, and critics within the church. Arizmendiarrieta did not act as a defender of co-op management, but returned to his belief in the connection between thought and action and the evolving reality of the cooperative system. In Azurmendi's view:

> Arizmendiarrieta had in his hands a concrete object [the Mondragon system], and a revolutionary one, but one certainly unable to be compared to a utopia or an ideal. After thirty years of defending himself from the right, in fighting in Mondragon against the capitalists and against ignorance, fear or the indifference of the people . . . Arizmendiarrieta had a difficult defense to make. At bottom, with his own position, he felt too close to the new critics. He respected too much their rebellion, their spirit of struggle and their love of liberty. He knew very well the necessity for all organizations to have elements of inequity, of demanding idealists, who bring about revulsion. . . . Arizmendiarrieta found himself divided, present on both sides.[43] The debate in 1974—between co-ops and strikers, co-ops and community, and the Mondragon system and ETA—involved intertwined threads of theory and practice, of revolutionary doctrine and tactics, and judgements about cooperative praxis and accomplishment. That the co-ops not merely survived but learned from this experience is a tribute to their commitment to the process of equilibrio that relies upon the strength of cooperative democracy.

Co-op democracy is taken much too lightly by radical critics. Marx wrote in 1844 that universal suffrage would lead to the abolition of both the state and civil society, since it would mean the overthrow of the property relations that sustain them: "It goes without saying that the right to vote is the main political interest of actual civil society. . . . Within the abstract political state the reform of the suffrage is hence a claim for the dissolution of the political state, as well as for the dissolution of civil society."[44] This appreciation of the possible revolutionary effects of universal suffrage was a major theme of such liberal thinkers as Mill and the framers of the U.S. Constitution (and the nervous holders of substantial amounts of wealth, property, and slaves in the new republic). That capitalism eventually found it could tolerate the semblance of universal suffrage, and even social democracy in power does not invalidate the aspirations and sentiments for liberty that animated the great social movements of the eighteenth and nineteenth centuries.

As the twentieth century draws to a close, the Marxists' critique of co-ops has been historically orphaned: there is no imminent revolution in advanced capitalist states for co-ops to defuse even in the face of the forces of postmodernism. This is further complicated by the idea that the era of the industrial working class as primary agent of social change has passed[45]—a fact that explains some, but not all, of the current discouragement of the revolutionary Left. The anxiety and ennui afflicting revolutionary Marxism does not in itself make cooperative efforts valid; it does suggest that such efforts as Mondragon merit serious consideration. This is "revolution" construed as a revolutionary kernel within an evolutionary and participatory historical process, something far different from a sudden seizure of power.

Marxism, certainly Marxism in power, usually has little to say about the forces arising from below that are transforming the existing society of industrial modernism in ways that bear little resemblance to the Marxist model. The present social menace is the destruction of the environment and human freedom and community. The world system of industrialism is consumed by the planning and conduct of war, the gross exploitation of nature and of people, the denial of freedom by national and international bureaucracies of state and corporate power. Mondragon cooperativism, through the democratic pursuit of equilibrio, represents the forces of revolutionary social transformation emerging in response to the world of late industrial modernism.

Cooperatives are certainly relevant to the course of the social transformation under way in the Eastern bloc and in China. In 1989, European Communist governments agreed to new political structures and to free elections, following on the heels of the Soviet Union's first contested and conditionally democratic voting in more than seventy years. Here, too, cooperative forms can play a crucial role in establishing the new independent organs of civil society that are transforming the practices of formerly Stalinist states.

Equilibrio, Cooperation, and the New Dialectic

I believe that the devolutionary forces transforming industrial modernism represent, in part, the impulses for nonviolent social revolution and the rise of an ecological postmodernism. The practitioners and theorists of such movements within, for example, Central Europe and Mondragon, are breaking new ground, but the world they are re-creating is outside traditional ideological boundaries. The concept of equilibrio could be said to represent a broadly dialectical logic, one that reflects the evolutionary processes of developmental indeterminacy (conditioned by deep social structures).

Mondragon's functioning admits the operation of classic evolutionary processes and feedback mechanisms typical of ecological systems. Evolutionary and dialectical mechanisms exist within the same social space, interact, and condition each other. The point is not that the Mondragon cooperators have repudiated the importance of class, of economics and power, relationships that influence the nature of their universe, but that they have stepped beyond the limitations established by a formulaic adherence to dialectical materialism. For the Mondragon cooperatives, forty years of experience in creating a social system has meant that the future is lived and re-created every day. This is in marked contrast to Marx's focus on cooperation as primarily a tool to multiply workers' productive power that made industrial cooperation central to the development of capitalism.

In *Capital*, Marx notes:

> From the standpoint of the peasant and the artisan, capitalist cooperation does not appear as a particular historical form of cooperation; instead cooperation itself appears as a historical form peculiar to, and specifically distinguishing, the capitalist process of production.

It is cooperation that he identifies as the central means necessary for capitalist exploitation and for the very creation of capital!

> It [cooperation] is the first change experienced by the actual labour process when subjected to capital. It takes place spontaneously and naturally. The simultaneous employment of a large number of wage labourers in the same labour process, which is a necessary condition of this change, also forms the starting point of capitalist production. This starting point coincides with the birth of capital itself. If then, on the one hand, the capitalist mode of production is a historically necessary condition for the transformation of the labour process into a social process, so, on the other hand, this social form of the labour process is a method employed by capital for the more profitable exploitation of labour, by increasing its productive power.[46]

Marx's critique of cooperation extends beyond this: he disparages it in tribal cultures and in agricultural communities where "the individual has as little torn himself free from the umbilical cord of his tribe or community as a bee has from his hive." He indicates in a footnote that "Linguet is probably right in his *Théorie de lois civiles* when he declares that hunting was the earliest form of co-operation, and that the man-hunt (war) was one of the earliest forms of hunting."[47] Of current concern to the future of industrial modernism is not Marx's failed predictions about proletarian revolution, but the determinism and exclusivity that drives

Marxian dialectical materialism as an analytic tool. As a social philosophy, Marxism assiduously follows the three basic principles of the steel triangle of industrialism, Progress–Hierarchy–Technique.

Marxism has a fundamental belief in progress—in this case progress toward communist utopia. Events, driven by class struggle, are seen to have an almost teleological bent toward fulfilling Marxist prognostication. Marxist theory celebrates the transformative power of technique, of science plus technology, and respects the order and discipline of the industrial enterprise. And, particularly in its Leninist incarnations, Marxism celebrates hierarchy—the discipline and leadership of the Party. Marxism is the application of the principles of "scientific" socialism to the task of liberating humans from capitalism, not from industrial modernism. In contrast, the search for equilibrio is based upon the exercise of freedom and community building, not some abstract notion of progress; embraces democracy before hierarchy; and encourages participation and dialogue before technique. The search for equilibrio is not simply an attempt to maintain a balance that serves the status quo; it is a dynamic, evolutionary process. Evolutionary change does not necessarily imply measured or linear change: evolution, whether biological or social, can be abrupt, punctuated by sudden and dramatic change.

In the complex and multivoiced relationship between individual and social choices, the search for equilibrio means, in practice, making social choices to limit the conduct of industrialism. These new social choices are the prerequisites for liberation. The search for equilibrio therefore establishes an inclusive social space to resolve the tensions between such social constructs as chance and necessity, free will and determinism, and idealism and materialism through action within complex and evolving structures. "Nonhierarchical" does not mean there are not different levels of structure and complexity. The lowly phytoplankton are fundamental to the entire ensemble of life; atomic phenomena seem to be governed by chance and statistical probability; physical, chemical, and social processes can lead to sudden and dramatic change, particularly in systems far from equilibrium. "Nonhierarchical" does reject, however, the idea of a great chain of being that decribes a hierarchical order ruled by humanity, along with a variety of weary monistic determinisms that rely upon a privileged, fixed, and ahistorical standpoint to render mechanistic judgement.

In the determinist doctrine, co-ops—even if they transcend the narrow enterprise consciousness of worker capitalism—mark the accommodation of working people with the capitalist system and thereby weaken the ultimately irreconcilable contradictions that will lead to revolutionary action by the proletariat. The doctrine relies upon class and economism, upon a determinism that makes empirical claims to validity.

158 *WE BUILD THE ROAD AS WE TRAVEL*

It thus tends to admit little or no ambiguity about the role cooperatives might play in social transformation.

The Mondragon record is startling and heartening. It makes no great claims, but it offers itself as the history of a social experiment. Alfonso Gorroñogoitia, writing a detailed review of the co-op system, sees

> Mondragon as a project in constant motion.... [O]ur cooperatives are an open process.... Equilibrio in motion. The static vision of the cooperatives can be dangerous for all. For those outside because they believe in a vision of utopia ... that doesn't exist. For those inside ... that want to say that the Mondragon Cooperative Experience has been finished.[48]

Mondragon's New Independent Organs of Civil Society

One manifestation of the cooperators' creative impulse over the years has been the development of a wide variety of cooperative structures, processes, and procedures. The co-op has not developed as a bureaucratic exercise of planning focused on the bottom line or on maximizing surpluses. Instead, there is participation in the pursuit of equilibrio and of cooperative entrepreneurship and in the making of new social choices in response to the needs and goals of groups of cooperators.

The process operates on the macro level with the development of democratic governance and such policy structures as the cooperative congress and on the micro level with decisions by individual cooperatives on the treatment of their social capital. Cooperative development extends to housing, health, social insurance, environmental planning, education, day care, and consumer and agricultural cooperatives, and it tends to become coextensive with the full range of activities conventionally considered to be the province of govenment or corporate power. Members are not driven by an abstract determination to create a co-op universe, but by the desire to fill perceived social needs within the Mondragon system. This section will explore a number of these responses.

Mondragon Surpluses and Community Reinvestment

The treatment of social capital is fundamental for the cooperatives, and not simply as a question of managing resources. It reflects the way the co-ops have transcended the economists' dour predictions of self-destruction. Not only have the Mondragon co-ops been able to decide to forgo short-term income for long-term economic benefit, but they have continually shaped their investment decisions with social considerations. The democratic control of surpluses, what Mondragon accurately calls "social capital," has evolved to a division of resources between retained earnings, member accounts, and social contributions that can be adjusted according to circumstances. Collectively, such capital, through the Caja Laboral Popular, has become available to help finance and support the evolution and elaboration of cooperative forms.

At first, the co-ops—after deducting retained earnings and making a social contribution—distributed their yearly share of surplus directly to the cooperators, who could spend or save it as they chose. When it became clear that this arrangement would not provide sufficient long-term capital resources for the cooperatives, they established the system of internal capital accounts. The funds in these accounts remain with the Caja Laboral Popular and may not be withdrawn before the cooperator leaves. (As noted above, up to 70% of all surpluses goes to cooperators' individual accounts, at least 20% is held as retained earnings, and a minimum of 10% is used as a social contribution.) As the amount of surplus increased, the formula that governed its distribution meant that the percentage held as retained earnings and for social contributions also increased.[49] This formula encourages reinvestment in the cooperative and in the community. Thus 90 percent of co-op surpluses were available, in practice, to help finance operations, either as retained co-op earnings or as accounts of cooperators in the CLP.

The economic stresses of the 1980s led to a change in the distribution of social capital as co-op groups varied the basic percentages to provide more discretionary funds for the individual cooperatives. For example, in 1987 Fagor had a basic distribution of a minimum of 45% to retained earnings (Fondo de Reserva Obligatoria), 10% to social funds; and a maximum of 45% to individual cooperator accounts. Another group allocated a minimum of 30% to retained earnings, 10% to social contributions, and a maximum of 60% to individual accounts.[50]

In addition, it was formally proposed in October 1987 that interest rates on individual cooperator accounts be set at 6% annually, plus a revaluation for inflation based upon 70% of the increase in the consumer price index, with an annual minimum interest of not less than 5%.[51] This would tend to penalize the cooperators in times of high inflation and subsidize co-op operation. In 1987, with inflation reduced to 5.2%, internal capital accounts did quite well.

Since the baseline for co-op "wages" has been the local prevailing wage (exceptions are discussed in Chapter 10), a cooperator in a successful Mondragon firm will earn approximately this wage plus a share of the surplus. Today, if co-op surpluses equal 5% of total sales (a typical figure), this would amount to a yearly average of $3,525 per member (depending on the percentage allocated to individual accounts). For a typical cooperator with a 1.6 job rating and a yearly salary of $19,064, this would mean an 18% annual bonus. This is a substantial benefit, but hardly the reaping of enormous personal wealth. In general, the short-term rewards for the cooperators are fair wages, a secure job, and the many ancillary benefits of the cooperative system.

The collective maintenance of social capital, mediated through the CLP, provides the community with resources to support the evolution of the system. The creation and democratic control of social capital is central to Mondragon and to the ability to make new social choices. As J. M. Mendizábal observes, "Cooperativism is for the poor; the rich already can organize themselves without cooperatives."[52]

The successful application of such solidarity in the treatment of social capital reflects the revolutionary social potential of the Mondragon system. Note that solidarity is not here simply a matter of class, but includes a complex relationship between class and ethnic identification that transcends a simple notion of Basque identity. Alfonso Gorroñogoitia comments that much of the theoretical and political writing about Mondragon shares a belief that "ethnicity and social class cannot exist in the same social space." But this is not the Mondragon reality:

> Specifically, in the Basque Country, it is clear that there exists a complicated and dynamic relation between social class and ethnicity, and that the same persons or groups can follow at the same time their interests as social class and as ethnic group. Therefore, the intention of explaining the origin and success of the co-ops by the fact that the Basques form an ethnic group, is to believe in a serious distortion of the reality and the complexity of the social forms that are expressed through the means of the cooperatives. Also inconvenient for such an analysis is that more than 25% of the cooperators in Ulgor are immigrants [to the Basque region] and that many of the Basque cooperators work in political parties that have a class orientation.[53]

Cooperative Congress and the General Council of the Mondragon Group

The first Mondragon Cooperative Congress in 1987 began a new era in the development of the system. The congress represents the firm consolidation of democratic control, making it clear that such powerful cooperative organizations as the Caja Laboral Popular, while of great significance to Mondragon, are merely a part of a democratically governed community.

The congress has broad powers to discuss basic policy issues of concern to the cooperatives, including treatment of work and capital, development of model rules and statutes, promotion of new cooperatives, scientific and technical investigation, business development and promotion, social insurance, formation of new entities to serve the cooperatives, development of common business practices, analysis of problems affecting the Mondragon group, and development of institutional relationships nationally and internationally.

But in the essentially consensus-seeking process of the Mondragon group, the power of the congress over individual cooperatives is largely advisory. The general assembly of each cooperative must approve such basic changes as rules and regulations that will affect the co-op and participation in new cooperative bodies established by the congress. The congress thus is a grand assembly—one that debates complex issues and makes broad policy decisions, but one that leads rather than rules; there is no recourse to coercive power.

The congress elects a president, vice-president, and secretary; candidates must be nominated by at least three co-ops. As with any large deliberative body, much its work is done in committee. The four major issues of the first Congress were adopting the ten basic principles, creating new regulations on treatment of social capital, discussing salary differentials, and determining the rules and regulations that will govern the FISO "rainy-day" fund.

The Council of the Mondragon Cooperative Group was established to coordinate and implement the work of the congress. It includes delegates from each cooperative group (usually the general manager) plus representatives of Caja Laboral Popular, the Empresarial Division, Lagun-Aro, Ikerlan, and Eroski. The council has a small administrative staff.

According to José María Ormaechea, who resigned as CLP general manager to serve as the first chairperson of the council, it will deal with issues of development and daily operation without making decisions on basic principles and policies. One major goal, according to Ormaechea, will be to find mutually satisfactory solutions to the problems the co-ops face in an increasingly complex political and economic environment, further complicated by the differences between the cooperative culture in the Mondragon area and the other Basque regions. The congress and the council, he says, are an opportunity to help achieve both logical economies of scale and synergistic benefits of cooperation.[54] For Ormaechea, who has a strong entrepreneurial bent, the congress and the council are not bureaucratic keepers of the status quo. Their "basic mission is that of promoting cooperativism in order to expand employment in the Basque Country and promote technological advances."[55]

Lagun-Aro and Social Insurance

In 1987, the Lagun-Aro social-insurance system, a voluntary superstructure cooperative, provided coverage to 140 member co-ops with 18,055 cooperators. That year, 46,333 people received health benefits, and 1,234 were paid retirement, disability, and survivor pensions. It includes a pension system, a variety of family benefits, health care, sick leave payments, unemployment insurance, company medical services (focused on preventive care), and job investigations for health and safety procedures, including ergonomic evaluations of jobs and sound-level studies. A separate fire-insurance cooperative has also been founded.

In 1988 the Basque regional government established a program of universal free medical care and will now pay for and operate the healthcare system; Lagun-Aro's operations will continue in all other areas. Contributions to Lagun-Aro are based upon the labor grade of the cooperators and the actuarial estimates of funds required. The system is intimate and accountable; it is designed to prevent sickness and injury and to serve the needs of friends and neighbors and of the community.

Environmental and Energy Issues

As part of the planning process for new co-ops or new development, Mondragon co-ops require an environmental impact statement, as well as consideration of the social and business implications of their activities. This was a path-breaking policy for the Basque country and for Spain, and it reflects the cooperatives' basic commitment, as part of the search for equilibrio, to move in ways that will strengthen the community and the cooperative system within it. It is a decision to consider not only narrow economic "rationality," which externalizes environmental problems, but to pursue appropriate long-run policies for the health of co-op and community in a world where such resources as clean air and water can no longer be considered as "gifts."

Thus the cooperatives' attitude toward environmental regulation has not been the typical corporate response of opposition, grudging acceptance, and foot-dragging to meet minimal legal requirements. As one division of Lagun-Aro studies jobs to eliminate worker hazards without government prodding, so environmental concern has become part of the co-ops' mode of operation. Historically, the steel and metalworking industries of the Basque country created significant water and air pollution—rivers were dammed to provide power for the mills and then used, like the sky, to dispose of and disperse industrial wastes. To help remedy this situation, cooperatives have contributed to the building of a water-treatment plant. While concern for the strikingly beautiful countryside is a cornerstone of Basque life, it has not been fully translated into abatement of industrial pollution. The Mondragon industrial co-ops tend to turn out consumer products and high-technology items that— although generally less polluting than, for example, foundries and smelters—pose certain environmental problems. The deep recession of the early 1980s also made it difficult to deal with existing pollution, and it must be said that the co-ops had not then fully come to grips with environmental concerns.

Energy is a significant interest of the Ikerlan research cooperative, which searches for new products, such as computerized heating-system controls, and new resources, such as wind and solar energy. Historically, wind energy and hydroelectric power have played an important part in the development of Basque industry; unfortunately, the climate and topography are not as promising for solar development as in lands further south. Ikerlan engineers have also been engaged in energy conservation studies on public buildings for the Basque government.

A strong grass-roots antinuclear and environmental movement existed in the Basque region even before the Chernobyl catastrophe. (One symbol was of a smiling sun saying, in Euskara, "Nuclear Power, No Thanks.") A proposal to construct a reactor in the Basque country was actively opposed and brought to a standstill by tactics that included the assassination of plant management by ETA. Yet, one small co-op manufactures a condensate-monitoring system for reactors. Mondragon did not have a clear policy (at least in the pre-Chernobyl period) in opposition to nuclear energy.

In sum, the environmental record of the co-ops is mixed, but it is evolving in a positive direction. The environment has clearly been recognized as a major factor in the search for equilibrio. Most significant is that environmental concerns have arisen from below and have not been imposed by the state: the co-ops have been leaders, not followers. Mondragon is not ecotopia, but co-op processes are clearly ecological in the broadest sense and these will lead the co-ops—through self-management and not regulation—toward heightened environmental concern as part of everyday life.

Agricultural Co-ops

The eight constituents of the Erein Cooperative Group are involved in farming, dairy operations, forestry, food processing, selling fruits and vegetables, animal breeding, and producing animal feed and fertilizer. Mondragon's agricultural efforts, therefore, involve both farming and agribusiness, and current plans include new co-ops and projects in sheep raising, fish processing, and cereal grains. Agriculture was, at first, an unconventional interest for Mondragon, given the cooperatives' industrial experience, but involvement has become increasingly natural.

William and Kathleen King Whyte point out that the operations of the agricultural co-ops (such as the large dairy co-op, Lana) provide a creative and fair balance between the interests and power of farmers and processing plant workers supported by the financial and marketing expertise of the co-op system.[56]

The agricultural co-ops are supported by structures that include the Eroski system, which, with its hundreds of stores and support facilities, provides not only a consumer-oriented retail sector and a natural market for co-op consumer products, but incorporates a governance system that respects the interests of the cooperators and customers, has made itself available to consumers, and has undertaken a varied and innovative consumer-education program.

Housing and Construction Co-ops

The fifteen housing cooperatives, a response to the housing shortage in the Basque region (whose terrain often makes residential property quite expensive) also provide a natural market for the six cooperative construction companies, which are engaged in a variety of work, from residential construction to major industrial and institutional projects.

Conclusion

The evolution of Mondragon represents the growth of multifaceted social system, a growth that reflects the community's social needs and the cooperators' creative entrepreneurial efforts—all in the context of the increasingly broad pursuit of equilibrio that conditions the exercise of freedom and the social choices made by the cooperators.

Chapters 8 and 9 review the economic record of the cooperatives and their response to hard times and structural economic change. Keep in mind, however, that the social and financial roles of the cooperatives are not separate entities connect only by chance. Social and economic successes not only potentiate and facilitate one another, but reflect the democratic search for equilibrio. The spheres of Mondragon life interpenetrate and are governed by broadly similar dynamics and choices, with the economic tending to become merely one aspect of a dynamic social system.

Notes

1. Quoted in Azurmendi 1984, p. 369.
2. Quoted in Azurmendi 1984, p. 294.
3. Wittgenstein 1983, p. 234.
4. Illich 1973, p. 25.
5. Mill 1968, pp. 47–49.
6. In Warner, New Hampshire, the Merrimack County Telephone Company has 5,213 customers. It is one of 1,380 independent phone companies (including 200 cooperatives)

Social Structures **165**

in the United States. It still calls to remind me to pay my bill and asks if I need more time to pay. It is a revelation to deal with the phone company as a community institution.

7. Quoted in Azurmendi 1984, p. 221.
8. Azurmendi 1984, p. 211.
9. Quoted in Azurmendi 1984, p. 231.
10. Olabarri, quoted in Azurmendi 1984, p. 184.
11. Quoted in Bookchin 1977, p. 154.
12. Quoted in Krimerman and Perry 1966, pp. 413–15.
13. Max Stirner (pseudonym of Johann Kaspar Schmidt), quoted in Krimerman and Perry 1966, pp. 171–72.
14. Quoted in Horvat, Markovic, and Supek 1975, p. 88; emphasis in original.
15. Azurmendi 1984, p. 186.
16. Quoted in Azurmendi 1984, p. 190; emphasis in original.
17. Fagor Informe Anual 1987.
18. These include CAD/CAM (computer-assisted design/computer-assisted manufacturing); programming and use of Aurki numerical controller for machine tools; quality control of production processes; programming in Pascal; architecture and operation of sixteen-bit microprocessor systems; data acquisition; industrial design; accounting analysis; financial accounting; and marketing.
19. Iranukor, Programa de Actividades: Curso 86–87.
20. See Henningsen n.d.
21. Photograph in Bookchin 1977, p. 292. The caption reads: "The people in arms. A truckload of armed CNT workers in Barcelona during the July, 1936 fighting against the insurgent garrison."
22. Bookchin 1977, p. 280.
23. "La Pasionaria also represented the idea of revolutionary womanhood, a strong force in a country which had given the Virgin a special place in religion. As long ago as 1909, women in Barcelona had been the most eloquent, daring and violent among strikers." Thomas 1977, p. 9.
24. Clark 1979, p. 126.
25. Azurmendi 1984, p. 301.
26. Dale Spender's concept of the dominant and the muted indicates that the deep structure of such language means that women remain trapped within "male encoded registers" of understanding. Spender 1985, pp. 83–84.
27. Quoted in Spender 1985, p. 83.
28. Quoted in Azurmendi 1984, p. 301.
29. Clamp 1986, p. 192.
30. Quoted in Azurmendi 1984, p. 309.
31. Interview with María Asún González, Auzo-Lagun personnel director, July 1985.
32. Clark 1979, p. 168.
33. Whyte and Whyte 1988, pp. 91–92.
34. There have been contradictory reports on the number of strikers dismissed. The figures used here are from Azurmendi 1984, p. 629.
35. See Gutiérrez-Johnson 1982, pp. 264–97; Whyte and Whyte 1988, pp. 91–102.
36. Gutiérrez-Johnson 1982, p. 296.
37. Clamp 1986, p. 187.
38. Lembcke 1982, pp. 56–57.
39. From LCR-ETA-VI, a pamphlet produced by one of the factions formed from the sixth assembly held by ETA; quoted in Azurmendi 1984, p. 629.
40. Compa 1982, p. 300.
41. Quoted in Warner 1984, p. 13.
42. Quoted in Azurmendi 1984, pp. 742–43.

43. Azurmendi 1984, pp. 642–43.
44. Marx and Engels, *Werke* (Berlin: 1963), vol. 1, pp. 326–27; quoted in Avineri 1968, pp. 36–37.
45. Gorz 1982.
46. Marx 1977, p. 453.
47. Ibid., p. 452.
48. Gorroñogoitia 1987, p. 32.
49. The formula for distribution of surpluses is d = Y ÷ (Y + Z), where d is the percentage of funds allocated to collective reserves and social funds, called the "alpha coefficient"; Y is the surplus; and Z is the total of payroll costs plus interest payments on own resources, called "computable base." From Thomas and Logan 1982, p. 150.
50. Ginto 1987a, p. 9.
51. Ibid., p. 5.
52. Mendizábal 1984, p. 2.
53. Gorroñogoitia 1987, p. 31.
54. Ginto 1987b, pp. 12–13.
55. Ibid., p. 14.
56. Whyte and Whyte 1988, p. 195.

8
Economic Performance: Considering Mondragon's Record

The Mondragon cooperatives have an outstanding record of economic performance. In the thirty-two years from the founding of Ulgor in 1956 to 1987, the cooperative system has thrived and adapted successfully to the exigencies of the marketplace.

Introduction

The co-ops' founding coincided with the start of the great Spanish economic expansion of the late 1950s, and growth was spectacular during the boom of the 1960s and early 1970s; it continued despite contraction of the Spanish and global economies in the 1970s. Today, the Mondragon cooperatives have completed major restructuring and again are prospering in a newly dynamic Spanish economy.

Mondragon's economic record is not a fairy tale about the infallibility of cooperative business procedures. Rather, it is a sober and inspiring document of the construction of a system in the capitalist market that transmutes Schumpeter's "creative destruction" to cooperative creative renewal. The Mondragon record is the performance of an integrated social system of considerable depth, diversity, and complexity, and its economic success is a community phenomenon made possible by the exercise of new social choices. The cooperatives' health cannot be viewed conventionally, as the triumph of a group of firms in the marketplace. Social and economic development are inextricably connected in the co-ops' history.

For Mondragon, it is the reality of the social choices that demolishes traditional "rational" economic assumptions about cooperatives in action—assumptions predicated on the idea that the cooperators will pursue individual interests. Economist Jaroslav Vanek, who has developed a rigorous mathematical model for the effectiveness of a labor-managed economy, distinguishes between a "narrow" income-maximizing goal and a "broad" motivating principle encompassing diverse objectives:

> The true objective of the participatory firm is complex and multidimensional. If we insisted on reducing it to a single variable, we could not do otherwise than to say that the single variable is the degree of satisfaction of the individuals within the collective. Of course monetary income may be an important ingredient of the satisfaction, especially in very poor environments, but it is definitely not the only one. The working collective can, for example, sacrifice some money income in exchange for additional leisure time, lesser intensity of work, better human relations—or even a kinder managing director. If this is so, all the alternatives mentioned must be considered as a part of the participatory firms's objective, and thus a component of the moving force of the labor managed economy. In fact, the broader interpretation of the motivation base can include even objectives which normally would not be included under the heading of "self-interest" such as giving employment to others in the community, preventing unfavorable external effects such as air and water pollution and many others.[1]

Reviewing the co-op record through 1979, economists Henk Thomas and Chris Logan note that "[c]rises are characterized, as Vanek has argued, by a slowing-down of growth rates, not by downswings which result in the firing of workers and closing of factories, as occurred on a large scale in the Basque provinces during the 1970s."[2] They conclude: "Efficiency analysis has proven that a group of cooperative factories, provided it has access to credit sources and management services, can develop strongly during times of economic boom and also during a recession."

It is not surprising that even Vanek, as an economist and a maker of mathematical models still inclines toward a universe defined by the inclinations of a hypothetical economic human—a more cooperative human in his case, but one not yet fully conditioned by the dynamic human potential that stands behind Mondragon's social reality. As Alec Nove, with uncommon sense, notes of economic models, "A certain lack of realism is a legitimate price to pay for theoretical rigor. But one must never forget the extent of the abstraction that has been made from a necessarily complex reality."[3]

An economic analysis of the Mondragon cooperatives is a daunting task: their fortunes are obviously more complex than those of a single cooperative firm in the capitalist sea. Mondragon is a cooperative sector in the Basque economy, but not one in the usual sense—that is aggregated from largely unrelated firms. Mondragon is an integrated and coordinated system, but its level of integration is deliberately less than that of a typical industrial group or modern conglomerate. Within the system, co-ops, co-op groups, and their individual members maintain their independence and remain at risk. But cooperative independence does not simply mean economic accountability. Real power flows from below and is expressed formally as democratic control and informally as a consensus-seeking decision-making process. Such independence can be a burden during times of economic difficulty. The general manager of a small co-op complained in 1982 that "the symbol of the CLP is not recognized anywhere. . . . And the bank today has considerable potential as a bank and as an industrial group. If we were to consider it, the cooperative group, as an industrial group . . . it would be within the top twenty industrial groups of Spain."[4]

The tension between impulses for centralization and impulses for independence—a familiar theme for the Basques—is recast within the co-ops, where the pull toward centralization, in the name of efficiency and control, must be balanced with the countervailing imperatives for freedom, self-assertion, and independence. The dynamic balance between the two forces is central in shaping the development of the cooperative entrepreneurial system in ways that transcend the balance sheet. For Mondragon as a social system, this process is the expression of the integration of freedom and community.

The dynamic flux between centralization and autonomy is directly related to the co-ops' superior business performance. It provides a natural prod to entrepreneurial activity and to careful analysis of and adjustment to its effects. The tension is also reflected in the humanity of Mondragon and in its relative lack of sentimentality—not a surprising lack, because for the Mondragon system business success is a necessary survival skill. While failure can mean destruction, success is socially meaningful to the extent that it is shaped by the cooperators' social choices; they do not simply identify business success with the creation of a humane social reality.[5] Mondragon's restraint is not sentimentality. As Vanek suggests, the social values of Mondragon, crucial to its identity and survival, have become a part of the decision-making process for the monetized business of the system.

Co-op business operation is characterized by open exchange of information and by dialogue. The same dynamic appears in the development of cooperative organizational forms as they evolve to meet and balance the interests of various parts of the cooperative universe. For example, the cooperative congress establishes clear democratic governance from below, while the council of groups promotes greater coordination. The more complete integration of the cooperatives within particular groups improves efficiency and supports individual cooperatives, but at the same time it serves as a decentralizing counterbalance to the power of the Caja Laboral Popular. Clamp notes that co-op groups "are an important innovation for insuring the system's accountability at the local level while enabling the system to continue to grow."[6]

Our economic analysis, then, must be conditioned by an understanding of the practice of cooperative business, the evolution of cooperative organizational forms, and the reality of cooperative social practice. Mondragon in action is not scientific management, applying power or treating people as objects and the world as consumable resources. The cooperative entrepreneurial method is the antithesis of Taylorism: it is much less concerned with measuring the time required to get from one point to another than with the process of setting the boundaries of action—and with the human spirit that sustains the journey. Nor is this cooperative community animated by the modern faith in the deities of scientific method and positivism. Instead, cooperation in action attempts to discover what is needed for the health of community, no more and no less. That community is obviously imperfect: women are not equal, the environment suffers, and the cooperators still labor east of eden. But what a grand and hopeful struggle.

This chapter will consider the flexible strength of the co-ops' performance in the capitalist market. Chapter 9 will examine Mondragon and the transition to a postmodern economy.

Mondragon in the Market place

In 1987, the Mondragon cooperatives had annual sales of 180,000 million pesetas, or about $1.57 billion; exports amounted to 20 percent of sales, or $310 million (see Chart 8-1). As noted, the growth of sales and employment, considered together, generally reflect an S-curve: there is a take-off period of modest growth, followed by rapid acceleration, and then a slowing of growth, to be followed, it is hoped, by renewed growth as the cycle begins again.

Changes in business fortunes for the Mondragon cooperatives reflect three broad factors. The first is an internal dynamic of the birth, expansion, and maturity of the cooperative system, shaped by historic conditions and business opportunities. The functional choices made by the cooperatives—their focus on consumer durables, intermediate goods, and certain types of capital equipment—were natural and rational, given their experience and the state of the economy. But the development of the cooperative system followed a unique trajectory, conditioned by the social choices the cooperators made.

The impact of the general business cycle is also important. For better or for worse, the co-ops were influenced by cyclical fluctuations of growth, recession, and recovery that helped shape demand for their products. Cooperative practice was able to respond to the economic challenges posed by cyclical downturns and to ameliorate the social

Chart 8-1. Mondragon Annual Sales, 1970–87 (In actual and constant 1985 Pesetas)

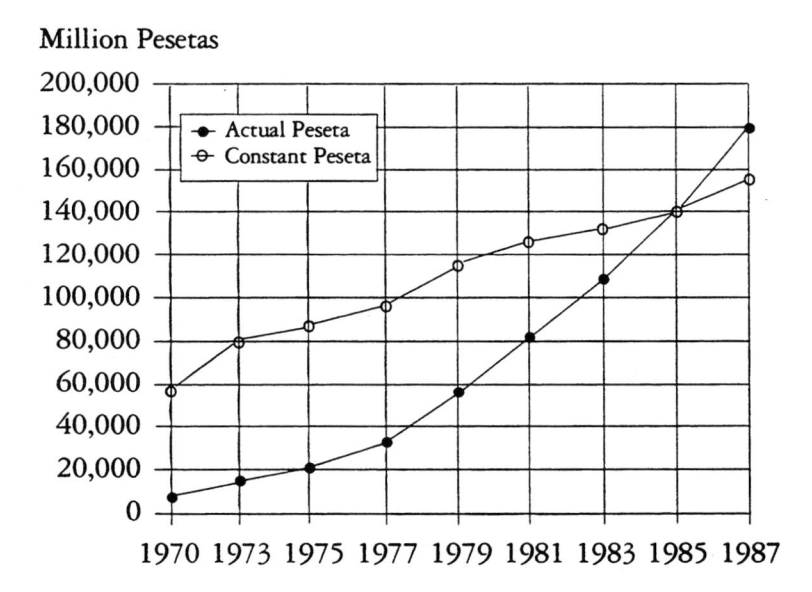

Sales data are from Caja Laboral annual reports (1972, 1985, and 1986), and from *T. U. Lankide* (1988). Inflation are from United Nations (1985); *Boletín de Estadística*, Sept.–Oct. 1985; and from Spain (1988).

At 115 Ptas/$, 1 million Ptas=$8,696. 140,000 million pesetas in 1985=$1.217 billion.

effects upon the cooperators and their communities. Finally, the transformation of the cooperatives came about in response to long-term economic trends affecting the industrial and service sectors of the economy. In the 1980s, the co-ops became accutely aware of a related complex of so-called structural changes reshaping the economy that were not simply connected to a cyclical downturn, but reflected longer-term developmental and evolutionary processes influencing both the local and world economies.

The Primacy of Jobs and the Growth of Employment

Economic analyses of Mondragon's first thirty-two years often overlook, or treat as an afterthought, the most striking facts about the cooperative system for working people in market economies: the virtual elimination of long-term unemployment and job loss; and the minimization of business failures.

At ground level, Mondragon's concern for human dignity, for the intangibles that are translated into community, is revealed in its practices of employment creation and maintenance. The contrast with the surrounding economy is startling: even as the Basque region and Spain recovered from deep recession, Basque unemployment in 1986 was still at 23%. In 1986 and 1987, the Mondragon system created about 1,800 new jobs, and there are now 21,000 durable jobs in the firms.

Given the co-ops' orientation, growth of employment has proven to be a generally valid indicator of economic condition. That is, economic surpluses and positive cash flows are usually translated into new jobs for new cooperators. In times of economic contraction and retrenchment, job creation may slow sharply. From the founding of Ulgor in 1956 to 1972, 10,055 jobs were created. In the next fifteen years an additional 10,945 jobs brought total employment to 21,000. But this growth was not uniform: overall, expansion was particularly rapid from 1960 to 1980 (from 395 to 18,733 positions, despite the impact of global recessionary pressures on the Basque and Spanish economies in the 1970s).

From 1980 to 1986, the number of cooperators increased only by 936 (to 19,669) as the co-ops devoted their energies and resources to retooling and restructuring under the reconversion plan developed in response to the economic downturn and to the increased competitive pressures anticipated as a result of Spain's entry into the European Economic Community (see p. 206). Then, in 1987, the number of positions increased to about 21,000 as co-op operations expanded as a result of the positive economic effects of the reconversion plan and the expanding Spanish economy.[7]

The industrialized Basque region had been a leader in the great Spanish economic boom, attracting migrants from other parts of Spain. But in the recession, Basque unemployment became chronic, exacerbated by the unfortunately familiar tendencies of older industries to erect new plants to the south, a trend perhaps encouraged (or at least justified in the press) by the ETA's practice of levying a revolutionary tax upon local industry to support nationalist activities.

At the end of 1985, according to a detailed report prepared by the Caja Laboral Popular for the Basque government, the total Basque work force (employed and unemployed) was just under 1,000,000 workers. Of these, 228,000 were unemployed. Industrial-sector employment was 322,000 workers; service-sector, 431,000; agriculture, 61,000; and construction, 67,000. The 228,000 unemployed included 116,000 members of the work force not classified by sector and therefore presumed to be chronically unemployed.[8]

The co-ops, which account for about 6% of industrial employment in the Basque country, have adopted as a goal (beyond their own economic health) the creation of at least enough new jobs to eliminate a share of Basque country unemployment that is equal to the total percentage of workers employed by the co-ops. This would mean an increase of about 5,000 jobs relative to the approximate 2% co-op share of the total regional workforce. As the 1986 CLP annual report states:

> The time which has elapsed over the last decade has clearly shown that social and economic life undertaken in solitude have no assured future. The right to work, a prerogative which is vainly pursued nowadays by one in every four people able to work, constitutes a fundamental piece of equipment to make society simply possible to live in. . . . The cooperativists of the associated Group, all of them, have come through the critical decade 1976–1986 without ever losing their jobs nor—of course—their remuneration. If we were to think that the merit was attributable on an individual basis we would be making a tremendous mistake and clashing head on in contradiction with the idea of "being more, acting better, giving more of oneself."[9]

The interactive choices made by the cooperators that have structured the business and employment policies of the cooperative system include, as discussed in earlier chapters:

1. A fundamental commitment to the creation of new jobs and new cooperatives and viewing co-ops as enduring community institutions supported by reinvested social capital accumulated by the co-ops and cooperators
2. The strong and mutual support provided to co-ops at all phases of their life cycle, including the financial resources of the CLP and the expertise of the Empresarial Division, supplemented by

the pooling of economic results within cooperative groups and the FISO fund
3. Economic planning based on the idea of labor as a fixed cost to minimize unemployment
4. The ability to arrange transfers (because of the economic diversity of the system), at first within cooperative groups and then within the whole system, to help accommodate seasonal and short-term economic fluctuations
5. The establishment of a strong cooperative social-insurance system, coordinated by the Lagun-Aro co-op, with mechanisms to mitigate the effects of short-term and structural unemployment
6. A commitment to an interactive and flexible cooperative entrepreneurial system that can respond swiftly and creatively to economic downturns
7. Strong and active pursuit of product innovation and new technologies

Co-op Failures

Mondragon has faced severe economic trials but only three business failures. Two were relatively special cases: Copesca, a fishing co-op with twenty-four operator-owned boats, was begun in 1965 and abandoned in 1973. The owner-workers' contribution was only 5 percent of total equity; as 71 percent came from a very soft loan from the Spanish government and 24 percent came from a CLP loan. As reported by Thomas and Logan, the new boat owners were unable to discipline themselves either to divert enough of their cash from large catches to service their long-term debt, or to reduce their catches to help prevent overfishing. Under the circumstances, when the CLP found it was unable to restructure the failing co-op financially, Copesca was dissolved.[10]

In 1983, as a result of the deep recession, Labeko, a small chocolate factory converted from a captialist firm, failed, as did Scoiner, a furniture-veneering-machine co-op, which was a more typical Mondragon start-up but existed in a sector whose market was sensitive to the economic downturn and overcapacity.

The Co-op Economic Transformation of 1976 to 1987

The changing economic fortunes of the co-ops since the mid 1970s can be seen in average sales per cooperator, capital investment, and annual cash flows. In general over these years, the co-ops have instituted an economic restructuring based upon capital investment in new technology for improved productivity, complemented by a strengthening of the co-op groups, improved monitoring and intervention by the Empresarial Division of the CLP, and a series of economic sacrifices and adjustments by the cooperators.

The increase in capital intensity and the commitment to new technologies puts the co-ops in the mainstream of an industrial evolution that depends upon the increasing use of computerized automation and such new technologies as lasers and robotics. But this has been done within the context of the cooperatives' commitment to employment and community: the goal was to maintain and then to expand the existing system. Despite economic pressure, the co-ops did not attempt to turn to low-tech and low-wage methods, either to maintain jobs or to provide them for the masses of Basque unemployed.

Mondragon, moving forward with the momentum of twenty successful years, continued to expand employment and overall sales even as the general economic crises deepened in the later 1970s. But average sales per cooperator dropped sharply between 1970 and 1976 (see Table 8-2 and Chart 8-3 on p. 176). In short, there were more co-op workers and not enough business, and the expansion of the late 1970s did not generate enough income to change this. The downturn was not merely a short-term fluctuation: expansion slowed dramatically. Both co-op surpluses and cash flows dropped sharply in the later 1970s and early 1980s. As a result, co-op investment first lagged, then new investment meant increasing co-op debt as cash flows could cover a smaller percentage of investments. The Mondragon system was in trouble.

Through the constellation of measures under the reconversion plan (detailed below) the co-ops responded successfully. Real sales per member increased sharply to a level much above that of the 1970 to 1975 period, reflecting the new capital investment in retooling and construction of new factories. By the later 1980s co-op cash flows had strengthened sufficiently to cover new investments—and that led to the rapid creation of new jobs in 1986 and 1987.

The successful conclusion of this restructuring depended, of course, upon the durability and resources of the Caja Laboral Popular. Co-op sales and CLP resources tracked each other closely until the late 1970s, when the deepening economic crisis slowed sales (see Chart 8-3). Surprisingly, the co-op bank confounded the popular wisdom and continued its strong growth. This has proved important to the co-op's ability to respond to economic challenge and reflects the business acumen of the bankers. There was no run on the co-op bank as the recession deepened and Basque unemployment soared. In fact, quite the opposite occurred: the Caja Laboral Popular maintained the confidence of tens of thousands of small depositors in the bank and in the long-term health of the industrial cooperatives with which it is identified.

Table 8-2. Sales per Cooperative Member (Figures in millions, constant 1985 pesetas)

Year	Value	Year	Value
1970	6.73	1980	6.34
1971	6.37	1981	6.85
1972	6.94	1983	7.13
1973	6.72	1984	6.97
1974	6.77	1985	7.36
1975	6.76	1986	7.40
1976	5.71	1987	7.45
1977	5.88		
1978	6.08		
1979	6.33		

Sales Mean = 6.71 million pesetas/cooperator/year (in constant 1985 Ptas)

Data are from CLP annual reports (1973, 1985, 1986); *T. U. Lankide*, 1988; and Thomas and Logan (1982). Inflation data are from United Nations (1985); *Boletín de Estadística*, Sept–Oct. 1985; and Spain (1988).

Chart 8-3. Growth of Mondragon Sales and CLP Total Resources*

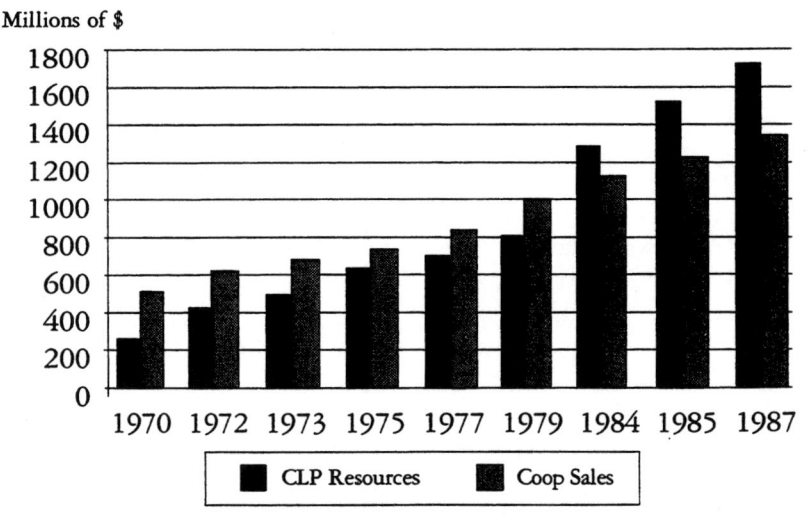

Millions of $

[Bar chart showing CLP Resources and Coop Sales for years 1970, 1972, 1973, 1975, 1977, 1979, 1984, 1985, 1987, with values ranging from approximately 200 to 1800 million dollars]

*This chart is useful for comparing the relative scale of co-op operations over time and the relationship between co-op sales and CLP resources.

Actual sales and financial resources (in pesetas) were first converted to constant 1985 pesetas and then to dollars at 115Ptas/$.

Data are from CLP annual reports (1972, 1985–87 and from Thomas and Logan 1982).

A brief examination of the data helps clarify the broader picture. In 1987 cooperative sales were approximately $75,000 per cooperator, or—excluding the personnel of the CLP, Lagun-Aro, and Eskola Politeknikoa—about $86,000 per cooperator. In comparison, 1977 sales, adjusted for inflation and converted to 1987 dollars, were $58,500 per cooperator. Chart 8-5 on page 178, using a statistical measure (Z-value), shows the clear trend for increasing average sales per co-op member from 1976 on (in constant 1985 pesetas. The 1983-84 decline reflects a recession.).

While average sales per member were increasing, net co-op surpluses dropped from their high levels of the mid 1970s (a peak of 10% of sales in 1973; 8% in 1974; 6% in 1975; and 7% in 1976). In fact, co-op surpluses were negative or close to zero in the early 1980s; some co-ops were clearly operating at a loss, and the entire system was struggling to break even. But co-op surpluses and cash flows became positive again in the late 1980s. In 1987, for example, the Fagor group had sales of $2.496 billion (31.5% of the Mondragon total), with a positive cash flow of $50.8 million and a net surplus of $25.2 million (5.1% of sales.)[11] Table 8-4 shows that cash flows were unable to fully finance new investment without possibly destabilizing increases in debt. In 1979, as the impact of the recession became clear, investment plunged, and it only recovered

Table 8-4. The Balance of Mondragon Cash Flow and Investments (In constant 1985 pesetas)

Year	Cash Flow	Co-op Investments	Cash Flow as Percentage of Investments	Surplus (Profits) as Percentage of Sales
1971	1,325	1,450	0.91	4%
1976	2,820	3,600	0.78	7%
1979	4,585	2,300	1.99	2%*
1985	5,900	7,490	0.79	
1986	8,791	10,395	0.98	

Data are from CLP annual reports (1973, 1985, 1986); *T. U. Lankide*, 1988; Thomas and Logan (1982); and Whyte and Whyte (1988).

*There is some uncertainty about profit data for 1979. The 2% figure is from a graph presented by Whyte and Whyte (1988) based upon a 1982 CLP document, *Reflexiones para el Cambio en Torno a la "Experiencia Cooperativa."* Thomas and Logan (1982) cite 4%, based on CLP data. I believe the latter document is accurate.

as the reconversion plan took hold. By 1987 co-op cash flows amounted to 98 percent of a substantial level of co-op investment.

The success of the investment program has been translated into recovery of co-op surpluses based on the high level of sales per cooperator required by the increasing investment in retooling and new technologies under the reconversion plan. As the capital intensity of the industrial cooperatives increases, the sales per co-op worker must also increase. Fewer workers can produce more at lower unit costs.

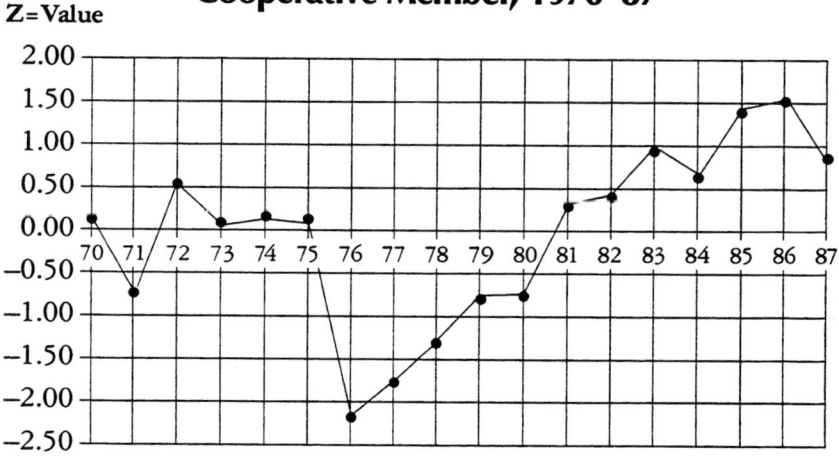

Chart 8-5. Growth of Sales per Cooperative Member, 1970–87

Z=Value

---

*In constant 1985 pesetas, based upon sales data from CLP annual reports (1973, 1985, and 1986), T. U. Lankide, 1988; and Thomas and Logan (1982). Inflation data are from United Nations (1985); Boletín de Estadística, Sept.–Oct. 1985; and from Spain (1988).

Z-value is a statistical measure of the difference of each year's sales/member from the average (mean value) in terms of the standard deviation. The formula is:

$$Z = \frac{(\text{Year's Sales/Member}) - \text{Mean}}{\text{Standard Deviation}}$$

In this case: Mean Yearly Sales/Member = 6.69 million Ptas (in constant 1985 Ptas)[a]
   Standard Deviation = .465 million Ptas

For example, in 1981, sales/member = 6.85 million Ptas, therefore:

$$Z = \frac{6.85 \text{ million Ptas} - 6.69 \text{ million Ptas}}{.465 \text{ million Ptas}}$$

Z = +.344

---

[a]At 115 Ptas/$, 1 million Ptas=$8,696. 6.85 million Ptas sales/member in 1981 = 59,565.

Mondragon in Operation as a Community Economic Sector

The long-term stability of both the cooperative firms and cooperative jobs is no accident. It reflects deliberate social choices—and not ones made through a simple trade-off between jobs and an efficient economic system; on the contrary, they are major factors in the dynamism and success of the Mondragon system. Cooperative entrepreneurship has demonstrated operational efficiency and the ability to manage social capital in response to market signals. Mondragon operates as an integrated social and economic system with well-considered goals that increase the operating efficiency of the individual cooperative firms and of the whole system.

Mondragon represents a clear departure from the baleful practices of conventional capitalist corporations and government bureaucracies. For the co-ops, people and their communities are central, not incidental to plans for profit and power. Older factories are not milked to divert cash into stockholders' pockets and then abandoned. Instead, there is systematic and strategic reinvestment. For Mondragon, investment in retooling and in automated technologies did not mean laying off workers; instead, change followed planning that preserved jobs and that was predicated upon an overall increase in employment. The system does not subsidize failing firms to save jobs, but pursues management and investment strategies that take full advantage of existing community strengths and human and social "capital"—including the owner-workers' knowledge, experience and commitment. Neither individuals nor communities are "resources" that can be declared redundant and summarily discarded. Everyone and everything are enlisted in the democratic, consensus-seeking process of cooperative entrepreneurship to respond to the realities of the capitalist market.

At the same time, co-op business practices do involve what may be termed "opportunity costs." Clearly, Mondragon has pursued long-term social and economic stability, sometimes at the expense of short-term profit. The co-ops have refused to use their economic weight to buy and sell firms, or to expand opportunistically; nor do they use large numbers of seasonal or temporary workers to enrich core members. Instead, they have the discipline to understand the greater economic and social benefits to be gained by not pursuing certain types of short term income.

Today, arguing the need for economic efficiency and the right to manage, conventional corporations often use increased profits, not to reinvest or diversify, but to disinvest in search of short-term "paper profits." Such gains can yield bigger dividends for stockholders and bonuses for corporate managers, but not a secure future for workers and their communities. Profits can mean not revitalization and diversification, but the acquisition of other firms to, in effect, buy profits; or the construction of new plants in areas with low wages, low taxes, and few regulations to protect workers and the environment.

For transnational corporations, by and large, workers are simply a disposable factor of production. In the United States, corporate public-relations figures prattle about regaining "competitiveness" in the world market (as deindustrialization proceeds at home) and gush about enhancing output and profits by combining computer automation with the efforts of a small number of highly trained—and "cooperative"—workers (see Chapter 9).

Mondragon Employment Policy and Economic Efficiency

The success of the Mondragon process of creative renewal effectively assaults one of the last bastions of the neoclassical critique of cooperative functioning: that co-ops are overly fond of maintaining jobs at the expense of the economic "efficiency" enjoyed by owners or managers of capital to transfer assets quickly and freely to more "profitable" investments. This process, it is argued, is more "economic" and socially beneficial, since in the aggregate it creates more wealth.

In addition, it is often maintained that cooperatives' managers will inexorably choose to pay themselves higher wages, turning co-ops into "cash cows" at the expense of reinvestment and long-term economic health. Why cooperators whose livelihood and communities are strictly dependent upon the existence and prospects of their co-ops should be less inclined to reinvest than absentee corporate owners is not explained. It seems at least as likely for cooperators to save by reinvesting in their co-ops and their future.

The assertion of the purported efficiency of the untrammeled mobility of capital (responding to market forces) is in practice often little more than a gloss to justify greed at the expense of working people and their communities. Thus, proponents suggest that the rust belt, redlining, decapitalization and deindustrialization, the hollow corporations, the corporatization of farms, and the globalization of capital are ultimately all for the good—that a rising tide lifts all boats.

But this notion of the blind supremacy of capital confuses short-term maximization of income from any source with the creation of real wealth. Quick, enormous profits can be generated by financial manipulation and speculation—for example, by buying and selling international currencies and by manipulating markets—and these have more appeal than investments that may take many years to be profitable. Today, almost any corporation can swiftly become a takeover target, not just to eliminate competition but also when corporate income (and therefore dividends and stock prices) decline. The bottom line jitters of U.S. corporate managers have worsened under the tireless examination of megaspeculators who look only at the ratio of the market value of a corporation's assets to the present total value of its stock.

One popular takeover scam, in simplified form, works this way. A hypothetical firm, Northland Paper, makes newsprint at its $25 million mill in Northland, New Hampshire. The company owns 50,000 acres of forestland that is managed for a sustained and renewing yield of trees to supply enough pulpwood to meet the demands of the mill. The timberland is valued at $300 per acre, or $15 million overall. The company also owns logging and delivery trucks worth $2 million and an office building in Boston worth $1 million, so total assets are $43 million. The company is the major employer in Northland; its 750 workers are unionized and earn a living wage. Logging is done by small contract entrepreneurs who hire 100 loggers and pay them on the basis of how much timber they cut.

Unfortunately, there are fewer newspapers, and the newsprint market is contracting. Recycling is increasing, but the Northland mill cannot handle recycled paper pulp. The company is still profitable, but long-term prospects are not outstanding, and Northland is actively considering diversifying by adding a new $10 million production line to manufacture toilet paper. There are 1 million shares of Northland stock outstanding, selling at $36 per share for a total value of $36 million. This is less than the market value of its assets of $43 million; however, this does not necessarily make Northland a takeover target. Almost all its assets are in the mill and the surrounding timberland, and the only potential buyers would be other paper companies—who would face the same problems as Northland. If, however, a speculator bought blocks of Northland stock at $36 per share in a manner that created a rumor that the company was a takeover target, stock prices might climb and he or she could bail out with a quick profit.

Or say an arbitrageur, driving through Northland on the way to his ski condo, passes the mill and the miles of undeveloped timberland and begins to see condos, a four-season resort, shopping centers and the like. He sees at least half of Northland's $300 an acre timberland might become $3,000 an acre development land worth $75 million; he could scrap the mill and sell the land, the trucks, the office building for perhaps $90 million. His syndicate tenders an initial offer of $50 a share for Northland's stock. The company, the town, and the people are now "in play."

This short-term versus long-term question is not, at bottom, one of enlightened ("good") capitalists and greedy ("bad") capitalists who will eventually be sorted out by the market. The real issue is conflict between today's absolute necessity for socially beneficial and productive investment and the belief that investment and income are value free and will eventually help establish social equilibrium through the long-term effects of the price system. The gathering environmental and political catastrophe has made it all too clear that income from polluting and destructive industries, or from parasitical speculation, will not redeem us and will not be corrected soon enough, if ever, by the operation of market forces.

The flexible adaptation of the Mondragon cooperatives to economic hard times suggests the power of the cooperative solution to industrial modernist dissolution.

Notes

1. Vanek 1971, pp. 13, 14.
2. Thomas and Logan 1982, p. 167.
3. Nove 1983, p. 218.
4. Interview, Sept. 1982 in Clamp 1986, p. 155.
5. "Humane" as an adjective is in danger of falling into disrepute as reflecting a destructive "humanism" or an anthropocentrism at the expense of the earth and other creatures. For me, "humane" connotes an inherently ecological perspective. To suggest that "humanism"—like sexism and racism—is identified with the destructive practice of industrial modernism is to adopt a facile view that removes humanity from nature and identifies it with evil, instead of condemning some of its social practices and behaviors. The very process of objectifying humanity as "other" in relation to an otherwise harmonious Nature is thoroughly suffused with the perspective it is attempting to escape. Such notions can incline to a variety of violent, obscurantist, and stringent solutions, none of them healing or integrative. "Humane," in my view, connotes the best qualities of humankind—kindness, tenderness, mercy, sympathy. . . .

Standing up for "humanism" as a respectable term is not part of an effort to enter into the currently popular disputation between "social ecology" and "deep ecology." We need important aspects of both ecologies if we are to effect the transition to an ecological postmodernism. The war of words among ecologists, and between factions of the Green political movement, is troubling. While the Green movement in the United States is developing a local presence of some vitality, as a national entity it is long on talk and short on performance. Some of the talk is important talk, but the Greens would be well advised to heed Arizmendiarrieta's injunction that Mondragon should be judged more by its actions than by its words.

6. Clamp 1986, p. 252.
7. Data from CLP annual reports, 1972, 1985, and 1986; *T.U. Lankide* 1988; and Thomas and Logan 1982.
8. Economía Vasca: Informe 1985, p. 449.
9. CLP Annual Report 1986, p. 5.
10. Thomas and Logan 1982, pp. 31–32.
11. Informe Anual 1987, Fagor.

9
Economic Transition and the Mondragon Response to Change

The Mondragon system's response to recession is a useful model of the cooperators' ability to enlist economic and social resources in the development of appropriate and creative actions. The changes in the co-ops that began as the economic downturn became severe in the late 1970s were not found in any plan book or text. They were developed and shaped as a collective response by the Mondragon community, as a cooperative evolution and adaptation to economic and social forces that went beyond a simple cyclical decline in demand.

The economic crisis was not experienced as something that happened like a natural disaster, and the Mondragon "plan" did not spring full blown from the offices of the CLP, as Athena sprang completely armored from the head of Zeus; rather, there was planning, thought, and dialogue on every level in, for example, round tables organized by the Caja Laboral Popular and seminars presented by the Ularco Group (now Fagor).[1]

Questions of Value: The Search for Equilibrio

Underlying the sometimes difficult process of making hard decisions that affected people's lives was the search for consensus as free women and men, an attempt through dialogue to find equilibrio. This was not based on a narrow economistic view: economic necessity conditions but does not determine Mondragon's actions. For the cooperators, after the economic factors are boiled down there is still a residuum that cannot be explained away. Reviewing Mondragon's response to recession in a World Bank discussion paper, economists Keith Bradley and Alan Gelb are moved to conclude that "a cooperative community–firm economy can overcome some of the moral hazard and informational problems which plague the social safety net in conventional economies.... Unemployment is negligible despite generous insurance."[2]

In hard times, Mondragon's members choose the long-term health of the cooperative community, even if offered substantial unemployment benefits. They are not inclined to become "free riders" on the cooperative dole; they seek neither to minimize personal effort nor to maximize personal income. They search instead for equilibrio, which brings the well-being of the individual into harmony with that of the cooperative community.

In their economic restructuring, the cooperators have broken the stereotypes of "capitalists" and "workers." It is not sufficient to give a sigh of relief that cooperatives in the Mondragon mold can succeed; rather, the power of the Mondragon postmodern initiative lies in the cooperators' willingness to abjure the pursuit of wealth for its own sake, not on the grounds of moral superiority but in the interest of cooperative community.

Our own Mondragons will be constructed in our own social context and translated into our own vernacular. As a point of departure in looking for value that respects both our individuality and collective social reality, we can hypothesize that Mondragon approximates, to some extent, Jane Jacobs's view of a dynamic and protean economic life. For her, "the order at work is more like biological evolution whose purpose, if any, we cannot see unless we are satisfied to think its purpose is us."[3] If "the purpose is us," we are nudged ever so gently to entertain our existence as human beings, as social beings, not as abstracted "economic humans" or as deconstructed products of capitalism or patriarchy. We are alive—intimately connected social beings whose nature is to pursue human values for human ends.

Economic Transition and the Mondragon Response to Change 185

Human value is not only removed from monetary value but from use value. Use value, although it is posed in opposition to monetary value, still implies a relationship to a world of things and objects to be consumed and manipulated, to be "used," as clean air and clean water are used. In contrast, the concern of community is not use or objects, but people, people as coparticipants in a seamless web of ecological community.

The exchange value of a chattel slave and a wage slave is monetized: we know how much money we "make" in exchange for our efforts. But what is the use value of a human being? Norbert Wiener, founder of cybernetics, had an accurate appreciation of the megamachine of social systems and of the world of technique:

> I have spoken of machines, but not only of machines having brains of brass and thews of iron. When human atoms are knit into organization in which they are used, not in their full right as responsible human beings, but as cogs and levers and rods, it matters little that their raw material is flesh and blood. What is used as a machine, is in fact an element of the machine. Whether we entrust our decisions to machines of metal, or to those machines of flesh and blood which are bureaus and vast laboratories and armies and corporations, we shall never receive the right answers to our questions unless we ask the right questions. ... The hour is very late, and the choice of good and evil knocks at the door.[4]

Value for ecological postmodernism transcends Wiener's belief in the need to simply ask the right questions, essentially the task of the machine's managers and creators; for example, "we must know as scientists what man's nature is and what his built-in purposes are, even when we must wield this knowledge as soldiers and as statesmen; and we must know why we wish to control him."[5]

Wiener and the scientists gaze down from the pinnacles of power and knowledge. In contrast, the values of ecological postmodernism are plebeian, but they are the basis for constructing social orders and for modifying deep social structures. The social relations of freedom and community arise from below, from the Mondragon cooperators' search for equilibrio.

The set of human values of this search underlies cooperative adaptation and economic transformation, its ethics informs the cooperatives' actions and choices. Their response to economic contraction and structural change has the requisite nuts and bolts—contradictions, difficult choices, hard compromises, speaking truth to power. And it also has an irreducible residuum of human spirit. It is in times of stress that the reality of Mondragon cooperative behavior is disclosed and the worth of the human process of cooperative entrepreneurship becomes clear.

Matters of Practice

Our examination of the co-op response to recession and its implications focuses first on six basic areas:

1. The proactive role of the Caja Laboral Popular
2. The cooperators' individual and collective economic responses
3. A collective and adaptive approach to employment problems
4. The development of new organizational forms to respond to change
5. An increased opening to Euzkadi and to the world
6. The development of a retooling and reinvestment strategy

Since the changes that emerged in the recession also disclose the fundamental forces influencing social and economic change, we will then examine some of the broader forces conditioning the future of the Mondragon cooperatives and the global transformation now under way.

The Proactive Role of the Caja Laboral Popular

While the CLP's financial resources and management skills were crucial to cooperative adjustment, it was not a simple case of the CLP's riding to the rescue with bags of money. It did reduce interest rates, provide new loans, and forgive loans when essential, but CLP support decidedly went beyond being the lender of last resort.

Economic stress led to an elaboration and strengthening of connections between all levels of the cooperative system, not just between co-ops and the Caja. It became clear that improved communication, a fuller sharing of resources, and prompt and effective monitoring of relevant information were all crucial for the future of the system. In classic Mondragon style, the process was designed to provide assistance and to eliminate inefficiency while avoiding bureaucratization and maintaining local responsibility and autonomy.

One critical element in strengthening organizational infrastructure was expanding the capabilities of the Empresarial Division. A new intervention area, working with the auditing and information area, carefully systematized and computerized the monitoring of co-op operations and developed an intervention process for co-ops in economic difficulty (see Chapter 6).

During the economic restructuring, a staff of ten special management consultants worked with co-ops at risk through a formalized four-part intervention process involving: diagnosis of the problem; development of a recovery plan; reorganization, as needed, of co-op structure, personnel, and finances in accord with the plan; and implementation and adjustment of the recovery plan.

Intervention, according to José Gárate, director of the intervention area, is designed to help economic recovery and to strengthen the self-management and governing capabilities of cooperatives for the long haul. Financial support for co-ops in trouble comes from the CLP, from other co-ops (through the Lagun-Aro social-insurance superstructure), and from government and other autonomous organizations. Gárate notes that the "Caja Laboral supports unconditionally these recovery actions, supplying the necessary funds on very favourable conditions compared to the market."[6]

In an interview conducted with a visiting team from the Industrial Cooperative Association in November 1984, Gárate said the approach is to see need for intervention as an accident and a temporary measure, although it may last for several years. The intention is to support and strengthen co-op management, although at times the intervenor will recommend replacing the general manager or the chair of the governing council.

The intervention area does not act as a banker, but as a counselor who makes recommendations. The co-op must apply directly to the banking division of the CLP for new loans, interest-rate reductions, or other financial restructuring, and the division will decide based on its judgement of the economic viability of the co-ops' plans and of the financial resources available.

As part of the intervention process, the CLP can: reschedule existing loans for new seven- to ten-year terms; finance investments needed for the recovery plan and provide sufficient working capital; reduce co-op interest rates (to 0% if necessary); cancel co-op debts; and extend personal loans to cooperators, with five- to ten-year terms, to help finance co-op restructuring.

Intervenors also work systematically with the co-ops to explore and develop needed modifications in marketing and business practices, new-product development and retooling, and management practices and personnel; they may also recommend additional capital contributions and other financial sacrifices by cooperators and when necessary, transfers and layoffs. The Whytes, describing the particularly difficult struggles between 1983 and 1986 to reorganize Zubiola, a small co-op producing woodworking machines and tools, conclude that,

> the process of intervention at Zubiola was painful for everyone involved. Although it was full of conflict, the leaders and the members were able to work their way through the most severe differences in their dedicated efforts to find solutions that would provide some balance between economic necessities on the one hand and their social values on the other.[7]

The net result of the intervention process has been the return of the Mondragon cooperative system to financial health.

The Cooperators' Individual and Collective Economic Responses

Just as the Caja Laboral did not simply come to the aid of troubled co-ops with a blank check, so the restructuring of the system was also not merely a matter of making new business plans in line with the CLP's recommendations. Cooperative adjustment also required the cooperators to make a series of individual and collective financial sacrifices, permitting the co-ops to reduce labor costs and increase their available capital to support restructuring while minimizing short-term layoffs and long-term unemployment.

This practice of self-financing and wage cuts in response to hard times raises some basic questions. Are cooperatives merely a means to facilitate give-backs and to undermine worker solidarity? Do co-ops become a venue for self-impoverishment when worker savings are quickly wiped out by demands for more capital?

For the cooperators acting as owners, the decisions to reduce *anticipos* ("wages") or to make additional capital contributions could be viewed simply as a trade-off: reducing current consumption and increasing capital investment—in effect, moving money from one pocket to another for long-term benefit. But while this was technically true, it was not seized upon as a convenient way to escape from the broader political significance of the matter. The solidarity question was an explicit concern of the cooperators—and it was addressed, as we shall see, in an innovative fashion that included participation of Basque unions and other social movements. The decision-making process as a whole can be seen as the assertion of economic rationality with a human face.

In any case, the decision to make economic sacrifices (politically correct or not) was not a simple one, especially when success was not at all certain. At a meeting of the general assembly of Ulgor in 1981, members discussed making a second a capital contribution despite the fact that they had already been able to produce more at lower cost. "Where do these solutions take us," a woman cooperator asked, "if this year's sacrifice will only generate another for the next year?"[8] It was the validity of this question in the minds of the cooperative's membership, and of the managers of other co-ops and of larger cooperative structures, that shaped the extensive process of discussion and decision making about financial sacrifices.

For example, assume that there is a need to raise $2 million in additional capital. This is a very different matter for the five hundred owner-workers of a co-op who agree to a one-year, 20 percent wage cut from $20,000 to $16,000 from what it is for twenty investor-owners with yearly incomes of $250,000 and hundreds of thousands in the bank to each put up an additional $100,000.

The Mondragon cooperators, searching for *equilibrio*, acted to defend their basic social policy of full employment, the long-term economic viability of their cooperatives, and their solidarity with other Basque workers. While each cooperator made a sacrifice—by choosing to capitalize wages and make additional capital contributions—the political action was not one of surrender, but of empowerment.

The Ularco Group's Approach to Anticipos

The complex wrestling with the issue of *anticipos* by the co-ops of the Ularco group is a model of the Mondragon system in operation. By the late 1970s, when it became clear that the economic downturn would not quickly correct itself, the Ularco co-ops were suddenly in unknown territory. Their ability to cope with this issue indicates a growing sophistication in the wake of the Ulgor strike, which was triggered by questions involving job classifications—an issue that would seem to be somewhat less fraught with potential conflict than the situation faced by Ularco five years later.

In the Basque country, the impact of the mid-1970s recession was felt in the general economy before it began to have a marked effect upon the cooperatives. During the long boom, it had been a relatively simple matter for co-ops to maintain wage rates comparable with those in Basque industry for most owner-workers. Wage solidarity did not, however, extend to certain management and skilled technical personnel whose *anticipos*, capped by the 4.5 to 1 maximum pay differential, were often considerably below wages in conventional firms. [In practice, by 1980 actual Ularco pay differentials were much narrower than 4.5 to 1. For most workers the spread was only 2.5 to 1, and the maximum pay differential was 3.2 to 1, since there were no workers paid at the 1.0 level: the lowest-paid Ularco worker was at salary grade 1.4 (the average being 1.625).[9] Recall, too, that the 4.5 level was only paid to those who put in additional hours, traveled, or had special skills.]

However, stagflation and rapidly growing unemployment in the Basque economy began to lead to a divergence between co-op *anticipos*, annually adjusted for inflation, and wages in the surrounding economy. By 1979 *anticipos* for the lowest-paid cooperators were 10 percent higher than for persons in comparable Basque industry. Lower social-insurance costs for the owner-workers made the effective pay differential even greater.[10]

In the larger Basque economy, layoffs, then plant closings, became more common as the economic situation worsened. From 1975 to 1983 the region lost 20 percent of its jobs—a result not only of the recession, but of private capital's inclination toward deindustrialization. As in the United States, business had little interest in investing in new plants and modernization, instead transferring jobs to sites where unions were weaker and such incentives as tax rebates were easy to obtain.

As the industrial economy shrinks, new jobs tend to cluster in the low-wage, low-skilled service sector, and worker solidarity is undermined. In this atmosphere, splits tend to emerge between the employed and the unemployed—with the burden of unemployment falling most heavily upon the young who have never held jobs or who are first to be laid off under seniority policies.[11]

In such a context, Basque wage rates became very much a politically mediated issue. Spanish law made it costly to lay off workers and difficult to reduce wages. Thus, in recession Basque industry tended to take the course of permanently closing or relocating plants instead of mandating seasonal or indefinite layoffs for some workers; when possible, it used capital investment to replace workers and thus minimize social insurance costs.

The direct economic and political action exercised by the Mondragon owner-workers contrasts with the position of workers in conventional Basque industry, who had to deal with absentee corporate owners and their hired managers. The influence these employees wielded was largely indirect and political, the product of their collective power expressed through government policy.

By the late 1970s, it no longer made sense for the co-ops, themselves under financial stress, to continue to base *anticipos* simply on equivalence with surrounding Basque industry.

Ularco Decisions on Anticipos 1978–1979

Ularco was a complex organization of co-ops with more than six thousand members, and there was considerable tension and a great deal of debate and uncertainty in the process of dealing with this problem. This is nothing like the mythical, conflict-free "quality circle," in which individual workers discuss their concerns and insights with management, which acts, in due course, with the requisite paternalist wisdom.

The formal Ularco process began from above at the end of November 1978. The governing council proposed a new means of calculating *anticipos* to start in 1979. The council argued that general economic conditions, poor Ularco cash flow, and a 31 percent increase in *anticipos* as percentage of total sales—contrasted with a 20 percent increase in productivity (based on value added in 1969–1977)—justified this modification. The new plan was sent to the central permanent commission (CPC) of the Ularco group, composed of representatives of the social councils of all member co-ops of Ularco, which sits as a sort of super social council for the group, and of the governing councils of all member co-ops.[12]

Under the plan, *anticipos* would still be adjusted annually in line with the cost of living, but they would also be connected to the co-ops' economic performance to some extent. In addition, the plan suggested that there was a need to reduce *anticipos* as a means to help finance (capitalize) the economic restructuring of the co-ops.

To calculate the cost-of-living adjustment, new Spanish law on cooperatives required one generally technical adjustment: co-ops had to use the Spanish consumer price index (CPI) as the basis for adjusting wages. The CPI replaced an internal Mondragon index (called "Index B") that determined inflation by comparing the general price index for Spanish metal products over two years, presumably because metal production was the predominant area of co-op activity.

Index B was considered more "rational," since it would tend to more closely reflect changes in co-op income than changes in the general Spanish consumer price index. The CPI would more closely track the cooperators' actual cost of living than the cooperatives' cash flows. In times of slack demand and inflation, the metal-price index might lag behind the CPI if sales of such co-op products as consumer durables and machine tools lagged; in this case, the cooperators' *anticipos* would rise less than if they were based on the CPI. Similarly, in boom times demand might push metal prices ahead of the CPI and benefit cooperators more than the CPI-based adjustment.

The Ularco governing council's proposal began a complex process that lasted for fifteen weeks. It illustrates what Gutiérrez-Johnson calls Mondragon's "infrastructure of participation" and reflects the dynamic and open nature of cooperative democracy.

The central permanent commission (CPC) of Ularco responded to the governing council's proposal with a detailed "Critical Report." The CPC objected to the council's failure to include it in considering major policy changes of the sort that required the early participation of the CPC. The CPC also questioned the methodology and formula proposed and wanted the council to present alternatives. The "Critical Report" led to an open and frank dialogue between the two groups.

The CPC polled all Ularco members on their opinions about the governing council's proposal: 68 percent of members responded, and 90 percent of them supported in principle a change in the calculation of *anticipos*.

The CPC developed training and educational materials for social councils and sent representatives to help explain the proposal and its economic significance and to obtain member responses. These discussions lasted for several weeks. During this period co-op members organized interest groups that included participation by the Basque trade union ELA-STV ("Solidarity of Basque Workers") and another group that coalesced around a number of Basque political organizations and other unions.

In all, four alternative proposals to that of the Ularco governing council were developed: one by the Copreci Co-op social council; another, by a group connected to ELA-STV, the "Solidarity Proposal"; a third by a faction connected with Basque political groups and other unions, the "Coalition Proposal"; and a final one, by members calling for no change in the system.

All but the last of these accepted the basic logic of the governing-council proposal, with some modifications. For example, Coalition and Solidarity were more oriented toward a formula that would lead to higher *anticipos*. The Coalition, Solidarity, Copreci, and Ularco governing council proposals were submitted to the social councils for an advisory vote. The Coalition proposal won a plurality, followed closely by that of the Ularco governing council. Only a small percentage voted to abstain and therefore, presumably, rejected any change.

The governing council also suggested revising by-laws to implement changes in *anticipos*; alternatives to these were also developed and submitted to social councils for an advisory vote. Here, the Coalition proposal won an absolute majority.

The Ularco governing council then adjusted its proposal to more closely reflect member preferences.

In the final and binding vote, the co-op general assembly was asked to choose between the modified governing council proposal and "no change"; the former received the required two-thirds majority and was adopted. Members then voted on amendments to the suggested by-laws.

The Ulgor social council reviewed the decision-making process and expressed concern about the future need for early participation by the CPC; the low level of involvement of women members in the process; and the time pressure on the CPC, which led to decisions that sometimes lacked support.

This four-month decision making process is characteristic of an empowerment model whose nature was shaped by concerns that arose from below, within the basic context of cooperative institutions, rather than of a bureaucratic process established from above. The CPC's attitude toward the governing council was sometimes heated but it remained within the spirit of consensus seeking and the search for equilibrio as the dialogue proceded, and the governing council recognized the validity of the cooperators' assertions. The process, after discussion, was opened to the active participation of Basque unions and political groups, who contributed specific suggestions and plans to debates over questions of co-op member equity and of solidarity with Basque workers. The CPC did not act as advocate, developing a "members' " position in opposition to that of the elected governing council, but as facilitator, allowing the exploration and careful articulation of alternative positions that ultimately shaped the final proposal.

The system functions much more as an extended and inclusive process of discussion and modification than as a process of exclusion based on voting and the exercise of power. The CPC responded initially with its "Critical Report," entered into discussions with a responsive governing council, and polled the membership. This is an excellent example of the social council's ability to function neither as trade union nor company union but as a crucial actor in an essentially consensus-seeking process.

The effort led to an agreement on the three assertions made by the Ularco governing council in its initial proposal. First, economic rationality should govern the adjustment of *anticipos*. That is, the formula for setting them is linked to a combination of changes in the consumer price index as required by Spanish law and to the cash flow of the cooperatives.

Next, the co-ops should have autonomy from the setting of wages based on political agreements made with the Spanish government. Solidarity as a concept now includes the creation and maintenance of jobs by the co-ops and a relationship to wages in a broader context. Finally, the new procedures should be modified as the situation changes and are therefore governed by the principle of temporality.

The system for setting *anticipos* detailed in Table 9-1 is no magic formula, but it is a process that takes into account the cooperators' experience and economic judgement and their willingness to make compromises between current income and the financial strength of their co-ops. The "Self-Required Range" of annual cash flow of between 11 percent and 13 percent of sales is considered the basic goal and baseline for financial health leading to an increase of *anticipos* of the CPI plus 1 percent.

Changes in the method of calculating *anticipos* for other Mondragon co-ops did not necessarily duplicate the Ularco formula, though it did provide the basic model of connecting them with co-op economic performance. Bradley and Gelb indicate that in general *anticipos* were permitted to vary, depending on co-op financial status, at between 80 percent and 110 percent of the level of *anticipos* paid by the CLP, which is taken as the co-op standard.[13]

Table 9-1. Ularco Formula for Adjusting *Anticipos*

Cash Flow as Percentage of Sales in Previous Years	Percentage Increase in *Anticipos* for This Year
6	CPI minus 4%
7	CPI minus 3%
8	CPI minus 2%
9	CPI minus 1%
10	CPI
The "Self-Required Range"	
11	CPI plus 1%
12	CPI plus 1%
13	CPI plus 1%
14	CPI plus 2%
15	CPI plus 3%
16	CPI plus 4%

Source: Gutiérrez-Johnson (1982), p. 387.

Ularco Additional Capital Contributions, 1980–1981

As the recession continued, adjustments to *anticipos* were, by themselves, not sufficient to provide adequate internally generated working capital for a co-op in difficulty. Ularco found itself having to turn to its members for additional capital contributions.

This question had a different political and emotional dimension for cooperators from altering the formula for determining *anticipos*. While the issue of *anticpios* had immediate political impact with potential major long-term economic consequences, additional contributions would clearly place an immediate economic burden upon the cooperators.

In this instance, the Ularco decision-making process was facilitated by the experience of the *anticipos* question. Again, there was a proposal by the governing council; a detailed report of the CPC contesting the council's assertion that additional capital contributions were necessary; the opening up of the process to the social councils and to outside union participation; and, finally, a vote by Ularco membership on the question. What differed substantially was that while in 1980 the Ularco general membership rejected the governing council's proposal for additional contributions, it accepted such a plan in 1981 as the nature of the economic situation became clearer.

As with the *anticipos* question, discussion was sometimes heated but generally respectful. The CPC, the social councils, outside groups, and much of the general membership found it possible to disagree with the plan of the governing council even after its leadership attempted to make the question an issue of whether or not the membership trusted their judgement.[14]

For the cooperators, beyond agreeing to the need for additional capital funds on a one-time, extraordinary basis, three questions needed to be answered.

How would the amount of contributions required from each cooperator be set? The required contribution was scaled on the basis of the cooperator's *anticipos* index: for example, someone with a 3.0 pay level would contribute twice as much as a person with a 1.5 rating. The average contribution per cooperator would be about $600 per year for three years to attain the $12 million required by Ularco. Contributions were added to a member's individual capital account and treated in the normal manner. Cooperators could appeal on the basis of personal hardship for a partial or complete abatement of the contribution.

How would the funds be raised? The cooperators choose to make the capital contributions from a combination of withholding from *anticipos* and withholding interest payments normally received as cash on the internal capital accounts. This was made less painful because cooperators receive fourteen monthly payments of *anticipos*—in effect, there are two semiannual bonuses. Half the contribution was to come from withholding portions of the extra *anticipos*; half from interest payments due on internal capital accounts that are also paid semiannually. Since the Ularco co-ops had a long record of earnings, most members' internal capital accounts were quite large and interest payments were substantial. For newer members without large capital accounts, withholding from *anticipos* would be increased to create the required amount. For the Ularco cooperators overall, the plan meant a reduction in income of about 11 percent for three years. In addition, a number of other minor steps were taken. Members were no longer able to transfer capital accounts to their children or relatives; all new members who were joining the co-op had to make their own capital contributions. Further, there was a (relatively slight) reduction in overtime pay. Finally, a mandatory retirement age of sixty-five was instituted. This was only marginally significant, since most workers retired then in any case. Clearly, mandatory retirement makes jobs available for younger people (who generally start at lower pay), but it also carries the inescapable connotation of ageism.

Finally, will the sacrifice in fact solve the problem, or just lead to further demand for funds? The additional capital contributions were just one element in a complex of measures taken by cooperators to maintain control of their destiny and to strengthen their cooperative community. Additional capital contributions were agreed to only after it had become absolutely clear that the prolonged recession required collective sacrifice in the context of detailed plans for organizational and economic restructuring—that the contributions were not a panacea, but a necessary step.

Give-Backs or Worker Empowerment

The Mondragon cooperators' response to proposed financial sacrifices was conditioned in part by their reluctance, even as owner-workers, to sacrifice current income for possible long term benefit and by skepticism that co-op management's claims reflected real economic conditions.

But where economists speak of "sticky wages," what is usually at work in the general economy is that working people fundamentally lack democratic economic power. To gain some measure of control over their economic lives they must take collective action through unions and the political system. "Sticky wages," far from being the product of union strength or a political response to the interests of working people, is precisely the lack of power over fundamental management and investment decisions in both capitalist and state-owned firms.

Capitalists and state bureaucrats are most unwilling to yield the fundamental prerogatives of their "right to manage," and that ultimately rests upon their ability to control investment decisions: to sell, to close, to move, and to expand, shrink, or change the business. When pressed by unions and political parties, management may yield on questions related to wages or benefits for the unemployed, but these issues, while of considerable importance to working people, are peripheral for the conduct of business as usual for capitalist and state managers.

Thus in Spain the government has become involved in setting wages, and the law makes pay cuts difficult and layoffs costly. But these are not effective remedies for the fundamental lack of worker economic power. The dissatisfaction of Spanish workers is reflected in a growing estrangement between the Spanish labor movement and the nominally socialist government. The Mondragon response described above rests upon the basic difference in economic power between owner-workers and those in conventional business, and this becomes particularly apparent in recessions. The capitalist reality is that workers have little power to influence events: businesses fail, workers are unemployed, capital is shifted to more promising investments— more promising for the investors, that is. A community's economic base may be destroyed as definitively as if the area had been bombed.

The Mondragon experience also differs substantially from the trajectory of state intervention and from other economic options in time of decline that include:

- Demands by management for unilateral worker give-backs in order to keep their jobs at lower pay;

- Union efforts to exchange wage give-backs for some corporate stock ownership by workers, sometimes combined with gaining a union seat on the corporate board, such as the agreement made by Eastern Airlines workers with management that did not prevent further souring of labor-management relations;

- Institutional proposals, such as those by economist Martin Weitzman for a "share economy," whereby wages would fluctuate within a predetermined range based on a firm's economic fortunes.

Give-backs obviously transfer losses to worker wages and are seldom balanced by "take-backs" when the firm's economic fortunes improve. Trading give-backs for stock and union board membership as a one-time deal may be preferable, but as Eastern Airlines workers have demonstrated such arrangements do not fundamentally address the issue of the power that hostile management continues to wield, often at the expense of workers and their unions.

The so-called share economy offers workers a possible share of profits in exchange for assuming a definitive share of losses; it structurally undermines worker wage agreements. The share economy is a rough counterpart to the flexible rate home mortgage, where interest rates are tied to the prime lending rate: these do offer homeowners some relief if interest rates drop, but they primarily serve to lock in a rate of return and profits for the lender. A share economy likewise will help lock in investors' profits by quickly being able to overcome the political and institutional barriers (e.g., unions and labor law) that lead to "sticky wages."

Working people might benefit in the share economy by a decrease in layoffs and business failures, and perhaps receive a greater share of a firm's income in good times (though, depending upon the formula negotiated, this may not exceed the level wages would tend to reach anyway in boom times). At Mondragon the cooperators are not offered, at best, a bigger slice of the pie. Together they not only prepare the recipe and bake the pie—they own the pie.

The Mondragon system's ability to institutionally link its compensation scheme more closely with economic performance and to draw additional capital contributions reflects of the operation of cooperative democracy, the commitment to the cooperative community, and the search for equilibrio—not the acceptance of a share economy.

A Collective and Adaptive Approach to Employment Problems

Unemployment could pose a fundamental challenge for cooperative systems. On one hand, the creation and maintenance of community jobs is central to the purpose of cooperatives; on the other hand, cooperators may be drawn to choose to preserve their own jobs rather than act to ensure the firm's long-term stability. But at Mondragon, the cooperators, in the search for equilibrio, have developed—or more accurately, thrashed out—a singular approach to employment-security questions that balances the cooperative principles of stable community jobs and fair and just treatment of the cooperators.

The deep recession of the seventies meant that co-op unemployment could no longer be resolved by such simple remedies as seasonal short-term transfers between co-ops or avoided by accumulating inventory or cutting prices. What the co-ops recognized as structural unemployment began to appear: jobs in such industrial sectors as machine tools were being permanently lost as productivity increased while market demand slackened. Some co-ops required complete retooling or development of new product lines. As the recession deepened, the individual cooperatives also found that their reserves, given declining income, were no longer adequate to provide the very substantial unemployment benefits that had been paid to cooperators (and that were economically insignificant during the years of expansion). As a result, unemployment costs and benefits became a collective responsibility, calling on the combined resources of the individual co-ops, the cooperative groups, and the system as a whole.

The co-op definition of unemployment includes cooperators transferred to other co-ops who are considered "underemployed," those still on the co-op's payroll but whose work was not considered to be necessary, termed "hidden unemployed," and those on temporary layoff. In 1985, with unemployment in the Basque country over 20%, the co-op reported an unemployment rate of 6.9%, affecting 1,197 cooperators. Of these, only 104, or .6%, were actually not working and receiving unemployment payments.[15]

Data for 1986 indicate that 26 of the 140 member cooperatives in Lagun-Aro (19%) received unemployment assistance from the group; the remaining 114 paid into the system. By far the largest group of co-ops in difficulty was that manufacturing furniture and tools, parts, and equipment for manufacture of furniture and other wood products. A scattering of co-ops in capital equipment and machine tools received unemployment-benefit payments, as did the construction co-op Ulma.[16] Total 1986 payments, which include unemployment benefits based on 80% of *anticipos* plus 100% of social-insurance contributions, relocation expenses, severance pay, and early retirement payments amounted to about $4.5 million.[17] Table 9-2 summarizes unemployment policies.

Table 9-2. Mondragon Unemployment Policies

Description	Amount	Period
1. Unemployed cooperators	80% wages (*anticipos*) + 100% social insurance	For twelve months in any two-year period; may be extended if more than 25% of a co-op's members are unemployed.
2. Co-op closes	8% wages (*anticipos*) + 100% social insurance	For two years
3. Transfers outside co-op group	a. Permanent: Lagun-Aro pays only special costs	Individual circumstances
	b. Temporary: Lagun-Aro pays travel, per-diem expense, makes up salary difference (if less in new co-op)	For length of transfer
4. Structural unemployment	Co-op determined, as affected by structural unemployment	
a. Early retirement	Between 58 and 65 a member receives 60% regular pension, plus 100% social insurance; full pension at 65.	Members who have received twelve months' unemployment are eligible
b. Lump-sum payment	For members under 58; payment equal to one year *anticipos* + one month for each year over five that they have been co-op members.	

Co-op Eligibility: Co-ops who have been members of Lagun-Aro for eighteen months; co-ops that are hived off from existing co-ops are eligible immediately.

Source: Whyte and Whyte (1988), pp. 150–54.

The Lagun-Aro unemployment tax assessed on co-op *anticipos* in 1985 amounted to 2.35% of the total payroll, an increase from .5% in 1980, when the tax was instituted.[18] Compared to the usual assessment in the United States this is rather low, reflecting both the low level of co-op unemployment and the fact that part of the costs is borne directly by the co-ops and co-op groups.

True unemployment in Mondragon tends to be below 1% because, as noted above, cooperators are transferred and possibly retrained; layoffs are the last resort. Transfers may be short term or permanent, depending upon the co-op's condition. Lagun-Aro pays relocation expenses for transfers and special expenses for permanent reassignments. Temporary transfers may not make up more than 10% of a co-op's work force.

But the search for equilibrio does not simply involve reassigning workers. Transfers could create tension the worker's own co-op and in the co-op to which she or he is transferred. In a "white paper," some Ularco members objected to the arbitrary nature of transfer policy, arguing that co-op management "can determine who works a lot or not, based on whether one talks or not."[19] They claimed that blue-collar workers were transferred before their white-collar counterparts and that white-collar personnel were not transferred to blue-collar jobs. Management, recognizing the legitimacy of these concerns, agreed to involve the social councils to develop a fair and clear procedure that would include blue-collar as well as white-collar workers.[20]

In addition, as Basque unemployment soared, some co-ops objected to taking in cooperators transferred from outside the immediate area. As the manager of a small co-op told Christine Clamp in 1982:

> I want to make clear that the motivation of the group of twelve people that formed the cooperative here was to seek a solution to the unemployment in these three municipalities. . . . [W]ith 30,000 inhabitants, there are 1,500 unemployed. . . . This year there will be more. The people from here ask that we hire local people. The cooperatives ask that we do otherwise.[21]

One response to this problem has been a commitment to create new jobs—as noted in Chapter 8, the Mondragon co-ops have established a goal of creating, at a minimum, enough new jobs to eliminate that portion of Basque-country unemployment that is equal to the co-ops' percentage of the total work force. This commitment has been assisted by new policies of the Basque government. Since 1985, co-ops in such areas as furniture and machine tools manufacture, faced with technological unemployment, have also received aid from a Basque government program established to increase investment in new and competitive technologies and to help provide lump-sum payments for underemployed cooperators who are hard to transfer, primarily because of their age. By November 1987 the program had reportedly assisted thirty-one co-ops and provided $15.6 million in grants and $13 million in guarantees (compared to a total planned co-op investment program through the CLP of $40.1 million). This has been a significant help in the economic restructuring of these cooperatives.

The Development of New Organizational Forms to Respond to Change

The evolution of cooperative organizational forms was accelerated by the effects of recession, but the ensemble of changes should not simply be viewed as part of a process of rationalization or adaptation to the exigencies of economic contraction. These changes are not mere artifacts of a response to brute economic necessity, separate from the basic course of Mondragon history and the forces that have shaped the search for equilibrio.

Again, the underlying dynamic is part of the fundamental tension between freedom and community. As we have seen, this is a prime mover for the Mondragon system and for the emergence of ecological postmodernism. As Javier Mongelos, director of the Ularco group, notes, "[following] a period of progressive adaptation and re-adaptation of the organization, the bodies of managment—social and technical—have been developed in such a manner that an equilibrium has been reached between the opposed tendencies of centralization and decentralization."[22]

Thus, as the Mondragon system continued to mature, to grow and become more diverse, new levels of structure evolved to balance the impulses for freedom and community, and new democratic organizational forms developed. Among the new central bodies of coordination and decision making are the cooperative congress, to address fundamental policy issues; a council of cooperative groups to address basic issues of economic coordination and development; the FISO fund; and the Lankide organization, to assist co-op exports. New intermediate levels of structure and coordination (e.g., cooperative groups) are designed to balance the power of such central coordinating bodies as the Caja Laboral Popular and to create more diverse and effective means for local coordination and action than those available to individual cooperatives.

Some aspects of this process, such as the pooling of profits and losses by members of a co-op group, appear to be steps away from co-op autonomy for the sake of economic rationality, but this evolutionary process should not be viewed through such a narrow lens. Of far greater significance is the democratization of power through the congress, and the establishment of durable, community-based cooperative groups as effective economic and political institutions.

Organizational evolution has encouraged the rise of new levels of planning more closely linked to the cooperative groups' local communities in such areas as job creation, housing, and city planning. The new system functions at the expense of both the development of a unitary bureaucracy attempting to administer a two-hundred-co-op system and the entrepreneurialism of individual cooperatives. Co-ops that belong to a group are still individually accountable and make their own decisions, but the context of the cooperative group is integral to their planning and support. The standardization encouraged within a group obviously removes some of the idiosyncracies of individual co-ops that set their own bylaws and whose practices varied within the broad compass of the contract of association with the CLP and Lagun-Aro.

But it is not the transition from independence to group membership that is most significant. Essentially, through this process the great economic power of the Caja Laboral Popular clearly remains subordinated politically to the democratic community base of the Mondragon system. The CLP continues to operate as a bank in accord with its cooperative "vocation" and is in fact strengthened, since it can concentrate on its role as a bank and not upon the micromanagement of the cooperative system.

The cooperators thus averted the danger of creating a bureaucratic hierarchy, ruled by an economic technocracy concentrated in the CLP, which would operate as a merchant bank in control of an industrial conglomerate. The separation of the Empresarial Division (LKS) from the CLP, planned for 1991, also makes it clear that the cooperators have embraced a model that supports a diverse and decentralized cooperative ecology that can reflect a democratically controlled community where basic power flows from below. The LKS will add its own independent voice and perspective to the pursuit of equilibrio. The CLP still ties the Mondragon system together, but the Mondragon group is clearly not the creature of the CLP.

Co-op groups are emerging as recognizable entities. The Ularco group, now called Fagor (the brand name of some of its most popular products) is recognized internationally through its exports, which include computer numerical controls for machine tools and turnkey refrigerator plants. With about one-third of Mondragon members and total sales, Fagor will be considered in detail below. Here, we should note that since 1977, when Ularco (formed in 1965) was still the sole co-op group, eleven regionally based groups have been founded (see Appendix 1-3). There are also co-op groups, such as Maherco and Haltzari, organized on an industrial or sectoral basis that coordinate marketing, technological product development, and other business plans but that lack the social character of the integrated regional groups. A co-op may belong to both a regional and an industrial group.

Regional Cooperative Groups' Structures and Functions

Cooperative groups assume a number of planning and coordinating functions for their regions and their member co-ops. Although broad social goals that transcend basic business and entrepreneurial functions are integral to the role and significance of the groups, some operations are of particular relevance to the economic reshaping of the cooperatives.

Through "reconversion of results," for example, cooperative groups pool the surpluses and losses of member cooperatives, thus providing them a greater margin of support. Council of cooperative groups chair José María Ormaechea notes that co-op groups pool "their economic results so that they have been redistributed in an act of solidarity which we call 'Reconversion of Results.' "[23]

Groups can decide the level at which surpluses and losses will be pooled (it may vary from 30% to 100%) by decisions of the member cooperatives. Such pooling by a diverse group of cooperatives provides further protection from the effects of short-term market fluctuations and their attendant problems for individual co-ops.

Industrial reconversion is a second specialized operation. Co-op groups work to facilitate the transfer of cooperators between member co-ops to eliminate unemployment as discussed above.

Another group function is regional planning (Planes de Largo Plazo). Regionally based groups formulate long-range economic-development and entrepreneurial plans for their operations that supplement, complement and expand upon the work of the Empresarial Division. Sophisticated group planners consider investments to develop new products and new technologies, solutions to marketing problems, and questions of information management.

Finally, group central service organizations are designed to eliminate duplication of efforts by member cooperatives and to take advantage of appropriate economies of scale. The central service organizations operate in three areas. Promotion works roughly like the promotion and product departments of the Empresarial Division, but it focuses on the needs of the group and region in helping found new co-ops, doing feasibility studies, securing product licenses, and marketing. The economic-financial sector deals with loans from the CLP, financial planning for the group, and auditing and tax questions. Third, the human resources area provides personnel services that coordinate employment and human-development programs, as well as deal with issues of recruitment, organization of work, health benefits and social insurance, education and training, organizational structure, and job evaluation. (While the operation of central services has remedied some of the problems faced by individual co-ops, the system has not been entirely satisfactory. Improved coordination and effectiveness is one concern the new Council of the Mondragon Groups is attempting to address.)[24]

Co-op Group Development and Mondragon Evolution

Over the long term, the development of co-op groups clearly potentiates the dynamic development and elaboration of additional co-op constellations within the Mondragon universe. Each regionally based group is a vehicle for more intensive and decentralized cooperative development; they can help individual co-ops continue to grow in scale and complexity while maintaining the balance between centralization and autonomy, between freedom and community.

With the regional groups, it is reasonable that a 170-co-op system can grow to several times its present size and still maintain the conviviality characteristic of Mondragon. As groups expand, they will likely reach a point where it is desirable to hive off new regional groups, as co-ops have hived off divisions, to maintain an appropriate scale. There is as yet no clear sense of the maximum effective size for cooperative groups. Similarly, as the Mondragon system itself continues to evolve it may reach a point of complexity where it naturally decides to divide into a number of independent or semi-independent and cooperative entities.

This cooperative evolutionary process is an example of the benign transformative forces of ecological postmodernism in action. The essence of ecological postmodernism is the elaboration of the particularity and diversity of human society embedded in the natural world. Such a community is the product of choice, and such choice cannot long be separated from the practice of democracy and practical equality—expressed not simply through formulaic measurement but through the practice of solidarity. Cooperative evolution does not mean the absence of tension or struggle; indeed, it is motivated by resolving the healthy tension between autonomy and centralization, freedom and community.

Cooperative evolution is an ordinary process with potentially extraordinary results, one of historical change and human choice that resolves the uncertainty in the lived present. The judgements we make are inextricably connected to human value—not the producing-consuming unit of reductionist doctrine, but the creature of exquisite complexity arising from the deep social structures that support our culture and define the nature of our individual and collective experience. Deep social structures go to the bottom. Deep social structures support not simply such complexities as values and ethics, but shape and condition human perception and knowledge, social phenomena embedded in the web of culture and history.

The conscious perception of the action of chance, necessity, and choice in the creation and codetermination of reality is the postmodern moment.

It is a rough cognate in the lived human present to the collapse of waveforms in the microworld of physics that brings forth physical reality from the realm of possibility. History happens.

Cooperative evolution is characterized by an appreciation of the diversity and interconnection of individuals and the social and natural world from which they are inseparable. It is opposed to the "rational" constructs that, in practice, justify hierarchies and the application of power. The reality of the Mondragon system—as a complex human entity, a result of historical processes, and a part of living history—is inconvenient for theories that seek to abstract historical archetypes from history itself. Mondragon's peculiarity is not limiting, but precious; it is a singularity that will help us recognize the diversity and splendor of our world and the human possibilities for change.

An Increased Opening to Euzkadi and to the World

For many years under Franco's dictatorship, the Mondragon cooperators shunned publicity, shielding themselves from the embrace of many who could have been sympathetic to their purposes and enthusiastic about their accomplishments. As members of a movement with profoundly political implications, they attempted to characterize themselves in a profoundly apolitical manner. Both inclination and necessity led the cooperators to let their only propaganda be that of the constructive deed: there was little to be gained and much to be lost by calling attention to the fundamental nature of the cooperative experiment. It was relatively easy to remain hidden in the mountains of Guipúzcoa, to take advantage of the obscurity of the Basque language. However, in the last decade, there has been a progressive opening from Mondragon to Euzkadi (the Basque nation) and to the world. This reflects of a number of related factors.

First, the Franco era has ended, and an apparently durable parliamentary government dominated by the Spanish Socialist party (now mostly socialist in name only) has emerged. While considerable tension still exists between Madrid and the Basques, the hostility has abated considerably. The capital has been willing to look favorably on some co-op ventures, such as the decision to assist Ulgor in its retooling after a government consultant's judgement that they were one of the Spanish firms likely to succeed following the country's entry into the European Economic Community.

Another factor is the granting of a considerable degree of local autonomy to Euzkadi by the central government and the successful establishment and growth of an elected and nationalist Basque assembly. The Basque leaders have proven sympathetic to the accomplishments of the Mondragon group in a time of deep unemployment and corporate disinvestment. In this climate, most Basques and their political groups (except some factions of ETA) have agreed to wage an essentially political and economic struggle for national rights within the context of conditional autonomy. Thus, in the deep recession the Basque government could turn to the co-ops for technical assistance and extend to them some financial support for creating new jobs and new technologies. The CLP's Empresarial Divison produces a detailed yearly analysis of the Basque economy; Ikerlan technical institute researchers are now partially supported by government fellowships and scholarships. In a variety of areas, co-op leaders and expertise have become part of the public policy discussions of the Basque leadership. Finally, the Basque government P.R.E. (Plan de Relaizationte Excepcional) provides grants and guarantees to help new investment, as well as social-insurance payments for underemployed workers in co-ops threatened by technological unemployment.

Third both Euzkadi and the cooperatives have become increasingly comfortable with the idea of participating politically and economically in the international arena, both for what each may gain and for what the Basques have to contribute. There is political space now to engage in activities that a few years before would have been unthinkable. For example, in October 1987 the World Cooperative Congress was held in Bilbao with the active participation of the Mondragon cooperators. In the summer of 1989, the annual international convention of END (European Nuclear Disarmament), a coalition of independent peace groups, was held in Vitoria in the Basque Country.[25]

In the past, information about the co-ops and access to individual members was typically available to those who had the good fortune to establish a personal working relationship with the cooperators. (In my own experience, this was not hard to accomplish, as the Basque people extend warmth and hospitality to the interested visitor.) However, certain specific information remained unobtainable as recently as 1985. Now, the co-ops have established a new policy of much greater openness toward visitors and the outside world and have made themselves more accessible in a variety of ways. For example, the Ikasbide training center now offers two-week summer seminars in a number of different languages for people interested in learning about the nature and operation of the Mondragon cooperatives.

Finally, the contraction of the domestic market and the increasing importance of co-op exports, combined with the need to be globally competitive when Spain enters the European Economic Community has led the co-ops to regard the whole E.E.C. as their domestic market. More than 20 percent of total co-op sales now come from exports, and some co-ops and co-op product lines focus on exports as their primary market. The cooperatives' attempt to use advanced technology and to institutionalize innovation and flexible production are part of their response to the globalization of the market. Jesús Larrañaga, one founder of Ulgor, looks to a future based on global economic interdependence and technological revolution in which "we cannot think that we in our cooperative 'microcosmos' can continue as in the past." He finds the regional and industrial co-op groups an appropriate means for international economic participation, but warns that there may be limits to self-development and that co-ops may have to enter into joint ventures and new forms of organization and participation.[26]

Chart 9-3 indicates the growth of co-op exports in terms of constant pesetas. Export sales in 1987 represented a 9.9 percent increase (not considering inflation) over 1986, but this was less than the projected expansion in what was a very good year in general for the co-ops.

Chart 9-3. Mondragon Exports, 1970–87 (In constant 1985 pesetas)

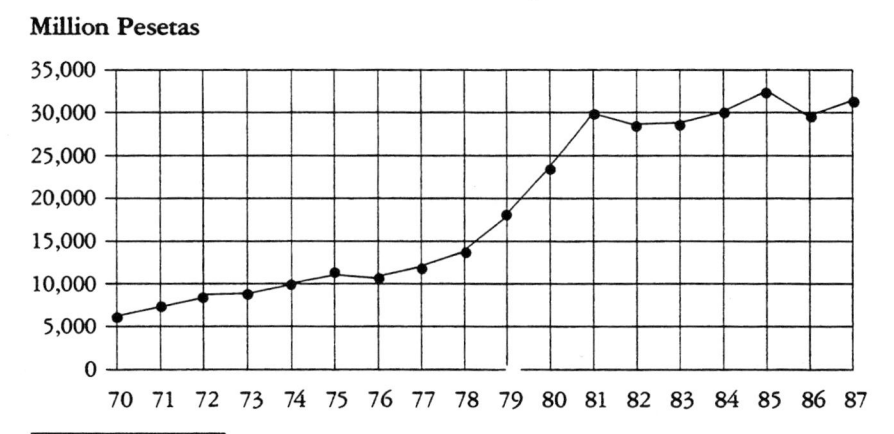

Million Pesetas

Data for 1986 and 1987 are based on use of value added tax (V.A.T.) that accompanied Spain's entry into the European Common Market (E.E.C.). This somewhat understates the total sales value compared with previous accounting procedures.

The Development of a Retooling and Reinvestment Strategy

New co-op investment has focused on selected product lines in high- and medium-technology areas. José Usatorre, one of the founders of Ulgor and now industrial-development advisor with the Empresarial Division, thinks the challenge facing the co-ops in economic restructuring was not essentially competition with Spanish industry but the impact of entry into the E.E.C. and the need to compete in a world market.[27]

This analysis—given the engineering background of the founding cooperators and the technological orientation and entrepreneurial spirit of most of the cooperative firms—led the co-ops to decide in principle to attempt to be on the leading edge of selected high- and medium-technology products and to remain or become competitive in a global market. Bringing this to reality was quite a different matter.

The success of the Mondragon technological initiative could be taken as a model of a program to restore "competitiveness"—a term given much lip service in the United States. The Mondragon program linked education, on-the-job training, research, product development, design, new production technologies, new organizational forms of work, financial restructuring, and domestic and export marketing. Technological change was an important aspect of these developments, but the accomplishment was not a triumph of hardware or engineering: the program succeeded because of a cooperative effort to implement the cooperators' social choices—choices involving quite a bit more than competitiveness and profitability.

By the late 1980s, the cooperatives' future began to be viewed explicitly as involving the emergence of a new postmodern social order. In 1987, Jesús Larrañaga wrote of an uncertain postmodern future shaped by a technological revolution that will require "room for liberty, for mobility and personal incentive." Cooperators saw aspects of this future reflected in the familiar mirror of technological change. In Larrañaga's view:

> The old admonition of Arizmendiarrieta that ideas separate us, necessities unite us, emerges as a concept that will guide and inspire not a few ideological and political movements. The shape of the future will intuitively be very different from that which was prophesied in the last century, the century of the ideologies that predicted the inexorable march toward a non-capitalist society. We cannot say what tomorrow will be, because the prophesies made regarding technological and social parameters have changed so radically that there must be a reimagination of the future society. No one is capable of stating what will be the nature of the society of postmodernism. We have given such a fright to the prophets, that for the moment some prefer to negotiate the terrain surrounding *perestroika*, while others explore the information age.[28]

The specifics of the Mondragon program detailed below are not responses to any technological imperatives. They are the product of social choices made to maintain equilibrio. These decisions are conditioned by the determination to place technology in the service of human value, of maintaining the dynamic social ecology of cooperative community.

Approaches to Diversification and Technological Change

The product-diversification and technological-development process is part of the integrated social, political, and economic strategy of cooperative change that is supported on a number of levels the financial and organizational initiatives discussed previously. These measures include:

- Market and product-selection research by the promotion department of the Empresarial Division and by the cooperative groups

- Advanced technical research in product development and production methods by the Ikerlan Technological Research Center (founded in 1977)

- Establishment of a sophisticated Institute for Industrial Design

- A comprehensive and evolving educational program that includes technical education by the Eskola Politeknikoa in Mondragon; continuing education, coordinated by Iranukor, in technical and business subjects for both graduates and co-op members (offered by E.T.E.O., the Escuela Universitaria de Estudios Empresariales in Oñati, and by the Eskola Politeknikoa in Mondragon); and co-op management training by the Ikasbide center. Other educational efforts include detailed study (through Saiolan) for young managers of all business and technical aspects of the development of a particular product and placement and assistance in advanced foreign technical-university training by Goeier (Goi Mailako Ikasketak Erbestean).

Marketing, Product Research, and New-Product Mix

Taking 1984 as an example, the Empresarial Division's product and market research included: computer software and peripheral equipment, computer services, industrial robotics, space electronics, precision and high-density plastics, specialized agricultural implements, forklifts, and conveyors. In the past, the CLP completed broad prefeasibility product studies on its own initiative, but 80 percent of them were not used. Preliminary investigations are now more carefully coordinated with the interests and plans of co-ops and cooperative groups.[29]

Market and technical research produced such high-technology icons as Fagor's industrial robot R-800, "Scara," introduced in 1987 and developed in conjunction with Ikerlan. It is designed to facilitate communication and integration with related computer-controlled devices and systems and can perform a variety of tasks. The Fagor group offers it as a turnkey product programmed and integrated into production systems for a specific factory. Fagor has also developed a flexible stamping center to enhance the diversity of its productive capacity and to reduce the inventory of raw-metal stock needed. This lowers the co-op's cost, since resources are not tied up in inventory.

Fagor

The work of the Fagor group provides an excellent indication of the thrust of recent cooperative technological-product development and investment patterns. The organizational and political dynamics that influenced the evolution from Ularco to Fagor involved not only Ularco, its member co-ops, and the Caja Laboral Popular but the Spanish government as well. The basic makeup of Fagor is indicated in table 9-4.[30]

The heart of the Fagor group is the consumer-products divison. The largest in its sector of the Spanish market, it includes five cooperatives: Ulgor (the first, and by far the largest, co-op) Fagor Clima, Lenniz, Radar, and Fagor Industrial. The new Ulgor refrigerator plant was opened in 1987, and new production facilities for washing machines and cooking ranges are under construction. These new white-goods facilities feature the integrated use of CAD/CAM (computer-assisted design/computer-assisted manufacturing), robots, and flexible manufacturing cells and are intended to make Fagor competitive in the domestic Spanish market as well as in the E.E.C.

The industrial components division (Copreci, Ederlan, Fagor Electrotécnica and Leunkor) is applying advanced production and quality-control techniques to making parts for appliances and to making casting, machining, and injection components for computers and automotive products. Electric motors are produced on a new and completely automated robotized production line (which includes automated and flexible set-up, production robots, automated movement and transport of materials, and real-time computer control of production). The division is involved in a research project with the U.S. Department of Energy's Batelle National Laboratory, and it has expanded into specialized markets in electronic semiconductors, producing zener diodes and signal-processing circuits; it has also entered the cable and satellite-television markets.

The engineering and capital-equipment division (Arrasate, Aurki, Uldata, and Ulmatik) is heavily involved in computer services and engineering consulting within Spain and in the international transfer of advanced and intermediate technology through turnkey production facilities, engineering services, and the sale of manufacturing licenses. In the Spanish market, the division consults in systems automation and plant engineering and provides data-processing, computer-programming, and software services. Aurki digital readouts and computer numerical-control devices are used extensively in Spain for computerized control of machine tools, internationally by General Electric, and have

Table 9-4. Fagor Group—1987

Employees: 6,602
Sales: 497 million dollars
Investments: 38 million dollars
Exports: 153 million dollars (31% of Fagor sales)
Surplus: 25 million dollars (5% of Fagor sales)

Consumer-Products Division

Ulgor—refrigerators, stoves, washing machines, dishwashers
Fabor Clima—water heaters
Lenniz—kitchen cabinets and equipment
Radar—stainless steel and aluminum cookware
Fagor Industrial—commercial food service and laundry equipment
Sales: $313 million (63% of Fagor Sales)
Exports: $ 64 million (42% of Fagor Exports)

Industrial-Components Division

Copreci—components for electric appliances
Ederlan—foundry for shaping and finishing iron and aluminum castings
Fagor Electrotécnica—electronic parts for transistors, TV, telephone
Leunkor—light machining and assembly, index drives
Sales: $128 million (26% of Fagor Sales)
Exports: $ 73 million (48% of Fagor Exports)

Engineering and Capital Equipment Division

Arrasate—machine tools
Aurki—numerical controls and electronic readouts
Uldata—minicomputer software
Ulmatik—engineering production analysis, feasibility studies
Sales: $56 million (11% of Fagor Sales)
Exports: $16 million (10% of Fagor Exports)

Data from Fagor annual report (1987) and from Whyte and Whyte (1), p. 167.

been licensed to the Shanghai Machine Tool Research Center of China and to India and Argentina.

Fagor has recently sold turnkey installation of a flexible stamping center to a French automotive-sector firm and an automatic assembly cell to a German clock manufacturer; in 1987 Fagor developed a new turnkey flexible manufacturing cell system.

The engineering and capital-equipment division has also been heavily involved, together with the cooperative Ikerlan Center, in the redesign and modification of the various Fagor production facilities. Outside the Mondragon co-ops, Fagor is involved in the application of a just-in-time production system for a rubber-products plant, developing a cloth-inspection process for a textile manufacturer, and working on printed circuits for an electronics firm.

Research and product development activities at Fagor involve a staff of two hundred and an investment of about $15 million, equal to 3 percent of total sales in 1987. Fagor's own investments are complemented by the activities of Ikerlan and the technical-education programs of the Eskola Politeknikoa and Iranukor, Saiolan's product-development training, and the work of the Industrial Design Center.

Ikerlan

Ikerlan was founded in 1977 as a second-degree cooperative. Today, with a staff of more than one hundred engineers, scientists, computer specialists, and students, Ikerlan offers services to member cooperatives, conventional Basque companies in noncompeting areas, and the Basque government. It was formed from the research staff at Eskola Politeknikoa and from individual cooperatives to concentrate on advanced technologies.

At first, Ikerlan was supported by a small set fee paid by each member of supporting co-op organizations plus contract fees for specific projects. In 1982, the Basque government, as part of its own industrial-revitalization plans, began to provide 50 percent of Ikerlan's budget. These funds are not used for general operating expenses, but to provide competitive research fellowships for scientists and engineers in the cooperative.[31]

Ikerlan's work is closely associated with the high- and medium-technology paths being pursued by the co-ops. Its projects are carefully designed and managed to provide short-term and long-term improvements in production methods and products. Ikerlan works on specific new product or production plans for co-ops or companies (37 in 1986) and on more general technology-diffusion and modernization plans (114 in 1986).[32]

A detailed outline of the co-op's research activities indicates the direction of Mondragon industrial development. Noncooperative firms pay a 50 percent higher fee than co-ops and an additional 50 percent for the right to two-year exclusive use of any Ikerlan development, or an additional 100 percent for permanent rights. When a project does not result in a successful specific application, Ikerlan splits the costs with the co-op or company in question.[33] Such projects are considered to be part of Ikerlan's research and to contribute to further understanding.

The cooperative is based in an attractive modern complex in Mondragon, down the hillside from the headquarters of the Caja Laboral Popular and near the Eskola Politeknikoa. The setting mixes physical and technological elegance and practicality: there are some marble floors, but the walls are cast concrete and lighting is by fluorescent strip fixtures. Staff members tend to wear lab coats over sportshirts with open collars. Their research on basic and applied projects ranges from work on industrial vision to improvements in CAD/CAM technologies to specific production technology for co-op factories. Ikerlan joined with the Aurki co-op engineers and the IAI national research center in Madrid to design the hardware and software for the Aurki numerical control device. Ikerlan research and development is divided into three basic areas: electronics, CAD/CAM, and energy.

Electronics

Industrial instrumentation—digital signal processing, image processing, automatic inspection, and pattern recognition

Microcomputing—design microprocessor-based products, multiprocessing, multitasking, and real-time computing; local-area networks (LAN); communications systems (IKERNET, IKERBUS)

Software—artificial intelligence (AI), analyze AI applications, AI in troubleshooting and planning, develop expert systems

Industrial automation—process control and controller design, process modeling and optimization, computer-aided control engineering tools, systems engineering, automatic guided vehicles

Testing—vibration, temperature, climate, electromagnetic interference, prototype design and assembly

CAD/CAM

Production systems management—flexible manufacturing systems (FMS), just-in-time systems (JIT), group technology (GIT)

Robotics—design of robotic structures, hardware and software development for robot systems, feasibility studies for robot applications

Analysis—design optimization and model analysis, structural analysis by finite-element method, strain measurement

CAD—solution of 2D and 3D problems, integration with CAD systems, computer graphics

CAM—numerical control programming applications, interfaces between programming systems and NC machines, design and integration of FMS, design of industrial prototypes

Energy

Renewable resources—solar energy, wind energy, energy storage

Energy systems—computer simulations of system operation, energy-management systems (EMS), equipment development

Services—computer monitoring of industrial processes, computer data acquisition in buildings

The Long-Term Consequences of Technological Change and the Rise of a Service Economy

The powerful industrial-production technologies and methods that the Mondragon system has used or adapted (and is now developing internally through Ikerlan, co-op research departments, and the allied educational system) will lead to an expansion of co-op industrial employment. But they are also clearly harbingers of economic transformation that will see the elimination of industrial jobs. Such technologies as CAD/CAM, flexible manufacturing systems, artificial intelligence, expert systems, robotics, automatically guided vehicles, integrated computer networks, and the like are creating a highly flexible and enormously powerful computer-integrated-manufacturing (CIM) production system that will require small numbers of highly trained workers. Thus, the trend is for capital investment in new technologies to result in a net loss of industrial jobs, as these technologies can allow fewer workers to produce more items at a lower price with greater flexibility. New positions tend to be in the area of services, either as highly trained specialists or as (in much larger numbers) low-skilled and low-paid workers.

Mondragon's attitude toward new technologies at first was the reasonable sentiment that robots should be used to perform such dangerous jobs as handling molten metal in foundries. However, the competitive impact of the new technologies has meant that automation cannot stop with the most hazardous or the most boring jobs. Thus Fagor has developed a completely automated line for flexible production of electric motors and is building new plants that use a variety of state-of-the-art production technologies. The cooperators believed that their future depended not only on manufacturing desirable products, but on technological innovations that permitted flexible production and allowed fewer workers to make more appliances.

In adopting computer automation and CIM systems, Mondragon tends to have a competitive advantage, all other things being equal, over conventional corporations. It is not burdened by layers of supervisors and managers who act as enforcers; instead, it has a talented, committed force of owner-workers who can successfully use the new flexible technologies. Mondragon puts a premium on decentralization, appropriate scale, and social intimacy. The modern corporation tends toward centralization and gigantism, such control mechanisms as specialized accounting procedures to measure "profit centers," and watchdog bureaucracies.

Still, the Mondragon cooperatives find themselves in something of a paradox in facing the job-eliminating and de-skilling potential of automation. The co-ops' owner-workers are actively involved in all levels of the process of automation—in planning and operation and in the organization of work. The new technologies are essentially viewed as tools to facilitate the cooperatives' work and ensure the health of the system— tools that enhance the workers' abilities, tools that are not used to de-skill workers or to make the production process "worker proof," controlled by the new managerial lords of the computer. But the long-term effects of computer automation are certain to transform the nature of work and the social dynamics of industrial society.

In many situations, managerial elites have been shocked and disappointed to find that their efforts to establish factories based on CIM procedures have often proven unsatisfactory. The superefficient, completely automated factory of "smart machines," controlled and integrated by computers, monitored by an industrial engineer and a programmer ensconced in a remote control room, is not a reality. At Mondragon, in contrast, the operators of numerically controlled machine tools are trained to program them. Persons who study machining at the Eskola Politeknikoa first learn the classic manual techniques, then are introduced to the use of the numerically controlled machines that are becoming the standard. Workers are retrained, not de-skilled. The Mondragon-produced Aurki machine has been designed to enable a properly trained machinist to program and reprogram it as needed, in contrast to models where programming is done by management or engineering personnel and the machinist becomes just a material feeder—and often a scrap producer.

Management control of programming, and the poor performance it leads to in flexible production systems, is consistent with Harry Braverman's classic argument that the development of technology and changes in the organization of work are driven by managerial imperatives to maintain power over workers and control of the production process in the name of "efficiency" and "rationality."[34]

The Aurki system relies upon a numerical-control model that reduces production tasks to numerical code. But as David Nobel argues, this is often extraordinarily difficult, particularly for work requiring subtle dexterity, eye-hand coordination, and responses to unanticipated changes in the nature of materials—all within the mastery of a skilled craftsperson. Nobel suggests a record-playback, or R/P, approach, in which the actual movements of the expert operator are stored on tape, then used to guide mechanical reproduction.[35]

The Aurki device is meant for the use of skilled machinists and reflects the experience that flexible production systems require on the factory floor, instead of remote control by managers. For example, a *The New York Times* front-page story notes, "Robot automation in factories has been disappointing; managers have found that the machines require smarter workers." *The Times* points to one success story in a G.E. electrical circuit board plant in North Carolina, where flexible computer automation and a highly skilled work force of seventy-six has allowed G.E. "to close five plants producing the same product, while gaining market share on its rivals. And the number of worker hours per distribution board produced has been reduced by two-thirds."[36] (It is quite possible, since G.E. is a major Aurki customer, that the plant uses Aurki devices.) The expectation, as computerized, flexible manufacturing systems lead to the up-skilling of workers and the elimination of positions, is that future jobs will be in the service sector.

Mondragon and Services

The Mondragon system is highly concentrated in industry. The agricultural area is growing, but still small, with limited potential for job creation since here, too, Mondragon's efforts involve applying sophisticated methods that reduce total employment. The service sector, however, is growing more rapidly, focused on the expansion of the Caja Laboral Popular and the Eroski retail co-op. This area includes a variety of small high-tech and low-tech co-ops such as Uldata, involved with minicomputer software; Ulmatik, which performs engineering production analysis and feasibility studies; and Auzo-Lagun's cooking and cleaning services.

Questions of economic value stand behind the talk of a "service economy" in the age of computer automation. The CLP is able to offer financial services because of the wealth created by the labor of the cooperators and other Basque savers and manifested in the products they have produced and in the buildings and the communities they have constructed. Eroski's retail services are not just a matter of marketing; rather, the monetized value of its work rests again upon the productive value of the goods that are sold, many of them produced by cooperators and by other local workers.

The impact of computer automation technologies in the office, the school, and throughout the service sector will likely tend to follow the trajectory of the industrial sector—first the de-skilling and rationalization of certain jobs (to increase output and profit without a corresponding increase in wages), followed by more powerful technologies that require fewer but more highly skilled people.

Paradoxically, the application of computer technologies has tended to industrialize former service jobs. This is clear in the movement toward automated data-processing workstations. In the era of "do not fold, spindle, or mutilate," traditional clerks became keypunch operators mechanically preparing cards for mainframe computer processing; keypunch operators then became electronic data-entry clerks whose accuracy and keystrokes per minute could be monitored in an office that more and more resembled a factory. And now satellite transmission allows firms to move data-entry tasks "offshore"—for example, using low-wage West Indians to process forms for U.S. companies. Optical scanning and reading systems, and robotic material-handling devices, can now replace data entry clerks as the central office becomes a decentralized series of largely automated workstations linked by a computer network, or alternatively the automated hypothetical General Data plant providing data-entry and data-processing products replacing armies of clerks with scanners, computers, and a small number of workers. Thus the long-term prospects for the number of service-sector jobs are uncertain.

Future Directions

Unfortunately, the story of the co-ops' successful adaptation to the complex of forces manifested during the long economic downturn cannot simply end with "and they lived happily ever after." Life goes on, and the forces transforming industrial modernism are intensifying.

The events from the late 1970s to the late 1980s showed that Mondragon was able to respond in a cooperative manner to economic and social stresses and to structural economic changes, while making needed adjustments for its own growth and evolution that have strengthened the decentralized and democratic nature of the cooperative system.

The Mondragon solution to problems, as we have seen, is a living social solution guided by the search for equilibrio and the pursuit of freedom and community, unity in diversity. It is a crafted, democratic, and participatory process, not a cookbook remedy that provides a sure and reproducible cure. An important part of the response has been a commitment to develop new technologies in a manner consistent with cooperative principles. But mere technological robustness is hardly the solution to the intertwined social, economic, and political problems of industrial modernism. What is to be done? It is clear that a future based on freedom and community, unity in diversity must be built, must be planned, cannot merely be the happenstance result of the forces of historical evolution, of technological determinism.

This chapter has explored Mondragon's economic and productive restructuring on the ground level and on the factory floor, and by considering technological development, financial measures, and democratic decision making. Such a view neglects the broader, long-term impact of political and social change upon the cooperatives—forces that reflect not only fundamental tendencies within industrial modernism, but within a Europe in dramatic transition. Chapter 10 will explore these broader issues.

Notes

1. Gutiérrez-Johnson 1982, p. 23.
2. Bradley and Gelb 1985, p. 32.
3. Jacobs 1984, p. 234.
4. Wiener 1967, p. 254.
5. Ibid., p. 250.
6. Gárate 1986, p.3.
7. Whyte and Whyte 1988, pp. 182–83.
8. Gutiérrez-Johnson 1982, p. 363.
9. From report of January 25, 1980, by Ularco management to group social councils on group self-financing; cited in Whyte and Whyte 1988, p. 141.
10. Gutiérrez-Johnson 1982, p. 338.
11. See Bradley and Gelb 1985, pp. 10–11.
12. Much of this account is drawn from Gutiérrez-Johnson, 1982.
13. Bradley and Gelb 1985, p. 22.
14. The process is detailed in Whyte and Whyte 1988, pp. 141–49.
15. Whyte and Whyte 1988, pp. 155–56.
16. Lagun-Aro, Memoria Ejercicio 1986, pp. 30–34.
17. Ibid., p. 23.
18. Whyte and Whyte 1988, p. 151.
19. Quoted in Clamp 1986, p. 161.
20. Clamp 1986, p. 167.
21. Ibid., p. 161.
22. Quoted in Gutiérrez-Johnson 1982, p. 236.
23. Ormaechea 1986, p. 4.
24. See Gutiérrez-Johnson 1982, pp. 236–45.
25. Some aspects of the END meeting have particular relevance to the cooperatives. One of END's basic themes is peacemaking and détente from below through the creation, in both East and West, of independent organs of civil society to act freely, both nationally and internationally, to help replace the war system and the bloc system with a peace system. The successful creation of such independent and interdependent organs of civil society is a fundamental contribution of the Mondragon system.
26. Larrañaga 1987, p. 17.
27. Interview with José Usatorre (January 5, 1984), Industrial Cooperative Association (ICA).
28. Larrañaga 1987, p. 17.
29. ICA interview, January 3, 1984.
30. Information on Fagor sales and activities are from 1986 and 1987 Fagor annual reports.
31. Whyte and Whyte 1988, p. 65.
32. Caja Laboral Popular 1986, p. 82.
33. Whyte and Whyte 1988, pp. 65–66.
34. Braverman 1974.
35. Nobel 1984.
36. *The New York Times*, October 17, 1988, pp. 1 and D-5.

10
Mondragon and Reimagining Future Society

> Technique alone, without any moral and ethical point of departure or aim, has brought us to the very edge of a universal catastrophe. . . . It is thus for every one of us . . . to help build toward a more human way of life. . . .
> —Hansel Mieth Hagel, Otto Hagel, and Marguerite Wildenhain

> The worship of money has unhinged an entire universe of people.
> —Joseph W. Bartlett

Mondragon has established its high-tech credentials, but what does this mean for the exercise of freedom and the building of community? What is the relationship between Mondragon's practice and the forces transforming industrial modernism? Does the Mondragon dynamic represent an opening to an emergent ecological postmodernism or is it just a footnote in the conduct of industrial modernism? This chapter will begin to address these issues in the effort, in the words of Ulgor cofounder Jesús Larrañaga, toward "a reimagination of future society."

Future Prospects and the Hazards of Prophecy

One characteristic of the gathering crisis of industrial modernism is a pervasive sense of a loss of personal and social balance. Hidden in the shadow of our discomfiture is a sorrow that struggles to find voice—the sorrow of the loss of unity, of wholeness. Together, the loss of balance and of unity are an expression of the social repression and attempted banishment of freedom and community that are central to industrial modernism.

The agonies of modern life are hardly news. But there is growing awareness that freedom and community are the social analogs of the ecological dynamic expressed as unity in diversity in the natural world. The assault upon freedom and community is increasingly understood as the social manifestation of the destructive conduct of industrialism toward nature—including human social systems. At bottom, there is no inherent separation between a social ecology and a natural ecology. The existence of human self-consciousness, the flexibility of human agency and technique do not mean that humanity stands outside of nature. Indeed, it is the conceit of industrialism that we can dispense with nature, internally and externally, in pursuit of the glib abstractions of money and power.

The global ecology movement, from the Greens in Germany to the rubber-tappers' union of the Amazon to the Clamshell Alliance of New England, is one facet of the social reclamation of freedom and community. Mondragon is another. The multifarious pursuit and defense of freedom and community will lead us toward the practice of what may one day be seen to be a true ecological civilization.

Unfortunately, there is no blueprint or guarantee that will predict the nature, timing, and course of social transformation. The prospects for catastrophe or for renewal are calls for human action. Industrial modernism has made clear its instability, and that we can no longer expect greatness to come from greed or from the wisdom of the managers. "Business as usual" must change, but the nature and timing of these changes are in question. Unstable systems can prove rather durable—the Roman Empire crumbled for centuries—but the pace of change engendered by industrial modernism makes it very unlikely that we will have such latitude. It is vain to hope that we can give a reliable forecast for either apocalypse or beneficial transformation.

Today, we experience wilder and more unpredictable swings of the megamachine: their effects are manifest, but their genesis and trajectory are matters of conjecture. The threatened disasters transcend mere human creations—we no longer even have confidence in the renewing rhythms of the seasons and the weather. The greenhouse effect and the destruction of the ozone layer, and cumulative assaults of industrialism upon the chemistry of the atmosphere have become matters of general consciousness and global complexity.

How can we distinguish between a global tendency and a local perturbation? On ground level, social choices often seem to run counter to expectations. For example, despite the nearly ceaseless propaganda about the labor-saving power of computerization and robotization bringing an era of leisure with 20- to 30-hour workweeks, in the United States the average increased from 40.6 hours in 1973 to 47 hours in 1988—for those working, while millions are unemployed and at least hundreds of thousands are homeless—as more and more two-wage-earner families struggle to maintain an unsustainable "middle-class" standard of living.[1] Is this merely a sign of the crumbling U.S. imperium and the rise of Japanese and European capital, or does it reflect deeper trends affecting a world choking on a glut of commodities and its own wastes?

For the majority of the world's peoples, whose poverty and destitution help sustain the industrial core of the privileged few, the issues are often much more immediate and elemental: war, mass starvation, epidemic disease, deforestation and desertification, dramatic social dislocation, and the growth of toxic megacities are their lot. And here the torment of one nation is visited upon its neighbors: the delta lowlands of Bangladesh now expect catastrophic flooding during the monsoon season because forests in the Indian highlands to the north have been stripped for wood fuel. Overwhelming human agony persists in the context of crushing debt, discriminatory terms of trade, and an average annual income per person less than one-tenth that of the industrialized countries. How can the intertwined agonies of the poor and the environment be considered as subjects for successful management by the industrialized nations that in large measure have created—and continue to profit—from them?

The Relevance of the Mondragon Model

The focus of Mondragon social practice upon the creation and maintenance of equilibrio is certainly germane to the crisis of industrial modernism. Clearly, Mondragon has accommodated itself to the practice of the industrialized world: it can exist, indeed thrive, within the context of the global capitalist market. But this does not mean that the Mondragon model represents either a kind of pallid reformism or a prophylactic to maintain the basic character of a system in chaos. The importance of Mondragon goes beyond industrial method or techniques;

as Arizmendiarrieta saw, the project stands for a revolution without violence built from below.

Change is central to the nature of Mondragon, but it is change conditioned by considered social choices made in the democratic pursuit of equilibrio. Arizmendiarrieta once commented that "the vitality of a People is not demonstrated by their lasting, but by their being reborn and adapting."[2] This rebirth and adaptation is not change for the sake of change, nor is it simply a churning of a moribund market whipping up a froth of profits to be skimmed by the few from the labor of the many. Rather, Mondragon represents currents moving toward coherence and the development of an ecological postmodernism.

Mondragon is not the limit of expression of ecological postmodernism, and we are not limited to attempts to merely copy or duplicate the experiment—indeed, as Mondragon is alive and evolving, we must try to transcend it.

Recognizing the fundamental importance and ecological nature of Mondragon's pursuit of freedom and community may assist and help catalyze the future development of the global Green movement, which has been too often unable to connect its critique of industrialism with a constructive program for change. The Mondragon model presents environmental movements with a logical way to connect means and ends—and, for Mondragon itself, greater attention to explicit environmental concerns will help broaden, deepen, and strengthen the cooperative community.

Distinguishing between the principles that inform Mondragon's practice and the specific conduct of the cooperatives is not just a way to ignore the concrete and obtain a theorist's license, but to recognize the protean strength, reach, and flexibility of the fundamental social forces expressed in the formation and evolution of Mondragon. We need not hold it up to a test of eternal function to recognize its importance to our own practice.

Equilibrio and the Creation of Civil Society

The Mondragon model offers us the prospect of the organic creation of a truly independent civil society, a path away from the destructive allure of industrial modernism and toward a social order that respects and fosters the unity in diversity of the natural world. This is not simply a society characterized by distributive justice, or predicated upon a formal permission to compete in the market. It is a society built day by day through democratic practice and making considered social choices to maintain equilbrio.

It must be understood that the search for equilibrio is an ecological phenomenon whose bounds are never clearly defined; to succeed, it must encompass the indissoluble connections between all of humanity and between humanity and the natural world. This is the spirit that informs the search for equilibrio in reality: human confusion, conflict, the fog of self-interest, and the burdens of history are part of it, as are long meetings, hard work, love, joy, struggle, and disappointment. Mondragon is a source of excitement and optimism, not because success is historically inevitable, but because it represents the emergence of a transcendent and accessible model that allows us to make constructive use of the energy of the great transformative forces at work within industrial modernism.

Transformational Structures

A basic postulate of ecological postmodernism and of Mondragon—the indivisibility of freedom and community, of unity in diversity—cannot be easily addressed by the liberal imagination as presently understood. While freedom is central to classical economic and political liberalism in theory, in practice it has been largely the activity of isolated and competitive individuals—and most important, of ever-grander and more abstract corporate "persons."

The attitude toward community is much more ambivalent. The state, by definition, is antagonistic to the liberal exercise of individual freedom. The collective community, particularly while exercising political power, is viewed as a potent threat to the rights of the minority—particularly that minority possessing private property and privilege. Thus, for liberalism and, particularly, for the corporate liberalism of industrial modernism, freedom and community are held to be largely antithetical entities. The community's exercise of political and economic democracy must be carefully circumscribed to ensure the most profitable and stable conduct of corporate liberalism. The protection of property and self-interest—justified by the essential protection of the rights of individuals from the state—underlies much of the applied philosophy of liberalism.

Of course, the importance of the converging dynamic of freedom and community is not simply a function of philosophical weaknesses in the ideologies of industrial modernism. The enormously powerful forces at work dislocating industrial society are a result of intertwined practices and beliefs that permeate and shape every aspect of our existence, that distort and maim our lives and our environment.

Yet freedom and community cannot be banished; the theme must reemerge, just as a powerful but repressed emotion will find expression. As a social force, this dynamic is generally viewed as one of centralization versus autonomy—but there is a tendency to avoid even these terms, perhaps from fear of encouraging political action and stimulating deeper consideration that may unearth the heart of the matter.

At the moment in the United States, the business press discusses centralization versus autonomy as a debate on the most efficient world—will it be characterized by more multinationals, or by smaller, entrepreneurial firms? Consider, for example, in the capital-intensive semiconductor industry, producers of the microprocessor chips that are the foundation of computerization. Some hold that independent, relatively small entrepreneurial firms are the engine for technological innovation and economic growth; others, led by MIT's Charles Ferguson, believe in the economies of scale possessed by multinational giants (in partnership, when necessary, with a supportive government bureaucracy).

Ferguson's prescription is another dose of the old medicine—untrammeled corporate power and a more effective and sophisticated mobilization of social resources behind it in the name of nationalism and collective self-interest—a variation on the theme behind the rise and durability of conservative governments in the United States and Britain.[3] As Ferguson observes:

> The United States can no longer assume that its technology leads the world or its economic health is guaranteed. Only long-term collective action and large domestic investments—in education, in reforming government procurement and tax policies, in R&D and capital formation—will ensure that the United States participates fully in the information revolution. Correspondingly, faith in the market [as manifested in entrepreneurial vigor] must give way to a more sophisticated view of strategic behavior, of the incentives effects of government action, and of the relationships among technology, management, and industry performance.[4]

Here the impact of industrial modernism upon the social debate is resolutely reductionist. The real issues of freedom and community go unmentioned, and the alternatives between centralization and autonomy are essentially reduced to slight variants of the relationship between corporate capital and the state, and thus become no real alternatives at all. Such reductionism affects the practice of capitalism, and of socialism in transition. It ignores the complex social choices that actually determine the nature of industrial organization, its efficiency, and its impact upon the world. The reality of industrial decisions is thus masked; effects are split off as externalities—the perpetrators do not bear the real environmental, social, or economic costs. This denial of reality in the name of efficiency is the antithesis of the search for equilibrio.

The Globalization of the Market

The paucity of ideas informing industrial modernism is strikingly apparent in the current concoction of the "global market." In broad perspective, such a project is an attempt both to accelerate the imposition of the developing model of corporate capitalism being consolidated in the North to the South and to manage and channel into traditional forms the devolutionary forces that are challenging the traditional nation-state.

The corporate model of the global market is relatively straightforward. It is a global monoculture, allowing the operations of transnational corporations to proceed unhindered. Giant merchant banks, integrated with the transnational industrial and service corporations, are to be nurtured by a "healthy business climate" and supported by national and international governmental and quasi-governmental structures. The power and profits of the transnationals circulate freely, and the common global reality becomes one of an ascendant commodity and media culture conditioned by unremitting commercial exploitation.

In this setting, traditional culture becomes anachronistic material that can be used to further prod demand. As Ted Levitt, editor of the *Harvard Business Review*, assures us:

> Everybody is attracted to the multiple possibilities of modernity, including, coincidentally and paradoxically, the preservation of deeply remembered traditions and loyalties. They are deeply remembered and strongly coveted precisely because so much modernity is so alluring and so unsettling. That helps explain the global eruptions of nationalistic, ethnic, and religious intensities. Humankind, said T. S. Eliot, cannot stand too much change or reality. It needs roots, remembrance, attachments, fantasy, and transcendence, while wanting simultaneously everything else that beckons within palpable reach.
>
> Expanding are the possibilities of people having exactly what they wish as they wish things, and at mass produced prices—prices that are low not so much because of improved or flexible manufacturing, but rather because of global scale economies.[5]

While in pretense "inclusive," the global market reaches into much of the South by accelerating the split between the rich and the desperately poor. Governmental—and, much more important, social—structures become increasingly hollow. The recent round of famine has included the ultimate savage tribute to the "free" market: families starve not because there is no food, but because they have no money to buy it.

In light of such suffering, Levitt's conclusion about the prerequisites for corporate triumph are grotesque, drawn from what might be taken as part of an apocryphal *Shopper's Manifesto*: "Success therefore becomes a matter of combining global reach with local vigor . . . and of developing new, efficient ways to address and serve the heteroconsumer who is so ambidextrously engaged in pluralized consumption."

Devolution and Survival

This impoverishment of national cultures, and the fact that part of the population is literally rendered surplus for commercial exploitation, is part of the transnationals' contribution to the devolution of the nation-state. To be sure, there is little to mourn in the passing of the modern nation, with its militarist and nationalist preoccupations, and nations may evolve into units that reflect more natural and freely chosen affinities among people. However, much of the self-assertion of such movements as those in the Basque country, Northern Ireland, Québec, and the Palestinian intifada is, unsurprisingly, in part rather conventionally and traditionally nationalistic. They draw strength as much from resistance to colonial-style exploitation of relatively homogeneous regions as from the shortcomings of the nation-state and the impulses toward creating a newly democratic civil society. In this sense, the Basques share concerns that are broadly similar to those of the indigenous Kanaks of New Caledonia, the Irish resisting Britain, or South African blacks.

All these struggles also share in part the impulses leading away from nationalism toward democratic, multicultural, open societies that will encourage freedom and community, unity in diversity. The Mondragon system represents a constructive means to harness and harmonize these energies, and the Basque movement for independence is clearly animated by these forces. But as political entities, they are intertwined with more traditional and potentially reactionary nationalistic impulses. It is too much to ask that these movements shoulder the full burden of dispelling the effects of nationalism while they are desperately working for political independence and the realization of their national social identities.[6]

The forces of devolution are ascendant today in Europe—the birthplace of the nation-state and of industrial modernism. A number of interrelated and interactive themes characterize the increasingly fluid political, social, and economic situation there.

Perhaps paramount among them is the rapid and accelerating disintegration of the two great blocs of the Cold War, whose leaders are exhausted economically and politically and whose reciprocal and implacable hostility is beginning to dissolve.

The growing economic and political integration of the European Economic Community, whose members will remove all economic barriers to trade by 1992, constitutes a second theme. This is complemented by the growing importance of transnational governmental initiatives, such as the formation of a popularly elected European parliament.

Although the current focus is upon an economically integrated "United States of Europe" as an economic superpower, such steps could mean more than simply achieving economic or political economies of scale. The dynamic growth of independent social movements and the creation of new social structures outside the orbit of governments and corporations is of potentially much greater significance. At this point, there is enormous uncertainty over the direction a united Europe will take in pursuing the very general goals of freedom of movement of goods, services, capital, and people. There is clearly the opportunity for constructive change of enormous import. An alternative to a Europe of nations is a Europe of the peoples—de facto independence for Basques, Catalans, Welsh, Tuscans, etc., within a transnational system—a common European home of some kind, if not necessarily that envisioned by Mikhail Gorbachev.

Another factor is the transformation of the societies of Eastern Europe, driven by the great social movements for freedom from below and complemented by ongoing citizen initiatives across both national frontiers and the dissolving boundaries of the Cold War. These efforts include plans for independent and international citizen assemblies. While in the Soviet Union *glasnost* and *perestroika* began as reforms initiated from above, the social forces now in motion are profound and have proved to be beyond the control of elite government functionaries.

Fourth, movements for social change in Eastern and Western Europe, such as Solidarity in Poland and the Greens in Germany, are converging on ideas that do not call for a seizure of state power but look to nonviolent change from below, such as Adam Michnik's "New Evolutionism" in Poland and the Greens' parallel emphasis on transferring power from the state to society—in Eastern European terms, the creation of the independent organs of civil society. There is also a rapid evolution of international cooperation among independent social-change movements. For example, a December 1988 meeting in Amherst, Massachusetts, brought together the European International Peace Communication and Coordination Center (composed of representatives of leading independent Western European peace groups) to help facilitate cooperation between European and U.S. peace activists.[7]

Another important theme is the increasing democratization of the societies of Western Europe, with the end of dictatorships in Spain, Portugal, and Greece and the rise of parliamentary institutions that have now demonstrated their durability. These changes represent what seems to be the final refutation of the authoritarian and fascist tendencies that erupted in the 1930s, attempting to solve the crises of capitalism and to face the challenge of socialism with militaristic nationalist states that adopted the ideological fig leaf of fascist populism to justify their defense of the status quo. The new democracies do not mark an end to social evolution, but a point of departure for future developments in concert with the democratic changes occurring in Europe and the Soviet Union.

Finally, there is deepening environmental crisis, accompanied by the rise of an environmental movement that is now a major and growing political and social force from Ireland to the Soviet Union. The environmental movement is catalyzed by singular events such as a chemical disaster on the Rhine and the Chernobyl catastrophe, but its task is to reverse the unremitting assault of industrial modernism upon the biosphere. It is decidedly not exclusively a creature of industrialized nations, but a global phenomenon essential to transcending the limitations of the nation-state for the sake of unity and diversity, freedom and community.

The excitement of social transformation is in the air. It would be a grave error for us to take for granted the sustainability of a world system moving further and further from equilibrium. We need not confer upon the poisonous writhing of industrial modernism the cachet of inevitability and durability for geologic time. Ecological postmodernism can offer us more than did the substitution of wage slavery for chattel slavery. The building of ecological postmodernism is not accompanied by the banishment of all struggle, pain, and want. Instead, we can find in the democratic pursuit of equilibrio a way to make new social choices and to re-create our world.

The Promise of Perestroika

In its early phases, *perestroika* has meant steps toward the introduction of market mechanisms to animate the ponderous Soviet system of state-owned and operated enterprises, complemented by the emergence of essentially isolated and independent capitalist "cooperatives" that are allowed to compete with the state firms. These cooperatives were first permitted in service sectors, such as cafes and restaurants, but they are now a possible venue for the entrepreneurial pursuit of industry, including high-tech fields, under the leadership of Soviet engineers and scientists (whose theoretical abilities are of the highest order). While the emergence of marginal neocapitalist restaurateurs and boutique owners is greeted alternately by socialist disgust and "we-told-you-so" winks, the perestroika co-ops in some form may be significant in the long run.

The forces now being unleashed in the East may suffer as much from ignorance of models like Mondragon as they do from the resistance of state and Party bureaucracies and from the state's unwillingness to allow sectors of countervailing social power. The impulses for the creation of civil society are too easily translated into calls for opening private stock exchanges and the rise of a new class of entrepreneurs and technocrats to mimic the "freedom" of the industrialized West. The Mondragon model has much to offer those exploring new directions as part of *glasnost* and *perestroika*.

Mondragon has participated in a number of recent trade fairs, technology seminars, and student exhanges in and with the Soviet Union. Fagor's construction of a refrigerator production plant in Shanghai and the visit of Chinese managers and economists to Mondragon is an example of the kind of activity that will help encourage the diffusion of cooperative ideas and possibilities to the industrialized world and to developing nations.

The People's Republic of China had been quite receptive, before the bloody suppression of the democracy movement in 1989, to the efforts of David Ellerman and Chris Logan of the Industrial Cooperative Association (working through a new private organization, ICA/China) to encourage the adaptation of the Mondragon model to Chinese circumstances. Dr. Ellerman reported from a 1988 China trip that

> [e]nterprises [in China] can roughly be sorted into: state (ownership by "the whole people"), collectives (theoretically owned by the workers in them) and private. The collectives are in fact run by levels of government between city and township. But the collectives are our main target to convert to a pure or hybrid form of worker ownership. There are 100 million workers in collectives. . . . [T]he reality is that the door is open to strongly influence the emerging model of a collective enterprise (100,000,000 workers) by working directly with the sympathetic relevant authorities.[8]

Ellerman declined an offer from an enthusiastic administrator to convert a sizable group of provincial factories to cooperatives quickly. The Mondragon model cannot simply be imposed by bureaucratic fiat; it can be encouraged by government, but it must essentially arise from the social choices made by present and future cooperators.[9] Clearly, the Chinese hierarchs, as they cling to power following Tiananmen Square, are little inclined to encourage self-assertion by Chinese workers. It is unlikely, however, that even the Communist mandarins of Beijing can indefinitely resist the currents of historic change.

The appeal of the Mondragon model to innovative thinkers in a Communist world in transition is understandable, given that the generally recognized options for a move away from bureaucratic socialism are clearly constrained by the limits of established capitalist practice. Ignorance of effective alternatives serves those who seek to maintain the basic imperatives of state power. The great changes in the Communist world need not follow a trajectory consistent with the oft-noted convergence toward state capitalism by "capitalist" and "socialist" states. The future can offer much more than substituting repressive corporate liberalism for the different, but equally barren prospects of bureaucratic socialism.

The New Alternative in Central and Eastern Europe

The peoples of Eastern Europe are in the process of building, through collective and democratic action, new social order from the wreckage of crumbling totalitarianism. In the midst of vivid moments of change, the old boundaries of the possible fade, and people discover themselves "doing things that don't even have a name yet."

In this atmosphere, the very meaning of the independent organs of civil society is in flux—a product of experiment, risk, and surprise. In the words of Yugoslav sociologist and peace activist Tomaz Mastnak:

> It is difficult to be precise because civil society should constantly be defined anew, ad hoc. Most generally, it is a sphere different and independent from the sphere of state activities and the political system. My own notion of civil society is quite similar to the ones developed by the Czechoslovak opposition—especially the ideas of parallel structures and culture; and it shares certain Polish ideas too, such as Adam Michnik's "New Evolutionism" (which put an end to the old idea of revolutionism).[10]

In this ferment, there are clearly openings to take up the Mondragon model. Refusing to embrace the socialist state need not mean adopting corporate liberalism; it can, instead, be characterized by the creation of an ecological postmodernism.

Social change here is not simply a reflection of the collapse of a sclerotic socialism, it is part of the broader crisis of industrial modernism. In the view of Václav Havel, writer and activist who became president of Czechoslovakia, totalitarianism includes much of what is the common essence, East and West, of industrial modernism:

> The fact is that the domination of a large group of powerless people by a small powerful group has long ceased to be its [totalitarianism's] most typical feature. Nowadays, what is typical is the domination of one part of each of ourselves by another part of ourselves. It's as if the regime had an outpost inside every single citizen. Consequently, "the regime" is something that is elusive and hard to locate precisely within a particular institution or social group. In an odd kind of way, the system pervades the whole of society, such as that everyone at the same time supports it and helps create it—by mutely acquiescing in its version of reality, by voting in formal elections, and by observing its various rituals and ceremonies. By doing this, not only do people support the regime, they actually help create it. But at the same time everyone finds themselves in opposition. . . .

In my view, Soviet totalitarianism is an extreme manifestation—a strange and dangerous species—of a deep-seated problem which equally finds expression in advanced western society. These systems have in common something that the Czechoslovak philosopher Václav Belohradsky calls the "eschatology of the impersonal," that is, a trend toward impersonal power and rule by mega-machines or colossi that escape human control. I believe the world is losing its human dimension. Self-propelling mega-machines, juggernauts of impersonal power such as large-scale enterprises and faceless governments, represent the greatest threat to our present-day world. In the final analysis, totalitarianism is no more than an extreme expression of this threat.[11]

The devolutionary forces in Europe are but part of a great global movement from below that is transforming the nature of industrial modernism. The instability of the system, and the passion of those working for constructive change represent a challenge to the existence of industrial modernism itself.

We need to place the present moment of crisis in historical perspective. What appears as the nearly omnipotent global reach and monolithic power of industrial modernism may, in retrospect, be as much a symptom of its transformation as of its longevity. The gathering forces resemble, in spirit, the forces undermining what seemed in the 1850s to be the irresistible institution of slavery in the United States. Following several political and judicial defeats, Wendell Phillips, a leading abolitionist, wrote in despair, "The government has fallen into the hands of the Slave Power completely. So far as national politics are concerned we are beaten—there is no hope. . . . The future seems to unfold a vast slave empire united with Brazil. I hope I may be a false prophet but the sky never was so dark." The proponents of slavery agreed; they "felt their system was as permanent as gravity. They did not know that the world was changing under them."[12]

The periphery collapses and breaks away first. Thus, as Ben Webb notes, the Communist governments of Eastern Europe increasingly resembled the final years of the Franco regime in Spain and that of Antonio Salazar in Portugal.[13] These were fundamentally nonideological governments based on maintaining power and characterized by "corruption and financial disintegration," with "[a]n irresponsible absolute rule firmly held by means of the army, the police, the monopoly of the press, the control of the judiciary, . . . long terms of imprisonment, ill treatment and torture of political adversaries" and an "open unashamed backing of the regime" by the military and financial resources of a superpower.[14]

These were the conditions in the Basque region at the creation of the Mondragon system. It is precisely at the point of ideological, spiritual, and material exhaustion that power, no matter how vast its armamentarium, no matter how formidable its secret police, begins to lose its grip and the ascendant evolutionary forces of freedom and community begin to find expression.

This is not simply hypothesizing that Mondragon-style structures shall arise in Eastern Europe, but a suggestion that the strains upon industrial modernism, of which the societies of Eastern Europe are an example in extremis, will potentiate the rise of appropriate social structures of ecological postmodernism of which Mondragon is an example. The "new thinking" of this homegrown brand of *perestroika* may even spread to the United States.

In considering the future we should not limit ourselves to extrapolating the dominant trajectory of endless growth and despoilation. It is on the fringes, at the periphery, that the alternatives for our future can be seen to take shape. As the pursuit of profits and power enters into what we can describe as the zone of impossibility—that point where the environment, human society, and available material resources can no longer sustain its conduct—dramatic change is both possible and likely in a system increasingly far from equilibrium.

In these circumstances, instability and social transformation alternately seem to promise either redemption through change or disaster. An apocalyptic vision inclines us—particularly at the core in the United States—to the role of spectators. Industrial modernism is essentially incapable of developing solutions to problems that are fundamental products of its conduct. This leads us to demand that "they do something" about the intractable crises we face and, nearly simultaneously, to despair of our ability to find solutions created by our technology and our society. We can sometimes agree that we can no longer afford to be mute witnesses to the bankrupt exercises of the status quo of Republican and Democratic parties, or of business as usual by transnational corporations, but the opportunities presented by the Mondragon system remain largely outside the conventional policy debate.

Reform Scenarios for Social and Ecological Renewal

One axiom of the environmental and social critique of industrialism is that unchecked growth of production, consumption, resource depletion, and pollution, combined with an expanding human population, is a recipe for disaster. Such a stand leads, however, to a wide variety of solutions influenced by differing genres of political economy.

It is tempting to judge systems merely on their apparent attitude toward growth and pollution. Industrial capitalism and socialism generally favor growth and propose to mitigate its difficulties through various forms of planning, regulation, or the mechanisms of the market. But capitalism and socialism do not exhaust the range of possibilities, even though each makes a claim to exclusivity.

Georges Bataille, for example, takes the position that we should not be concerned with how production is organized (capitalism, socialism, feudalism) but with how surpluses are expended.[15] Such a view is helpful in considering Mondragon as a kind of social system, not merely as a system of ownership. In this sense, a focus on Mondragon could be seen as a design for the sane disbursement of social product—for schools, housing, health care, social clubs, pensions, pollution treatment, and the like. The democratic pursuit of equilibrio is logically inclined toward producing goods and expending surpluses in a manner consistent with the fundamental ecological imperatives that shape the indivisibility of freedom and community, diversity and unity.

There is still an inclination to engage in prescriptive reveries that see relief from the pain of industrialism largely by mitigating the greed of capitalism through socialism—democratic or otherwise; and, alternatively, remedying the pain of socialism by introducing doses of the capitalist market. Industrial socialists by inclination, and capitalists by definition, are thoroughly taken with the romance of the machine, the liberating potential of technology, and the importance of economic growth. Socialists of whatever stripe generally unabashedly seek state power to right past wrongs; for capitalists, the liberal-democratic state is, in effect, part of the "public" property of private capital.

Capitalism offers us a pastiche of remedies. First, there is the creaking reliance upon the traditional market forces that somehow have not quite managed to work. A second layer is a new appeal to enlightened self-interest, ranging from the genre of peace through transnational penetration (the dream of selling oil for the lamps of China become Pepsi for the youth of Moscow) to the development of ethical and socially responsible capitalist business practices, New-Aged and otherwise. The final remedy is to apply a kind of planning, principally through regulation, that is generally limited to sustain the grasp and power of private capital and public bureaucracy.

The appeal of the pastiche is that its confusion reflects the strains within the system and promises, at least in form, most things to most people—and, above all, it legitimates the megamachine by helping maintain the illusion of freedom and democracy. But as an assemblage, the system is disinclined to change its fundamental parameters of hierarchical control and growth.

It is a hard time for reformers. We can act like World Watch or the nuclear-freeze movement, noting that time is running out and that environmental and social catastrophe will soon overtake us. Or we can propose a technical approach that allows the system to move toward greater stability, such as the "build-down" offered as a way for the United States and the Soviet Union to make newer and more accurate nuclear weapons as a path toward partial nuclear disarmament and arms control.

More boldly, we can even attempt to surgically remove from industrial modernism the central part in its ideology played by growth and offer a profound modification: an attempt to prevent the collapse of the megamachine by limiting expansion. Herman Daly's proposed "steady-state economy" is essentially a moral and technocratic reform, predicated upon the belief that the limits to economic expansion imposed by the geometric growth of population, resource depletion, and pollution are rapidly being reached and will tend to be irreversible.[16]

This is not to disparage reformers or the work of reform. Reform is desperately needed; it is often the best real alternative at hand, and it may even prove to be adequate or able to bring—through unanticipated consequences—greater change. Our collective fear and despair is that reform undertaken within the context of the megamachine of industrial modernism is insufficient for the task at hand. We must work to remedy the technological insanity of industrialism, work toward an economic and political system that begins to allow people, for starters, to feed, clothe, and shelter themselves, to drink clean water and breathe clean air. Can the strategies of democratic socialism and the mechanisms of a steady-state economy help us build such a world?

Democratic Socialism: Economic Growth and Environmental Quality

The desperate poverty of the majority of the world's people would appear to call for both the redistribution of income and economic growth. After all, those who have are supremely disinclined to transfer wealth to those who have not. Attempts to resolve the "Third World debt problem" that continues to crush the economies of the poor have led only to a glacially slow discharge of debts that can never be repaid.

Looking for the rehabilitation of industrial modernism, Barry Commoner believes that

> [we] can continue to hope that the USSR and the other socialist countries will, in the course of time, learn about not only the necessity of democratic reforms, but of technological reforms. But perhaps more immediately, I believe this task should be undertaken by the left in capitalist countries, and especially political parties that have already accepted the task of creating democratic socialism.[17]

However, the environmental record of the Western European democratic "socialist" governments of Spain, Italy, France, Greece, Germany, and Britain is not particularly encouraging.

Economic growth looks like a relatively painless to improve the distribution of goods, one popular with both capitalists and socialists; there is some truth to the cliché that a rising tide lifts all boats (happier than the cliché of struggling over the distribution of pieces of a shrinking pie). Since there are technological means to reduce pollution, why not opt for economic growth in a reformed capitalism and socialism? If we cease pursuing economic growth, do we freeze existing inequalities, leaving the majority of the global population in dire poverty while the industrialized world attempts to preserve those parts of the environment not yet destroyed? Barry Commoner, for example, identifies the five- to ten-fold rise in U.S. environmental pollution in the twenty-five years following World War II largely with technological decisions made on the basis of the pursuit of private profits.

We need to remember that questions about economic growth are raised in the context of an industrial system whose fundamental characteristic is dynamic expansion and global reach, a system that has created or helped to create the absolute misery of billions. Both capitalist and socialist industrialism are shaped by the conduct of power in pursuit of either private profits or social surpluses, which are used essentially to enhance the scope and reach of that power and only incidentally to strengthen human society and the unity in diversity of the natural world.

The Mondragon system, in contrast, focuses first on the social purposes of maintaining equilibrio and strengthening freedom and community. Cooperative entrepreneurship acts within the context of a system that can place limits on the conduct of industrial modernism. In creating both a social system and considerable material wealth, Mondragon has pursued an expansive policy characterized by growth, but it is an expansion focused on the scale of Mondragon operations—to provide more opportunity for jobs and participation within the cooperatives and to further elaborate their scope—while maintaining the basic distribution of wealth within the system by limiting wage differentials and the accumulation of personal wealth. The democracy and egalitarianism of Mondragon makes it extremely well suited to adjust to the imperatives of social change.

Benign Technocracy: The Steady-State Economy

It is sometimes suggested that we should directly assault the basic postulate of industrial modernism, the imperative for the limitless growth of production and consumption. Herman Daly notes that "[t]he apparent purpose of growth economics is to seek to satisfy infinite wants by means of infinite production. This is as wise as chasing a white whale, and the high rationality of the means employed cannot be used to justify the insanity of the purpose. Rational means simply make insane purposes all the more dangerous."[18]

Herman Daly suggests substituting various sorts of regulated stasis accounts for government to manage (along with market mechanisms) the conduct of industrial society. Daly's "steady-state economy" is ultimately a call for a sustainable, ecologically conscious, and morally responsible society. He proposes an intricate market system of entitlements (coordinated by government) to maintain a constant human population, a constant net stock of manufactured objects, and a reduction of the use of resources ("throughput of matter-energy"), with pollution cut to the lowest feasible level.

Daly focuses on the intensity component of growth and, by implication, the geographical expansion of industrial modernism. The basic issues of economic growth and of equity for the majority of the world's people, both those held in abject poverty and those rapidly industrializing, is put into question by the steady-state economy. It is a commonplace to note, for example, that the world could not tolerate a China, Brazil, or Soviet Union attempting to duplicate the U.S. automobile culture.

It is an error during a time of deepening ecological crisis to simply dismiss some form of market-based ideas, like Daly's, as totally at odds with the fundamental imperative of capitalist accumulation, which is predicated upon the creation of more—more wealth through more production, more consumption, and more services. Similarly, the rapid move toward market mechanisms in the socialist world certainly provides a venue, perhaps an even easier one, for acceptance of these ideas.

In general, Daly's steady-state economy can be viewed as a design for the technocratic management of a transition from industrial modernism to at least a relatively sustainable society. Such mechanisms might well be adapted by a kind of industrial global technocracy facing social and ecological disintegration. As political economy, the steady-state theory represents the sort of democratic reform from above that is thoroughly consistent with the nature of existing industrial modernism.[19] Stasis mechanisms could arise as a result of changes from below, but would likely bear little resemblance to the sort of technocratic management from above that essentially works to maintain existing power relationships—enshrined, in Daly's system, through the proposed auction of depletion rights. Those with power and money will get the rights.

Entropy and the Postmodern Future

Behind the justification for a steady-state economy is a type of global systems approach that equates industrial pollution and resource depletion with an increase in entropy—the irreversible tendency of closed systems toward increasing disorder and randomness. This suggests that our voracious consumption of the earth's nonrenewable resources and our contamination of the biosphere will place insurmountable obstacles in the path of our future. Pessimists (or, perhaps, realists) see that the world is being used up in ways we will not be able to remedy.

As a physical and philosophical concept, the principle of entropy can be used to justify what amounts to a sort of neomechanicism that views the world system either as a simple machine subject to the laws of classical mechanics or as a statistically enlightened, complex machine; both involve predictable cause and effect and generally linear change. A steady-state economy in these terms is a recipe for ultraregulation that extends from economic to political life, whose apotheosis is an integrated global technocracy—a neomechanicism thoroughly within the mainstream of industrial modernism, with its emphasis on order, hierarchy, and progress.

But this is not the only conclusion we can draw from the idea of entropy. We are not limited to construing the future as only the negation or the disintegration of modernism.

Ecological postmodernism has a science and a natural philosophy as well as a politics and a social philosophy. Let us examine briefly the work of the scientist Ilya Prigogine and the philosopher Isabelle Stengers on the role of fluctuations in the creation of order and harmony.[20] Their exploration of entropy theory describes an essentially ecological world of dynamic and sometimes dramatic change, where out-of-balance ("far-from-equilibrium") structures can form that may lead to sudden change that reestablishes system harmony.

In such a case, there is the irreversible direction of the flow of time provided by entropic processes, in contrast to the reversible nature of conventional physics and the potentially catastrophic nature of change as things become out of balance as entropy increases. It is at the margins, with systems under stress, that fluctuation and chance can have enormous impact. Prigogine and Stengers conclude that "nonequilibrium is the source of order. Nonequilibrium brings 'order out of chaos.'"[21]

The behavior of a world characterized by change can be viewed as the physical cognate of the social systems of ecological postmodernism. This is a nonmechanistic world "where the future is not given."[22] In its physics and in its social behavior, this is a world freed from the familiar tautology where future and past are contained in the present, deducible from existing conditions, and where the action of an individual is of only marginal significance.

The concern of such systems is the essentially ecological process of becoming and the maintenance of system equilibrium, or balance. This is a world characterized by "the creative science of change and circumstances."[23] This is a world in which we are freed from the tyranny of the object, both as material thing and as quasi-material data, and address ourselves once again to the fundamental relations of freedom and community, unity in diversity.

Techno-fixes and regulations are sometimes useful, even necessary, but neither is likely to redeem us. We must be profoundly skeptical of the excursions of the transnational corporation and the heavy dance of giant bureaucracies: the record has proven that neither can transcend their basic commitment to industrial modernism. The evolutionary "reforms" of ecological postmodernism rise from below.

An ecological civilization will become a solar civilization. It will apply the wisdom of analyses that understand that many environmental problems are the result of specific technological choices made on the basis of power and profit without regard to real effects. It will reflect the impossibility of infinite growth and realize the future price to be paid for present profligacy. But an ecological civilization can only be built through the embracing of freedom and the building of community by ordinary citizens where they live and work. Social change is a multidimensional process. It is essential for each of us to act in appropriate ways as citizens, as workers, as consumers, as voters, as individuals, and as members of families and communities.

What matters, when it counts, is not abstractions of intention or purpose, but the participation of people in matters that affect their lives and their exercise of opportunity for real democratic control. The construction of an ecological society is based upon the ever-widening pursuit of equilibrio that identifies in its practice the indivisibility of freedom and community, unity in diversity.

Mondragon and the Future of Freedom and Community

Despite their interest in technology, the cooperators' perspective is essentially social rather than technological. They sweat the details, but it is the human reality that supports the maintenance of equilibrio that underlies their accomplishments.

The cooperators have a predilection for discussion, planning, and considering steps needed to respond to the reality of the world and to shape the future. Their burden appears substantially heavier than that of a conventional enterprise in that their aims go beyond generating profits and administering social functions. But the record of durability and flexibility suggests that Mondragon's prospects have been enhanced by this task.

The reality of the system is the invigoration of social reality, individual and collective participation in the process of making and shaping the future. Cooperative reality is not a shroud shielding the cooperators from the world. The proliferation of the institutions of civil society of the Mondragon system is an intensification of participation in the reality of existence. In this sense, the reach of the cooperatives for the future is unbounded; in this sense, the Mondragon reality represents the integration and fusion of being and becoming.

The process of equilibrio is one of continual re-creation and actualization that absorbs the nature of being in the process of becoming. Industrial modernism concentrates on epistemological questions, upon knowing. Everything is reduced to two simple dicta: science is knowlege; knowledge is power.

Ecological postmodernism recognizes not merely the social creation of knowledge, but the social actualization and re-creation of being in the active process of becoming. The democratic pursuit of equilibrio is willed, it is intentional, it involves individuals; but it is not the lonely existential drama of individuals undertaking the task of Sisyphus in the shadow of the megamachine. Rather, it is an individual and social process of becoming that it re-creates a reality that is ineluctably social as well as individual.

Ecological postmodernism is not simply the substitution of a new set of assumptions to revivify modernism or the creation of new techniques to maximize performance. Equilibrio is the reestablishment of dynamic balance through the process of becoming, the process of creating and building the future. In this task, humanity can turn from the vanities of alienated power, from the futile attempt to conquer nature and thereby ourselves, and from the sterile divisions (within people, within society, within nature) spawned by the pursuit and exercise of power.

The future is uncertain. But uncertainty is the door to freedom that can lead to the end of the loneliness that is central to the life of industrial modernism. There is nothing mystical in understanding how the individual and social pursuit of equilibrio can help us dispel the miasma of loneliness that blights our lives. It is an everyday affair, a domain of action, not abstraction, the convergence of being and becoming.

Ambiguity calls for humility, not paralyzing despair. Uncertainty (and therefore freedom), the idea of a relativistic universe, of establishing equilibrium through fluctuation, are not elements of a brief against knowledge and human value but against closure and finality. They reflect a universe of continuous re-creation, one where reality and truth are neither external nor changeless, a social and moral universe where the fault is not in the stars but in ourselves. To recognize human agency is to recognize the fusion of being and becoming.

Mondragon is a system of voluntary and democratic social choices; its themes and concepts arise, in part, from the enormous complexity of the deep social structures that condition our actions. Mondragon's pursuit of freedom and community, unity in diversity, resolves the tension between individual human rights and the utilitarian desire for the greatest good for the greatest number. Its answer is not either/or, but both.

The belief in the end of history, the death of God, the collapse of philosophy, and the dissolution of the idea of progress are best understood as creatures of the nearly unbearable strains borne under industrial modernism. But these tumultuous currents of uncertainty carry the potential for the reintegration of the individual and the collective prospect for understanding a world in motion that is characterized by ecological postmodernism.

Such a view represents the reinvigoration of human value through the process of democratic choice and empathy, expressed in its highest form as love in action—as nonviolence. Ecological postmodernism re-creates the future through individual and social pursuit of equilibrio. Empathy underlies equilibrio; it first weakens and then dissolves the boundary between observer and observed, between self and other, and represents the ultimate lack of dissonance between freedom and community. For Mondragon at its best, empathy is practice. Mondragon asks What do we do? and How do we do it? These are not questions of technique, but of becoming; inquiries that flow from the underlying cooperative principles.

In their reimagination of future society, the cooperators have recourse to the fundamental social values that have given life to the Mondragon system; the future is not simply a matter of tinkering and optimizing, but pursuing what can be. As J. M. Mendizábal observes:

> Solidarity is not possible without a plan for the future. The dynamic element of solidarity is the plan, the objective, the action that is undertaken, the result that is sought.... Arizmendiarrieta's plan is not to become rich. His idea is the creation of liberty, of social emancipation that seeks the good individual in the good society and is subordinated to these. It is not only a business plan, it is also a plan for society and life. And at the same time it is not an individualistic plan.... To be a cooperator is precisely to be convinced that we strive for what is best for all.[24]

Thus for Mondragon, the past can only be seen as prologue. Prior accomplishments are not a mold. Jesús Larrañaga, for example, speaks of the co-ops embracing an expansive and internationalist model of "co-development" with a variety of partners. A 1988 editorial in *T. U. Lankide*, "Looking Toward 1993," discusses the potentially momentous changes the co-ops face in a "Europe moving toward its political integration ... progressively shaping the outline of a state formed by different peoples rising above the limits born of national belligerence" and warns that the future will require new attitudes that will facilitate "the opening to sincere cooperation, in order to undertake common strategic plans, with the abandonment of inertia" and of "sterile vanities." For the Mondragon cooperators in this new Europe, "the group will have practical value only if it 'crosses frontiers.' "[25]

Thus the future prospects for freedom and community, unity in diversity, involve the ability to cross frontiers—not only national borders, but the limits placed upon individuals and society by industrial modernism. This process has been integral to Mondragon, which began by opening the conversation about the future of industrial modernism to the Basque poor. Now, new voices must be allowed to join in the conversation—the voices of women, of people of color, of the majority of the world's people who are poor, of children, of the nonverbal but omnipresent voice of the biosphere. This imperative to transcend the boundaries of past practice as part of the ongoing re-creation of the future is both a model of the struggle we all face and a call to action.

It is a gentle call, but one that finds a resonance in the perilous balance with which we cling to our everyday lives. Above all else, the work of the Mondragon cooperators is a call to use our own particular gifts to overcome the pain that holds our world in thrall. The choice and the opportunity are our own. It is time for us to work, and to play, to embrace freedom and community, to rediscover the joys and renewal of unity in diversity.

Notes

1. Butterfield 1989, p. 12.
2. Quoted in Caja Laboral Popular annual report 1987, p. 6.
3. In contrast, the conservative government of the Federal Republic of Germany has generally maintained the social-democratic policies that have been resolutely dismantled or opposed under Reaganism and Thatcherism.
4. Ferguson 1988, p. 62.
5. Levitt 1988, p. 8.
6. Breecher 1987 presents an interesting discussion of the political dynamics of national devolution.
7. For a view of the Green prospect from a left perspective see Hawkins 1988.
8. Ellerman 1988, pp. 2–7.
9. Personal conversation with David Ellerman, Fall 1988.
10. Thompson 1988, p. 149.
11. Blair 1987, pp. 114–16.
12. Boyer and Morais 1974, p. 17.
13. Webb 1988, pp. 3–4.
14. de Madariaga 1958, p. 638.
15. Bataille 1988.
16. See Meadows et al. 1972.
17. Commoner 1985, p. 26.
18. Daly 1979, p. 77.

19. Ibid., pp. 67–94.
20. Prigogine and Stengers 1984.
21. Ibid., p. 287; emphasis in original.
22. Prigogine and Stengers 1984, p. 16.
23. Michel Serres, quoted in Prigogine and Stengers 1984, p. 304.
24. Mendizábal 1984, p. 2.
25. "Mirando Hacia 1993," *T. U. Lankide* no. 310, Jan. 1988, p. 2.

11
Mondragon Is Perspective

We live at a time of the exhaustion of the political, material and moral resources of industrial modernism, and in the midst of a gathering global ecological catastrophe that exacerbates the basic political and social disequilibrium of a world where nuclear weapons are increasingly commonplace and the major expenditure is for weapons and more weapons. There is too much to do and too little time, energy, and money.

Yet the gathering crises have not yet roused us from our collective lethargy. Most of us are thoroughly domesticated, like feedlot sheep awaiting their transformation into mutton. The piles of dead from the ongoing wars and the latest famine, after all, have an ancient if perversely reassuring context, just as the masses of the destitute are said to comfort the rich. But this time there is an undercurrent of difference, a murmuring of warning. In North America and Europe we have watched the forest begin to die; we remember the deeper greens, the fuller tree crowns of healthy and exuberant life. In the cities suddenly there is unbroken heat and haze, air that is almost unbreathable. We begin to realize that history and circumstance impel us to act, to use our humanity.

It is not predetermined that we will fall into an inescapable vortex of destruction. From the process of life flowers hope, the reality of choice, and the certainty of change.

We can act to heal the wounds, to reestablish balance. Although not a simple journey, it begins with simple steps. Mondragon cooperativism shows a healing and reintegrative path. When we make a choice for freedom and community, unity in diversity, we open a door to the future. We are faced with two basic alternatives: extinction or postapocalyptic barbarism; or some type of global technocracy or ecological postmodernism.

Extinction (which may include all life) or postapocalyptic barbarism (if some of us survive) is the sad and predictable end of industrial modernism. But, fortunately, life and history do not in general follow predictable trajectories. We can find solace in the fact that such despair is a creature of the world view of industrial modernism, where the sense of possibilities is incommensurate with the realities of human choice.[1] As to the prospects for an apocalyptic moment, there is no satisfactory general theory to connect and order the relationships involved in the operation of world systems under great stress, and it is highly improbable that such a theory could be found. It is one thing to pontificate about the course of history and the rise and fall of civilizations; it is another to determine whether or not an adventurer or a madman will decide (or be permitted by collective unconscious) to push the button and unleash nuclear holocaust.

While the apocalyptic moment is a distinct prospect, our efforts and energies in practice must naturally focus on the choice between global technocracy or ecological postmodernism upon which the future is conditioned. As individuals, as communities, as nations, as a global society, we must address the implications of the great social, political and environmental forces simultaneously at work. The real question is not whether fundamental change will occur, but how we will act as it transpires. We simply cannot continue lusting for more growth and expansion, mindlessly poisoning and destroying, reflexively building and using ever more destructive and sophisticated weapons. This is not utopianism. It is bedrock reality.

History is clearly not a chronology of conquests, nor an inhuman process of predestination or inevitability. History is the record of human choice and human experience. We must choose. We must participate. The system of industrial modernism cannot re-form itself, cannot save itself by decree.

Basic change comes from the whole of societies in motion, involved, in pursuit of individual and collective goals. We are not in the position of waiting passively for the judgement of God or Gaea, as if the future of our lives and our societies was somehow completely external to our actions. By our choices and actions we are are joined in the swirl of history, contributors and participants in the shaping of our destiny.

The social choices developed by the Mondragon system are basic material for creating a new reality. The exercise of freedom and the building of community, the social creation of unity in diversity, are central to the true social re-forming of industrial modernism. Arizmendiarrieta saw clearly that cooperativism represented both a means for economic gain and an ongoing "attempt to safeguard and guarantee the primacy of humanity and the supreme human values."[2]

The Mondragon "experiment" presents us with an example of an opportunity for re-creating social reality. It helps reveal the dynamics of the world system within which it exists. It is not merely a matter of public relations—cooperators refuse to characterize their experience as market socialism, humane capitalism, or a "third way"; it is an example of the possibilities of an integrative and ecological postmodern practice of freedom and community.

Mondragon is a direction and an opportunity, an affirmative choice and a possibility. It is a human endeavor, an act of creating something from nothing or, more accurately, the creation of a renewing social system from the available debris of the social and personal resources at hand. Martin Buber notes that "to create means to gather within oneself all elements, and to fuse them into a single structure; there is no true creative independence except that of giving form. Not where one finds a 'motif' but what one does with it is historically decisive."[3]

In three hundred years, the United States has been transformed from a vast and wondrous land of life in dynamic ecological balance, inhabited by human beings for a thousand generations, to an industrial empire. There is little to dispute in the sad observations in the call issued by the Iroquois Confederacy in 1978: "The air is foul, the waters poisoned, the trees dying, the animals are disappearing. We think even the systems of the weather are changing. . . . When the last of the Natural Way of Life is gone, all hope for human survival shall be gone with it."[4] From fear of the future, from anger at the violence done to earth and living things, from guilt at our participation in and gain from the process, can come a recognition of what was and what is, and a forgiveness that helps kindle our determination for change. Our future depends on our ability, individually and collectively, to overcome our inertia—inertia that keeps us divided, within ourselves and within our communities.

The Mondragon example is supremely relevant, since its history is precisely one of overcoming destitution, powerlessness, and despair through the exercise of the freedom of human choice and the building of community. These are times, for better or worse, that bid us to participate actively and humanely in the processes of life and of history. Action is called for. It is our choice. José María Arizmendiarrieta, who was participant and teacher, philosopher and explorer, put it simply: "We have realized that theory is necessary, yes, but it is not sufficient: we build the road as we travel."[5]

Notes

1. Reporter to Gandhi: "What do you think of Western civilization?" Gandhi: "I think it would be nice."

2. Azurmendi 1984, pp. 752–53.

3. Buber 1967, p. 63.

4. Akwesasne 1978, p. 52.

5. Azurmendi 1984, p. 481 (translation of "se hace camino al andar," by Ana María Pérez-Girones, from Whyte and Whyte 1988).

Appendix 1-1
The Mondragon Cooperatives in Detail*

Co-op Type, Name and Description	Jobs	Sales (million $)	Exports (million $)

I. Industrial Cooperatives

A. Casting and Forging

1. Amat (Guipúzcoa)   365   16.80   10.09
Iron and bronze fittings for various types of piping for water, oil, air, steam, gas.

2. Ampo (Guipúzcoa)   245   20.72   13.30
Steel casting and molding of piping products; valves of various types and steels.

3. Ederlan (Guipúzcoa)   708   40.77   19.75
Iron casting, aluminum casting (automobile and computer parts); machining (appliance and other parts).

---

*Data from a summary volume on the coops: *Caja Laboral Popular* (Bilbao: S. Coop. Elkar, 1987). The jobs, sales, and exports figures are for 1985, with peseta figures changed to dollars at exchange rate of 115Ptas/$. Note: this appendix does not include figures for either the CLP or educational co-ops.

Co-op Type, Name and Description	Jobs	Sales (million $)	Exports (million $)
4. Enara (Guipúzcoa) Special pipe flanges and fittings.	181	12.87	9.20
5. Funcor (Vizcaya) Special casting and molding; agricultural equipment, including feed processors, crop dryers, dehydraters, and silos; citrus processing.	215	10.23	2.54
6. Sakana (Navarra) Specialty iron parts and nickle alloys (ship motors and machine tools).	67	5.31	2.65
7. Tolsan (Vizcaya) Hot forging and stamping of steel and light alloy parts.	125	5.20	1.65
Subtotal: All Casting and Forging Co-ops	1,906	111.90	59.18

B. Capital Goods (Tooling)

	Jobs	Sales	Exports
1. Aurrenak (Alava) Foundry pattern equipment, including dies, plates, and coreboxes; molds and tooling for rubber-tire manufacture.	59	3.57	2.34
2. Batz (Vizcaya) Various types of dies for sheet metal work.	97	7.26	3.03
3. Doiki (Vizcaya) Checking and control devices, including parts for digital readouts and devices for dimensional checking and control, special welding.	46	1.76	—
4. Kendu (Guipúzcoa) Steel milling cutters for machining.	48	3.39	1.36
5. Latz (Guipúzcoa) Twist drills of various types and materials.	46	2.60	.56
6. Matrici (Vizcaya) Molds, dies, and models for various materials and large-sized metalworking tools.	350	17.15	11.61
7. Zubiola (Guipúzcoa) Various woodworking machine tools, drill bits, and cutters.	40	1.41	.07
Subtotal: Tooling	686	37.14	18.97

Co-op Type, Name and Description	Jobs	Sales (million $)	Exports (million $)

B. Capital Goods (Catering and Refrigeration)

8. Fagor Industrial (Guipúzcoa)   299   22.77   8.72
Ranges, fryers, convection ovens, dishwashers, washing machines, and dryers.

9. Kide (Vizcaya)   48   4.87   1.30
Industrial and commercial refrigeration rooms and cabinets.

Subtotal: Catering and Refrigeration   347   27.64   10.02

B. Capital Goods (Electrical and Electronic Equipment)

10. Aukri (Guipúzcoa)   249   17.96   8.00
Numerical control systems for machine tools, digital readouts, DC drives, industrial robots, and automatic-assembly machines.

11. Berriola (Guipúzcoa)   97   7.25   —
Industrial electronic process controls and automation; electric and electronic drives for hoisting machinery.

12. Bihar (Vizcaya)   18   .89   .03
Industrial process control, power electronics equipment.

Subtotal: Electrical and Electronic Equipment   364   26.10   8.03

B. Capital Goods (Miscellaneous)

13. Alkargo (Vizcaya)   79   5.22   .24
Electrical-distribution transformers, motors, and joints and connectors for rail-traffic signaling.

14. Gaiko (Navarra)   20   2.10   —
Steam generators, boilers, and engineering.

15. Guria Industries (Guipúzcoa)   110   27.79   9.95
Shipbuilding and repair of all types of steel boats (fishing boats, tugs, supply vessels).

16. Guria O.P. (Guipúzcoa)   228   39.49   .51
Construction equipment (excavators on wheels and treads, backhoes).

17. Irizar (Guipúzcoa)   361   21.38   4.67
Motor coach and bus manufacturers.

Co-op Type, Name and Description	Jobs	Sales (million $)	Exports (million $)
18. Ochandiano Talleres (Vizcaya)	62	6.00	.10
Conveyor-belt rollers, belts, packing tunnels, fish-processing installations.			
19. Oinakar (Guipúzcoa)	35	4.8	—
Battery and engine forklifts and material-handling systems.			
20. Urola (Guipúzcoa)	167	12.47	1.9
Extrusions and extrusion-blowing machines for plastic and synthetic materials.			
Subtotal: Miscellaneous Capital Goods	1,062	119.31	17.37
All Capital Goods Coops	2,459	210.19	54.39

C. Machine Tools (Abrasive)

1. Danobat (Guipúzcoa)	539	26.52	6.11
Numerical-control grinding machines and lathes, robots, flexible-production- system cells, and automatic-handling equipment.			
2. Izarraitz (Guipúzcoa)	75	2.74	.02
Reciprocating, band, and crosscut saws.			
3. Lealde (Vizcaya)	60	6.09	—
Numerical-control and cam-copying lathes.			
4. Soraluce (Guipúzcoa)	168	9.62	1.70
Numerical-control boring and milling machines, flexible systems.			
5. Txurtxil (Guipúzcoa)	57	3.17	1.10
Grinding machines and electrical-discharge machines.			
Subtotal: Abrasive	899	48.14	8.93

C. Machine Tools (Metal Deformation)

6. Arrasate (Guipúzcoa)	309	15.79	5.23
Shaping and bending lines, rolling mills, presses.			
7. Goiti (Guipúzcoa)	51	3.93	1.09
Numerical-control sheet-punching machines, eccentric and high-speed presses.			

The Mondragon Cooperatives in Detail 251

Co-op Type, Name and Description	Jobs	Sales (million $)	Exports (million $)

8. Ona-Press (Vizcaya)   81   4.30   .51
Hydraulic presses for metal, plastic, ceramics, and rubber, processing abrasives.

Subtotal: Metal Deformation   441   24.02   6.83

C. Machine Tools (Woodworking Machinery)

9. Egurko (Guipúzcoa)   113   5.43   1.57
Panel saws, dowel and hinge machines, tenon machines, sanders, borers, etc.

10. Ortza (Navarra)   38   3.01   1.05

Subtotal: Woodworking Machinery   151   8.44   2.62

     All Machine Tool Co-ops   1,491   80.60   18.38

D. Intermediate Goods (Plastics and Rubber)

1. Cikautxo (Vizcaya)   197   13.74   4.87
Injection molding of rubber parts, extrusions, cutting rubber pieces.

2. Maier (Vizcaya)   155   12.36   4.05
Mold construction, thermoplastics, surface finishes (chrome-plated, silk-screen).

3. Matz-Erreka (Guipúzcoa)   77   5.63   2.10
Screws, nuts, and miscellaneous metal fasteners; thermoplastics; electric motors for doors.

4. Matrici Plasticos (Vizcaya)   43   4.02   —
Molding reinforced thermoplastics.

5. Tajo (Guipúzcoa)   213   8.72   —
Mold construction for plastics and metals; thermoplastic injection.

Subtotal: Plastics and Rubber   685   44.47   11.02

D. Intermediate Goods (Mechanical, Electrical, and Electronic Parts)

6. Alecoop (Guipúzcoa)   335   7.62   .20
Electrical components for household appliances; electrical wiring for motor vehicles.

Co-op Type, Name and Description	Jobs	Sales (million $)	Exports (million $)
7. Copreci (Guipúzcoa)	1,049	42.34	22.56
Components for gas domestic appliances; thermostats for boilers and other heating devices; timers, switches, and controls for dishwashers and washing machines.			
8. Ederfil (Guipúzcoa)	52	9.63	1.81
Manufactures enamelled copper wire.			
9. Eika (Vizcaya)	138	8.69	6.04
Heating elements and boiling plates for ranges.			
10. Embega (Navarra)	86	3.77	1.29
Shaping and decoration of aluminum trim; screen printing and painting; gasket sealing.			
11. Fagor Electrotécnica (Guipúzcoa)	606	23.15	15.41
Semiconductors (various diodes and rectifiers), TV tuners.			
12. Orkli (Guipúzcoa)	190	10.97	4.65
Controls for heating systems, hot water, household appliances (motorized zone valves, ball valves, thermocouples, etc.)			
13. Zertan (Navarra)	224	6.52	3.70
Electric switches, thermostats, control devices.			
Subtotal: Mechanical, Electrical, and Electronic Parts	2,680	112.69	55.66

D. Intermediate Goods (Agricultural Equipment)

14. Aneko (Guipúzcoa)	12	.2	—
Precision seed drills.			
15. Goizper (Guipúzcoa)	134	11.24	4.65
Sprayers and dusters for agriculture, brakes and clutches, servomotors, scrapers for concrete mixers.			
16. Hertell (Guipúzcoa)	15	1.62	.47
Pumps for agricultural operations and manure tanks.			
Subtotal: Agricultural Equipment	161	13.06	5.12

D. Intermediate Goods (Medical Equipment)

17. Oiarso (Guipúzcoa)	39	1.59	.10
Blood transfusion and nutrition equipment, dialysis accessories.			

Co-op Type, Name and Description	Jobs	Sales (million $)	Exports (million $)
18. Osatu (Vizcaya)	18	1.04	.05
Cardiac monitors and defibrillators.			
Subtotal: Medical Equipment	57	2.63	.15

D. Intermediate Goods (Graphic Arts)

19. Bertako (Navarra)	83	3.49	—
Board for cartons, cartons, labeled packaging, marketing packaging machines.			
20. Danona Litografía (Guipúzcoa)	49	2.11	.03
Graphic design, printing, book publishing.			
21. Elkar (Vizcaya)	38	2.43	.29
Photocomposing, printing, binding.			
Subtotal: Graphic Arts	170	8.03	.32

D. Intermediate Goods (Miscellaneous)

22. Biurrarena (Guipúzcoa)	77	7.04	—
Sales and service of heavy equipment, manufacture of special mobile equipment.			
23. Coinalde (Alava)	33	4.43	.73
Wire nails.			
24. Etorki (Alava)	34	5.76	.09
25. Impreci (Guipúzcoa)	112	5.69	2.09
Gears, precision metal turning, brake levers for trucks and buses.			
26. Leunkor (Guipúzcoa)	70	2.15	—
Machining, indexing drivers, wire-welding products.			
27. R.P.K. (Alava)	73	5.07	.35
Springs of various types; copper coils for TV tuners.			
Subtotal: Miscellaneous Intermediate Goods	399	30.14	3.26
All Intermediate Goods Co-ops	4,152	211.02	75.53

E. Consumer Durable Goods (Furniture)

1. Basarte (Guipúzcoa)	13	1.29	.09
Chairs, sofas, sleepers.			

Co-op Type, Name and Description	Jobs	Sales (million $)	Exports (million $)
2. Coinma (Alava)	54	3.17	—
Lounge, bedroom, children's room, and office-furniture sets.			
3. Danona (Guipúzcoa)	384	21.06	4.45
Living room and bedroom furniture, stained wood panels.			
4. Herriola (Vizcaya)	37	2.50	.69
Designer lamps and suspended lighting for domestic and commercial applications.			
5. Lan-Mobel (Guipúzcoa)	116	5.53	.04
Living room and bedroom furniture.			
6. Lenniz (Guipúzcoa)	116	15.27	1.02
Kitchen furniture; custom appliance installations for the kitchen.			
7. Leroa (Guipúzcoa)	24	1.00	.05
Pine living room, bedroom, and office furniture.			
8. Maiak (Guipúzcoa)	36	2.60	.70
Living room furniture, children's furniture.			
9. Oihana (Navarra)	16	.91	—
Quality chairs for home and office.			
10. Uraldi (Vizcaya)	36	2.05	.10
Bathroom cabinets, mirrors, accessories.			
Subtotal: Furniture	832	55.38	7.14

E. Consumer Durable Goods (Domestic Appliances)

11. Fagor Clima (Guipúzcoa)	223	15.33	2.10
Gas and electric water heaters.			
12. Radar (Guipúzcoa)	125	13.50	.76
Kitchen goods (pressure cookers, frying pans, deep fryers, stainless steel trays, tea and coffee service).			
13. Ulgor (Guipúzcoa)	2,379	201.90	47.27
Cookers, ovens, refrigerators, freezers, washing machines, and dishwashers.			
Subtotal: Domestic Appliances	2,727	230.73	50.13

Co-op Type, Name and Description	Jobs	Sales (million $)	Exports (million $)

E. Consumer Durable Goods (Sports and Leisure)

14. Dikar (Guipúzcoa)   74   4.74   4.09
Muzzle-loading arms and replicas, ship models, gun sticks.

15. Eredu (Guipúzcoa)   39   4.90   1.04
Outdoor furniture, contemporary-design indoor furniture.

16. Gogar (Guipúzcoa)   13   1.51   —
Loudspeakers, hi-fi systems (amplifiers, tuners, radios, turntables, portables).

17. Ikus XXI (Guipúzcoa)   27   1.03   —
Eyeglass frames.

18. Orbea (Vizcaya)   169   13.70   —
Bicycles.

Subtotal: Sports and Leisure   322   25.88   5.13
    All Consumer Durable   3,881   311.99   62.40
    Goods Coops

F. Construction

1. Covimar (Vizcaya)   82   3.52   —
Cutting and polishing of granite and marble, fitting fascias on buildings.

2. Olarri (Guipúzcoa)
New co-op: no data available.

3. Orona (Guipúzcoa)   424   21.89   2.50
Elevators; electric drives; metal structural space frames for large-scale construction.

4. Ulma (Guipúzcoa)   470   30.61   2.97
Auxiliary metal structural parts (scaffolds, props, shoring systems, fences); greenhouses; machinery (wrapping and packaging materials, auxiliary equipment for bakeries).

5. Urssa (Alava)   250   12.87   1.97
Boilermaking; design, manufacture, and assembly of all types of steel structures (bridges, buildings, etc.).

Co-op Type, Name and Description	Jobs	Sales (million $)	Exports (million $)
6. Viviendas y Contratas (Guipúzcoa) Housing construction and promotion.		68	6.51
Subtotal: Construction*	1,294	75.40	7.44

Subtotal: All Industrial Cooperatives*

	15,183	1,001.10	277.32

II. Agricultural Cooperatives

1. Artaxa (Alava) Pig rasing and breeding.	6	.67	—
2. Barrenetxe (Vizcaya)	21	.64	—
3. Behi-Alde (Alava) Cattle for meat and breeding; milk production.	26	2.49	—
4. Coseheros Alaveses (Alava) Marketing Pioja Alevesa wines.	4	.47	—
5. Ian (Navarra) Canned and bottled fruits and vegetables.	45	7.61	.63
6. Lana (Guipúzcoa) Dairy (milk and cheese); forestry products (industrial packing, pallets, kits for do-it-yourself construction).	127	9.57	.85
7. Miba (Vizcaya) Preparation of mixed animal feeds; veterinary services; marketing agricultural products (tools, insecticides, milking and cattle-raising installations).	13	3.64	—
8. San Isidoro Labrador (Vizcaya) New co-op: no data available.			

Subtotal: All Agricultural Cooperatives

	242	25.09	1.48

(Based upon available 1985 data for co-ops operating in 1986.)

---

*Based upon 1985 data available from CLP for industrial co-ops.

Co-op Type, Name and Description	Jobs	Sales (million $)	Exports (million $)

III. Service-Sector Cooperatives

1. Auzo-Lagun (Guipúzcoa)   283   4.33   —
Women's cooperative for subcontracted assembly work; institutional cooking and cleaning services.

2. Ondoan (Vizcaya)   23   4.36   —
Design and installation of sewage and water-treatment systems; fire protection; HVAC installations.

3. Club Arkitze (Vizcaya)
Health club and gym. Data unavailable.

4. Uldata (Guipúzcoa)   91   6.27   —
Data-processing services; turnkey mini- and microcomputer systems for financial control and production; CAD-CAM (computer-assisted design/computer assisted manufacturing) systems; computer systems engineering and consulting.

5. Ulmatik (Guipúzcoa)   71   5.74   3.91
Engineering and assembly of industrial-automation systems.

Subtotal: All Service-Sector Cooperatives

   468   20.70   3.91

(Based upon available 1985 data for four of five co-ops in operation.)

Subtotal: Industrial, Agricultural, and Service-Sector Cooperatives

   15,983   1,046.89   282.71

(Based upon available 1985 data for co-ops in operation in 1986.)

IV. Retail Cooperative

1. Eroski (Vizcaya)   1,379   313.00   —
Stores throughout the Basque country.

Total: Industrial, Agricultural, Service-Sector, and Retail Cooperatives

(1985)   17,272   1,359.89   282.71

Appendix 1-2
Spanish Inflation Rates and Conversion to Constant 1985 Pesetas

Year	Index (base 1970)	Inflation Multiplier	Annual Inflation Percentage	Multiplier to Convert to Constant 1985 Ptas
1970	100.0	1.000	base year	8.129
1972	121.3	1.213	(data missing)	6.702
1973	137.3	1.373	13.1	5.920
1974	160.3	1.603	16.8	5.070
1975	188.9	1.889	17.8	4.303
1976	229.5	2.295	21.5	3.542
1977	285.4	2.854	24.4	2.848
1978	343.5	3.435	20.5	2.367
1979	401.8	4.018	17.0	2.023
1980	472.6	4.726	17.6	1.720
1981	535.8	5.358	13.4	1.517
1982	593.1	5.931	10.7	1.371
1983	665.5	6.655	12.2	1.221
1984	752.0	7.520	11.3	1.081
1985	812.9	8.129	8.1	1.000
1986	883.6	8.836	8.7	.912
1987	929.5	9.295	5.2	.865

Data on Spanish inflation were derived from United Nations (1985) for 1970 to 1982; from *Boletín de Estadística*, September–October 1985 and *Anuario Estadístico, 1984* for 1983 to 1984 and provided by Embassy of Spain; CLP annual report for 1985; figures for 1986 and 1987 came from newspaper sources.

Appendix 1-3
Regional Cooperative Groups

Group Name	Location	Year Founded	Member Cooperatives
Fagor	Leniz Valley	1965	Arrasate, Aurki, Copreci, Ederlan, Fagor Clima, Fagor Electrotécnica, Fagor Industrial, Lenniz, Leunkor, Orkli, Radar, Uldata, Ulgor, Ulmatik
Goilan	Goiherri	1978	Alttur, Ampo, Ederfil, Eredu, Irizar, Kendu
Learko	Lea-Artibai	1978	Cikautxo, Eika, Herriola, Kide, Lealde
Orbide	Donostialdea	1978	Biurrarena, Ekain, Gaztelu, Electricidad, Guría, Oirso, Orona, Scoiner, Vicon
Indarko	Mungialdea-Busturialdea	1979	Alkargo, Maier, Munko, Uraldi
Debako	Bajo Deba	1980	Danobat, Goiti, Soraluce, Txurtxil

Group Name	Location	Year Founded	Member Cooperatives
Nerbion	Gran Bilbao	1980	Bihar, Citamare, Elkar, Matrici, Matriplast, Ona-Pres, Ondoan
Naeko	Navarra	1980	Bertako, Embega, Gaiko, Ian, Oihana, Ortza, Sakana, Zertan
Urkide	Urola-Kosta	1980	Danona, Egurko, Gurola, Leroa, Maiak, Lan-Mobel, Zubiola
Urcoa	Alava	1981	Aurrenak, Coinma, Coinalde, R.P.K. Urssa
Berelan	Medio Deba–Alto Urola	1982	Aneko, Dormicoop, Impreci, Matz-Erreka, Gogar, Plásticos Urola
Onalan	Oinati	1983	Enmara, Oinakar, Ulma

Source: *T. U. Lankide* (1985); Fagor annual report (1986).

Appendix 2
Resources for Forming Cooperatives

These groups and organizations are a good place to begin if you are interested in starting a cooperative or need help with an existing co-op. Most have an orientation inspired by the Mondragon model, although some do not.

Industrial Cooperative Association (ICA)
20 Park Plaza, Suite 1127, Boston, MA 02116
(617) 629-2700

A nationwide technical assistance organization for worker cooperatives, the ICA has done much work in adapting legal and management aspects of the Mondragon system to U.S. conditions. It can provide detailed assistance for co-op conversions, start-ups, and management. The ICA offers a wide range of low-cost written materials, including model bylaws for Mondragon-type co-ops.

The Industrial Cooperative Association Revolving Loan Fund is an associated risk-capital fund that invests in worker cooperatives. It provides money for co-op start-ups, employee buy-outs of existing firms, and co-op expansion. The loan fund works to help co-ops leverage their own financial resources through a combination of financing from conventional public and private sources.

ICA staff, led by David Ellerman, is also involved in international efforts for democratic co-op conversion, working, for example, on a variety of levels in eastern and central European countries on cooperative restructuring.

Worker Owned Network (WON)
50 South Court Street, Athens, OH 45701
(614) 592-3854

This group, based in Appalachian Ohio, is inspired by a commitment to economic democracy and the Mondragon model. WON works with jobless and low-income people in an area where industries are moving away and coal mines are shutting down. WON helps with organizational skills and business management, as well as providing financial assistance. It focuses on "the skills necessary for workers to take action together."[1] Co-ops launched by the Worker Owned Network include a wholesale bakery, a Mexican-American restaurant, a cleaning services business, and a women's craft co-op.

Midwest Center for Labor Research
3411 West Diversey #10, Chicago, IL 60647
(312) 278-5418

This group offers direct technical and organizing assistance to unions, local and state governments, labor lawyers, educators, and community and religious coalitions to help save jobs and protect living standards. Assisting in worker buy-outs and forming cooperatives are just two of the areas in which the Midwest Center is active. They are involved as well in research against contract concessions, organizing and legal strategies opposing plant shutdowns, education, and expert-witness assistance. The center also publishes the journal *Labor Research Review*, which provides an accessible forum for labor and community activists who wish to exchange ideas and perspectives.

The Midwest Center for Labor Research advocates meaningful worker participation in management (as opposed to schemes that undermine workers' rights and unions in the name of "cooperation") and supports worker cooperatives that maintain both employment and labor solidarity.

There is much activity by unions in the use of ESOPs (employee stock ownership plans), resulting in varying degrees of worker control, cooperative formation, and worker buy-outs. The latter may range from building-trades workers taking over small construction firms to attempts to use leveraged buy-outs to gain control of major corporations such as United Airlines.

The United Auto Workers (UAW) has also been active in the effort for worker buy-outs. Contact the UAW, Solidarity House, 8000 East Jefferson, Detroit, MI 48214.

Institute for Community Economics (ICE)
151 Montague City Road, Greenfield, MA 01301
(413) 774-5933

This group provides technical help, information, and on-site assistance to urban and rural community groups and public agencies in developing community land trusts and community loan funds. Its work is informed by the belief that "[e]very local community should have a major role in planning the use of its land and resources and in developing the local economy."[2]

The work of the ICE is primarily in the formation of community land trusts and the acquisition of land and buildings for residences, which provide affordable and stable housing for communities permanently removed from the speculative real-estate market. Community loan funds also support worker-owned businesses. ICE's Revolving Loan Fund supports the acquisition and development of land and housing and assists worker cooperatives and other community-service organizations.

ICE provides a wide range of short-term and ongoing assistance to community groups in organizational, financial, and community-organizing areas. Literature and information are available at low cost.

Trusteeship Institute
Baker Road, Shutesbury, MA 01072
(413) 259-1600

A consulting firm specializing in the start-up of co-ops and in the conversion of existing businesses to cooperatives, Trusteeship Institute views Mondragon as a "third way," transcending conventional capitalist and socialist organizations.

In the words of Terry Mollner and Will Flanders of Trusteeship Institute:

> Father Arrizmendiarrieta's Third Way invites people to *freely* place the interests of society above those of one's self *within a context of freedom to choose the capitalist route*. The difference between capitalism and socialism and the Third Way—or "trusteeship" as we call it—is that the individual freely chooses to give priority to human society over individual interests.[3]

Trusteeship Institute has a particular focus on the human dynamics of cooperative formation, which it believes is of paramount importance.

> When assisting client owners to start or convert a company based on the Mondragon model, we have learned that our most important tasks are, first, to not limit anyone's freedom any more than it is already limited. Thus, in a conversion, we encourage the owner to assure all current employees that they will be free to remain employees for as

> long as they wish to remain with the company, and no one will be pressured to become a member of the cooperative. We call this model "a trusteeship cooperative."
>
> Secondly, although we inform the entire work force thoroughly and continuously, we work mainly with those who wish to become members of the cooperative to create it. For instance, in Nelco Mechanical Limited, a construction firm in Canada with over a hundred employees, we had only six employees become members of the cooperative initially. In this situation most of the employees were members of four unions which were opposed to the conversion, although they worked extensively with us to assure that it did not adversely affect their members and that they would be able to join. As the months have gone by, more and more union and non-union workers are becoming members of the cooperative.
>
> And, thirdly and most importantly, we give priority to teaching the work force the difference between the feeling of working together as a team and of not working together as a team. We teach that the essential skill to have the cooperative be commercially successful and enjoyable on a day to day basis is to be able to choose the feeling of a team at will.[4]

In addition to group dynamics, the Trusteeship cooperative-formation process emphasizes the creation of meaningful and effective cooperative bylaws.

> Clarity of agreements, as well as full understanding of them, is essential for an honest commitment among everyone. Meetings, particularly of the leadership chosen for the Conversion Committee (who may or may not become members), also provide opportunities for the teaching of the skill of choosing team feelings as a self-conscious and public activity.
>
> Since a cooperative is a partnership of people who have learned to be masters of themselves for the good of us all, we believe that if this is not taught a legal cooperative may exist, but it will exist in name only and have a short life.[5]

Notes

1. June Holley and Marty Zinn "Community Self-Mobilization at Ohio's Worker-Owned Network," in *The Entrepreneurial Economy: The Monthly Review of Enterprise Development Strategies*, November 1985.
2. ICE brochure.
3. From typed manuscript written for this appendix by Terry Mollner and Will Flanders, Trusteeship Institute, May 1988, p. 2.
4. Ibid., pp. 4–5.
5. Ibid., p. 7.

Bibliography

Akwesasne 1978. *Basic Call to Consciousness*, ed. Akwesasne Notes (via Rooseveltown, N.Y.: Akwesasne Notes, 1978).
Avineri 1968. Shlomo Avineri, *The Social and Political Thought of Karl Marx* (Cambridge: Cambridge University Press, 1968).
Azurmendi 1984. Joxe Azurmendi, *El Hombre Cooperativo* (Mondragon: Caja Laboral Popular, 1984).
Bartlett 1988. Joseph W. Bartlett, "The Real Business of *Bonfire*" [review of Tom Wolfe's novel *The Bonfire of the Vanities*], *Harvard Business Review* no. 4 (July–August 1988).
Bataille 1988. Georges Bataille, *The Accursed Share*, trans. Robert Hurley (Zone Books: 1988).
Berrigan 1987. Daniel Berrigan, *To Dwell in Peace* (San Francisco: Harper & Row, 1987).
Blair 1987. Erica Blair, "Living the Truth in Prague: An Interview with Václav Havel," trans. A. G. Brain, *New Politics* (new series) 1, no. 3 (Summer 1987): pp. 114–16.
Bookchin 1977. Murray Bookchin, *The Spanish Anarchists: The Heroic Years, 1868–1936* (New York: Harper Colophon, 1977).
Bookchin 1982. Murray Bookchin, *The Ecology of Freedom: The Emergence and Dissolution of Hierarchy* (Palo Alto, Calif.: Cheshire, 1982).
Boyer and Morais 1974. Richard O. Boyer and Herbert M. Morais, *Labor's Untold Story* (New York: United Electrical, Radio and Machine Workers of America, 1974).

Bradley and Gelb 1983. Keith Bradley and Alan Gelb, *Cooperation At Work: The Mondragon Experience* (London: Heinemann Educational, 1983).
Bradley and Gelb 1985. Keith Bradley and Alan Gelb, " 'Mixed Economy' versus 'Cooperative' Adjustment: Mondragon's Experience Through Spain's Recession," World Bank Discussion Paper, Report no. DRD122, April 1985.
Braverman 1974. Harry Braverman, *Labor and Monopoly Capital* (New York: Monthly Review Press, 1974).
Breecher 1987. Jeremy Breecher, "The 'National' Question Reconsidered," *New Politics* (new series) 1, no. 3 (Summer 1987): pp. 95–111.
Brenan 1960. Gerald Brenan, *The Spanish Labyrinth: An Account of the Social and Political Background of the Spanish Civil War* (New York: Cambridge University Press, 1960).
Buber 1967. Martin Buber, "The Spirit of the Orient and Judaism," in *On Judaism* (New York: Schocken, 1967).
Burkitt 1984. Brian Burkitt, *Radical Political Economy: An Introduction to Alternative Economics* (New York: New York University Press, 1984).
Bury 1952. J. B. Bury, *The Idea of Progress: An Inquiry into Its Growth and Origin* (New York: Dover, 1952).
Butterfield 1989. Bruce Butterfield, "Breadwinner's Lament: No Time to Enjoy It," *Boston Globe*, January 16, 1989, p. 12.
Caja Laboral Popular (Mondragon: CLP, 1987).
Caja Laboral Popular, "Annual Report 1972" (Mondragon: CLP, 1972).
Caja Laboral Popular, "Annual Report 1986" (Mondragon: CLP, 1986).
Caja Laboral Popular, "Annual Report 1987" (Bilbao: S. Coop. Elkar, 1987).
Carlyle 1969. Thomas Carlyle, "The Present Time" (1850), in *Latter-Day Pamphlets* (New York: AMS, 1969).
Clamp 1986. Christine Clamp, "Managing Cooperation at Mondragon," Ph.D. diss., Boston College, 1986.
Clark 1979. Robert Clark, *The Basques: The Franco Years and Beyond* (Reno: University of Nevada Press, 1979).
Commoner 1972. Barry Commoner, *The Closing Circle: Nature, Man, and Technology* (New York: Bantam, 1972).
Commoner 1985. Barry Commoner, "Economic Growth and Environmental Quality: How to Have Both," *Social Policy* (Summer 1985).
Compa 1982. Lance Compa, "The Dangers of Worker Control," *The Nation* (October 2, 1982), p. 300.
Daly 1979. Herman E. Daly, "Entropy, Growth, and the Political Economy of Scarcity," in *Scarcity and Growth Reconsidered*, ed. V. K. Smith (Johns Hopkins University Press, for Resources for the Future, 1979).
de Madariaga 1958. Salvador de Madariaga, *Spain: A Modern History* (New York: Praeger, 1958).
de Madariaga 1967. Salvador de Madariaga, *Spain: A Modern History* (New York: Praeger, 1967).
Economía Vasca: Informe 1985 (Mondragon: Caja Laboral Popular, 1986).
Edelman 1988. Gerald Edelman, *Neural Darwinism* (New York: Basic, 1988).
"El Congreso Cooperativo Fortalece el Sentido de Grupo," *Trabajo y Unión* no. 307 (October 1987).
Eliade 1957. Mircea Eliade, *Myths, Dreams, and Mysteries: The Encounter between Contemporary Faiths and Archaic Realities* (New York: Harper & Row, 1957).
Ellerman 1984a. David P. Ellerman, "The Mondragon Cooperative Movement," Harvard Business School case no. 1-384-270 (Boston: Harvard Business School, 1984).

Bibliography 267

Ellerman 1984b. David P. Ellerman, *Management Planning with Labor as a Fixed Cost: The Mondragon Annual Business Plan Manual* (Somerville, Mass.: Industrial Cooperative Association, 1984).

Ellerman 1984c. David P. Ellerman, "Entrepreneurship in the Mondragon Cooperatives," *Review of Social Economy* (December 1984): pp. 273–93).

Ellerman 1988. David P. Ellerman, "Memo: China Trip" (to Industrial Cooperative Association staff, photocopy, July 22, 1988).

Ellul 1964. Jacques Ellul, *The Technological Society*, trans. John Wilkinson (New York: Random House, Vintage, 1964).

Embassy of Spain. *Boletín de Estadística*, September–October 1985.

Embassy of Spain. *Anuario Estadístico, 1984*.

Fagor Informe Anual 1987 (Mondragon: Fagor, 1987).

Ferguson 1988. Charles H. Ferguson, "From the People Who Brought You Voodoo Economics," *Harvard Business Review* no. 3 (May–June 1988): p. 62.

Fondo. "Fondo Intercooperativo de Solidaridad," *T. U. Lankide* (May 1987): pp. 10–11.

Foty 1989. Caroline Foty, "Lesbian Space, Values, and Power," *Sojourner: The Women's Forum* 15, no. 1 (September 1989): pp. 45–46.

Freud 1950. Sigmund Freud, "Animism, Magic and the Omnipotence of Thoughts," in *Totem and Taboo*, trans. James Stachley (New York: Norton, 1950).

Galbraith 1975. John Kenneth Galbraith, *Money: Whence It Came, Where It Went* (Boston: Houghton Mifflin, 1975).

Gárate 1986. José Gárate, "The Support for Employment Intervention," visit of Rt. Hon. Kenneth Clarke, Q.C., M.P., Minister of Employment of the United Kingdom, September 10, 1986.

Gelderloos 1989. Orin Gelderloos, "Energy and the Bible," *ICE Melter Newsletter*, no. 36 (June 1989). [Interfaith Council on Energy, P.O. Box 26577, Philadelphia, Pa. 19141, tel. (215) 635-1122.]

Ginto 1984. Jesús E. Ginto, "Entrevista: Alfonso Gorroñogoita," *T. U. Lankide*, no. 273 (August–September, 1984).

Ginto 1987a. Jesús E. Ginto, "Tratamiento del Capital Social en Nuestras Cooperativas," *Trabajo y Unión Lankide* no. 304 (June 1987).

Ginto 1987b. Jesús E. Ginto, "Entrevista: José María Ormaechea," *Trabajo y Unión*, no. 306 (September 1987): pp. 12–13.

Gorroño 1986. Iaki Gorroño, "Our Experiment and International Cooperation," visit of Rt. Hon. Kenneth Clarke, Q.C., M.P., Minister of Employment of the United Kingdom (Mondragon, CLP).

Gorroñogoitia 1984. Alfonso Gorroñogoitia, President CLP (in *T. U. Lankide* no. 273, August–September 1984).

Gorroñogoitia 1987. Alfonso Gorroñogoitia, "El Grupo Asociado a Caja Laboral Popular (Mondragon) Como Fenómeno Típico Mundial," *Trabajo y Unión*, no. 308 (November 1987).

Gorz 1982. Andre Gorz, *Farewell to the Working Class: An Essay on Postindustrial Socialism*, trans. Mike Sonenschen (Boston: South End, 1982).

Gouldner 1980. Alvin W. Gouldner, *The Two Marxisms: Contradictions and Anomalies in the Development of Theory* (New York: Seabury, 1980).

Graham 1984. Robert Graham, *Spain: A Nation Comes of Age* (New York: St. Martin's, 1984).

Griffin 1982. Susan Griffin, "Pornography and Silence," in *Made From This Earth* (New York: Harper & Row, 1982).

Gutiérrez-Johnson 1982. Ana Gutiérrez-Johnson, "Industrial Democracy in Action: The Cooperative Complex of Mondragon," Ph.D. diss., Cornell University (Ann Arbor, Mich.: University Microfilms, 1982): pp. 185–86.

Gutiérrez-Johnson and Whyte 1977. Ana Gutiérrez-Johnson and William Foote Whyte, "The Mondragon System of Worker Production Cooperatives," *Industrial and Labor Relations Review* 31, no. 1 (October 1977).

Harris 1980. Marvin Harris, *Cultural Materialism: The Struggle for a Science of Culture* (New York: Random House, Vintage, 1980).

Hawkins 1988. Howard Hawkins, "The Potential of the Greens," *New Politics* (new series) 2, no. 1 (Summer 1988), pp. 85–105.

Henningsen n.d. Gustav Henningsen, *The Witches' Advocate: Basque Witchcraft and the Spanish Inquisition* (Reno: University of Nevada Press, n.d.).

"The Hollow Corporation," *Business Week* (March 3, 1986).

Horvat, Markovic, and Supek 1975. Brankoi Horvat, Mihailo Markovic, and Rudi Supek, *Self-Governing Socialism: A Reader*, vol. 1 (White Plains, N.Y.: International Arts and Sciences, 1975).

Illich 1973. Ivan Illich, *Tools for Conviviality* (New York: Harper & Row, 1973).

Irastorza 1986. Javier Irastorza, "Caja Laboral Popular: A Financial Enterprise within the Cooperative Group," visit of Rt. Hon. Kenneth Clarke, Q.C., M.P., Minister of Employment of the United Kingdom (Mondragon, CLP), Autumn 1986.

Jackobs 1979. Steven Curtis Jackobs, "Community, Industrial Democracy, and the Cooperatives of Mondragon," unpublished undergraduate thesis, Harvard College, April 1979.

Jacobs 1984. Jane Jacobs, *Cities and The Wealth of Nations* (New York: Random House, 1984).

Jakin, Koperatibak (EFA, Arantzazu: 1973).

Jameson 1984. Fredric Jameson, "Postmodernism, or the Cultural Logic of Late Capitalism," *New Left Review* no. 146 (1984): pp. 53–92.

John Paul II 1982. John Paul II, "On Human Work: Encyclical Laborem Exercens" (Washington, D.C.: United States Catholic Conference, Campaign for Human Development, 1982): pp. 37–51.

Kamata 1982. Satoshi Kamata, *Japan in the Passing Lane: An Insider's Account of Life in a Japanese Auto Factory* (New York: Pantheon, 1982).

Kaswan and Kaswan 1986. Jacques Kaswan and Ruth Kaswan, *The Mondragon Cooperatives—1986: Economic Democracy* (Berkeley, Calif.: Alternatives Center).

Krimerman and Perry 1966. Leonard I. Krimerman and Lewis Perry, eds., *Patterns of Anarchy* (New York: Doubleday, Anchor, 1966).

Kuhn 1970. Thomas S. Kuhn, *The Structure of Scientific Revolutions*, 2d ed. (Chicago: University of Chicago Press, 1970).

Lagun-Aro, "Memoria Ejercicio 1986."

Larrañaga 1981. Jesús Larrañaga, *Don José María Arizmendiarrieta y la Experiencia Cooperativa de Mondragon* (Mondragon: Caja Laboral Popular, 1981).

Larrañaga 1987. Jesús Larrañaga, "La Era del Co-Desarrollo," *Trabajo y Unión* no. 309 (December 1987): p. 17.

Lembcke 1982. Jerry Lembcke, "A Workplace Democracy Movement: A Success, but for Whom?" *Monthly Review* (October 1982): pp. 56–57.

Lévi-Strauss 1966. Claude Lévi-Strauss, "Overture to Le Cru et le Cuit" [*The Raw and the Cooked*], trans. Joseph H. McMahon, in *Structuralism*, ed. Jacques Ehrmann (Garden City, N.Y.: Doubleday, Anchor, 1966).

Levitt 1988. Ted Levitt, "The Pluralization of Consumption," *Harvard Business Review*, no. 3 (May–June 1988): p. 8.

Lovejoy 1960. Arthur Lovejoy, *The Great Chain of Being* (New York: Harper & Brothers, 1960).

Lutz and Lux 1979. Mark A. Lutz and Kenneth Lux, *The Challenge of Humanistic Economics* (Menlo Park, Calif.: Benjamin/Cummings, 1979).

McLuhan and Fiore 1967. Marshall McLuhan and Quentin Fiore, *The Medium is the Massage: An Inventory of Effects* (New York: Bantam, 1967).
Marx 1977. Karl Marx, *Capital*, vol. 1, trans. Ben Fowkes (New York: Random House, Vintage, 1977).
Meadows et al. 1972. Donella H. Meadows, Dennis L. Meadows, Jorgen Randers, William W. Behrens III, *The Limits to Growth: A Report for the Club of Rome's Project on the Predicament of Mankind* (New York: New American Library, Signet, 1972).
Mendizábal 1984. J. M. Mendizábal, "La Solidaridad Requiere Un Proyecto," *T. U. Lankide*, no. 275 (November 1984).
Meyers 1983. Milton L. Meyers, *The Soul of Modern Economic Man* (Chicago: University of Chicago Press, 1983).
Mill 1968. John Stuart Mill, "Bentham," in *Selected Writings of John Stuart Mill* (New York: New American Library, Mentor, 1968).
Miller and Estrin 1987. David Miller and Saul Estrin, "A Case for Market Socialism," *Dissent* (Summer 1987): pp. 359–60.
Mintegi 1986. Laura Mintegi, "New Directions in Basque Literature," *The Basque Studies Program Newsletter*, no. 34 (Reno: University of Nevada: November 1986).
"Mirando Hacia 1993," *T. U. Lankide* no. 310 (January 1988).
The Mondragon Experiment (Mondragon: Caja Laboral Popular, 1984).
The Mondragon Experiment (Mondragon: Caja Laboral Popular, 1985).
Nef 1964. John U. Nef, *The Conquest of the Material World* (Cleveland, Ohio: World, Meridian, 1964).
New York Times, October 17, 1988.
Nisbet 1982. Robert Nisbet, *The Social Philosophers: Community and Conflict in Western Thought*, concise ed., updated (New York: Simon & Schuster, Washington Square, 1982).
Nobel 1984. David F. Nobel, *Forces of Production: A Social History of Industrial Automation* (New York: Knopf, 1984).
Nove 1983. Alec Nove, *The Economics of Feasible Socialism* (London: Allen & Unwin: 1983).
Oakeshott 1978. Robert Oakeshott, *The Case for Worker Co-ops* (London: Routledge & Kegan Paul, 1978).
Ormaechea 1986. José María Ormaechea, *El Hombre Que Yo Conocí* (Mondragon: Fundación Gizabidea, 1986).
Parker and Slaughter 1988. Mike Parker and Jane Slaughter, *Choosing Sides: Unions and The Team Concept* (Boston: South End, Labor Notes, 1988).
Pert 1988. Candace Pert, "The Material Basis of Emotions," *Whole Earth Review* no. 59 (Summer 1988): pp. 109–11.
Plaskow 1990. Judith Plaskow, *Standing Again at Sinai: Judaism from a Feminist Perspective* (San Francisco: Harper & Row, 1990).
Prigogine and Stengers 1984. Ilya Prigogine and Isabelle Stengers, *Order Out of Chaos* (New York: Bantam, 1984).
Principios 1987. "Principios Básicos de la Experiencia Cooperativa de Mondragon," *T. U. Lankide* (May 1987), p. 4.
"Proyecto de Estatutos Sociales Cooperativos Grupo Ularco, 1986," Chart 25.
"The Realities of Profit Sharing," in *Economic Notes* 55, nos. 7–8 (July–August 1987).
Ryle 1988. Martin Ryle, *Ecology and Socialism* (London: Radius, 1988).
Sartre 1956. Jean-Paul Sartre, *Being and Nothingness*, trans. Hazel E. Barnes (New York: Washington Square, 1956).
Schumacher 1973. E. M. Schumacher, *Small Is Beautiful: Economics as if People Mattered* (New York: Harper & Row, Colophon, 1973).

Schumpeter 1950. Joseph A. Schumpeter, *Capitalism, Socialism, and Democracy*, 3d ed. (New York: Harper & Row, Harper Torchbooks, 1950).

Slaughter 1988. Jane Slaughter, "Auto Workers Find Companies' Drive for 'Flexibility' and 'Teamwork' Is International," *Labor Notes* (April 1988).

Sontag 1980. Susan Sontag, "Fascinating Fascism," in *Under the Sign of Saturn* (New York: Farrar, Straus, Giroux, 1980).

Spain 1988. Kingdom of Spain. *The Spanish Economy: Recent Developments and Prospects* (Madrid: Bureau of Economics and Finance, March 1988).

Spender 1985. Dale Spender, *Man-Made Language*, 2d ed. (London: Routledge & Kegan Paul, 1985).

Thomas 1977. Hugh Thomas, *The Spanish Civil War*, 2d ed. (New York: Harper & Row, 1977).

Thomas and Logan 1982. Henk Thomas and Chris Logan, *Mondragon: An Economic Analysis* (London: Allen & Unwin, 1982).

Thompson 1988. Mark Thompson, "Civilizing the System: An Interview with Tomaz Mastnak," *New Politics* (new series) 2, no. 1 (Summer 1988): p. 149.

United Nations 1985. *National Accounts Statistics: Main Aggregates and Detailed Tables, 1982* (New York: United Nations, 1985).

Urbach 1987. Ephraim E. Urbach, *The Sages: Their Concepts and Beliefs* (Cambridge, Mass.: Harvard University Press, 1987).

Vanek 1970. Jaroslav Vanek, *The General Theory of Labor-Managed Market Economies* (Ithaca, N.Y.: Cornell University Press, 1970).

Vanek 1971. Jaroslav Vanek, *The Participatory Economy* (Ithaca, N.Y.: Cornell University Press, 1971).

Warner 1984. Stanley Warner, "The Field of Workplace Democracy: Some Fundamental Issues," paper presented at National Employee Ownership and Participation Conference, Greensboro, N.C., October 12–14, 1984.

Washington Post 1988. *Washington Post*, "Soviet Union Planning a Foray into Cooperative Banking," *Boston Globe*, March 31, 1988, p. 9.

Webb 1988. Ben Webb, "Coping with 'Euphoria,' " *Peace and Democracy News* 3, no. 2 (Winter 1988–89): pp. 3–4.

Webster and Lambe 1986. Frank Webster and Keith Lambe, "Information Technology: Who Needs It?" in *Red and Green: The New Politics of the Environment*, ed. Joe Weston (London: Pluto, 1986).

Whyte and Whyte 1988. William Foote Whyte and Kathleen King Whyte, *Making Mondragon: The Growth and Dynamics of the Mondragon Cooperative Complex* (Ithaca, N.Y.: ILR, Cornell University, 1988).

Wiener 1967. Norbert Wiener, *The Human Use of Human Beings: Cybernetics and Society* (New York: Avon, 1967).

Wittgenstein 1983. Ludwig Wittgenstein, *Remarks on the Foundations of Mathematics*, trans. G. E. M. Anscombe, ed. G. H. von Wright, R. Rhees, and G. E. M. Anscombe (Cambridge, Mass.: MIT Press, 1983).

Wolf 1984. Robert Paul Wolf, *Understanding Marx: A Reconstruction and Critique of Capital* (Princeton, N.J.: Princeton University Press, 1984).

"The Work Taboo," *In These Times* 12, no. 9 (January 20–26, 1988).

Index

Acción Católica, 46
Admissions: open, 11, 97; of women, 147
Agricultural co-ops: and Caja Laboral Popular, 96, 115; description of, 68, 163-164, 256; sales of, 14, 256; size of, 13, 14, 216, 256
Alava: Basque province of, 6, 36; co-ops in, 13, 248, 253-256; politics of, 42
Alecoop co-op, 16, 251
Alfa co-op, 71
Alkargo co-op, 249
Amat co-op, 247
American Federation of Labor, 41
Ampo co-op, 247
Anarchist: education, 141-142; Movement, 151; unions, 51
Aneko co-op, 252
Arín, Father Joaquín, 43
Arizmendiarrieta, José María: and Caja Laboral Popular, 50, 101; on cooperation, 12, 51, 111, 135; on community, 131, 135-136, 208, 240; on cultural identity, 45; and education, 15, 46-47, 140-141, 142, 143; on empowerment, 131; and founding of Mondragon, 46-47, 48-49, 82; on law, 74; life of, 43, 46, 71; on Mondragon, 21, 109; philosophy of, 43-44, 263; on practice, 32, 56, 84, 109, 246; and social change, 36, 153-154, 222; on unions, 78; on values, 245; on women, 146, 147-148; on work, 44-45
Arkhipov, Viktor, 63
Arrasate co-op, 48, 210-211, 250
Artaxa co-op, 13, 256
Association of Women's Commissions, 147, 150
Aurki co-op, 117, 210-211, 213, 249
Aurki machine, 215-216
Aurrenak, 248
Austurias, 40, 51
Automation, 213-217
Auzo-Lagun, 147-148, 216, 257
Azurmendi, Joxe, 141, 142-143, 146, 154

Bacon, Francis, 2
Banco de Bilbao, 39
Banks, 86-87. *See also* Caja Laboral Popular
Barcelona, 51, 86, 141, 144, 165n
Barrenetxe co-op, 256
Bartlett, Joseph W., 219
Basarte co-op, 253
Basque: capitalism, 39, 67, 70; church, 37, 41-43, 54; culture, 6, 10, 12, 37, 45, 67-69; government, 38, 91, 94, 120, 162, 200-201, 205-206, 212; history, 36-37, 70-71; industry, 38-39, 162, 168, 190; labor movement, 78; language, 6, 15, 16, 37-38, 205; oppression under Franco, 10, 42-43, 141; peasant economy, 66-69; people, 36, 37, 70, 71; schools, 15, 16, 141; unemployment, 52, 95, 124-125, 172, 173, 198; women, 144-146; workforce, 173
Basque nation. *See* Euzkadi
Basque nationalism: and autonomy, 52-54; description of, 38, 41-42, 226; expansion of, 148-149; and methods, 145, 206; and Mondragon, 55. *See also* Basque Nationalist Party; ETA
Basque Nationalist Party; ETA
Basque region: class and ethnicity in, 160; co-ops in, 3; geography and natural resources of, 6, 36-37
Basque Nationalist Party (PNV), 41, 78, 145
Bataille, Georges, 233
Batz co-op, 248
Behaviorism, 138
Behi-Alde co-op, 256
Belohradsky, Václav, 231
Benefits, 18, 19, 161-162
Bentham, Jeremy, 139
Berrigan, Daniel, 83-84
Berriola co-op, 249
Bertako co-op, 253
Bihar co-op, 249
Bilbao, 144, 206
Biurrarena co-op, 253
Blanco, Admiral Carrero, 149
Blue-collar jobs, 147, 200
Bookchin, Murray, 5, 28, 133n-134n
Bradley, Keith, 62, 74, 184, 193
Braverman, Harry, 215
Brenan, Gerald, 37, 54, 67
Buber, Martin, 246
Bureaucracy: and co-ops, 63, 148-150, 202; and Industrial Modernism, 107; public versus private, 140; in relation to size, 13, 31, 127
Bury, J.B., 27
Business Week, 109

Caja Laboral Popular (CLP): accomplishments of, 87, 88-90, 91-92; assets of, 8, 86, 91; Banking Division of, 88; creation of, 49-51; distribution of surpluses by, 92-93, 193; functions of, 18-19, 85, 98, 159; governance of, 95-97; investments, 90-91; locations of, 13; membership, 88, 96, 97; position of, 160, 169; power of, 170, 201-202; in recession, 175, 184; relations with co-ops of, 94-97, 99, 161, 173; relationship to community of, 91, 94, 96; size of, 8, 13, 86, 216; and watchdog councils, 81; workers, 92; workings of, 50-51, 6, 10, 12, 37, 45, 67-69;

Caja Laboral Popular, Empresarial Division: functions of, 19, 81, 86, 98, 113-114, 115-116, 203; and intercooperative groups, 161; and intervention, 126, 129-130; location of, 87; and new co-ops, 116-121; organization of, 113, 202; during recession, 186-188; research of, 206, 209; staff of, 113, 207; strengthening of, 95, 97, 114
Capital, 156
Capital: and Caja Laboral Popular, 19, 49-51, 86, 97, 98; and co-ops, 159; in early cooperative movement, 48-50; expansion, 48-49; Mondragon definition of, 100; role of, in co-ops, 11, 77; shifting, 180-181, 196; social, 98, 158, 159, 161, 179; start-up, 47, 123-124
Capital accounts, internal: and Caja Laboral Popular, 92, 93, 94; workers', 50, 159, 195
Capital contributions, 187, 188-189, 194-196
Capital investment: and Caja Laboral Popular, 86, 97, 201; and conventional companies, 122; and co-ops, 47, 49-50, 128, 159, 180; decisions about, 158; and new jobs, 124, 173; in new technology, 174, 179; during recession, 175, 177, 186, 191; workers', 11, 124
Capitalism: Basque, 39, and cooperation, 62-63, 115, 151-152, 157; costs of, 23, 109, 224; and democracy, 154-155; failed businesses in, 114; and growth, 27, 106, 235; ideology of, 27, 104-108, 139, 224, 236; and industrial modernism, 2; and people, 179-180, 184; solutions for, 233; transnational, 107. *See also* Industrialism
Casas del pueblo, Las, 141
Cash flow, 177, 193-194
Catholicism, 37. *See also* Clergy
Centers for Promotion of Women, 144
Central Permanent Commision, 191-193
Centralization and autonomy: Basque, 10, 54, 152; in Mondragon system, 169, 170, 201, 204; politics of, 223-224; Socialism on, 54
CGT, 41
Charitable donations: Caja Laboral Popular's, 92, 93, 97; co-op's, 50, 158-159
China, 63, 229
Chrysler Corporation, 114
Cikautxo co-op, 251
CIM co-op, 87
Clamp, Christine, 147, 200
Clamshell Alliance, vii, 133n, 220
Clark, Robert, 145
Clarke, Kenneth, 100
Class: and co-ops, 151-152, 157, 160; and industrialism, 22, 70,

95, 104
Clergy, 42-43. *See also* Arizmendiarrieta, José María
Club Arkitze co-op, 257
CNT, 51, 144
Coinalda co-op, 253
Coinma co-op, 254
Cold war, 226, 227
Collective consciousness, 57, 59
Comet co-op, 48
Commoner, Barry, 25, 234, 235
Communism, 139, 145, 231
Community: in Basque life, 70; building, 56, 84, 157, 239; and Caja Laboral Popular, 50, 86, 90-91; co-ops' contributions to, 12, 50, 173, 206; co-ops' relation to, 3, 4, 39, 132, 200-201, 206; development, 65, 158, 200; and industrial modernism, 220; necessity of, 9, 50, 169; philosophy of, 131, 135-136, 185; support of co-ops, 206, 212; welfare of, 170, 172
Compa, Lance, 152
Confederation of Workers Committees, 51
Consensus: in Basque culture, 68, 69-70; between co-ops, 161; within co-ops, 77, 80, 192-193; process, 30, 71-73
Consumer Education, 143, 144, 164
Consumer Price Index, Spanish, 191, 193-194
Consumerism: capitalist and socialist, 138, 139; in Industrial Modernism, 26, 27, 138
Consumption, 236, 237
Conversion: of capitalist companies, 48, 70-71, 79; failures of, 117, 126, 174; U.S. resources for, 261-264
Cooperation: and capitalism, 151, 152, 156; and industrialism, 61-62; and social change, 63, 64-65, 82-84; and socialism, 156
Cooperative Congress: and Caja Laboral Popular, 95, 100; decisions of, 72-73; and democratic control, 158, 170, 201; description of, 9-10, 16, 19-20, 160-161
Cooperatives: in China, 229, 262; in U.S., 9, 152, 262-264; in U.S.S.R., 229. *See also* New co-ops
Copesca co-op, 126, 174
Copreci co-op, 192, 210-211, 252
Corporate takeovers, 180-181
Coseheros Alaveses co-op, 256
Council of Cooperative Groups, 16, 201
Council of the Mondragon Cooperative Group, 161, 204
Counting, 136-138, 139
Covimar co-op, 255
Creative destruction, 107-109, 113, 168
Cultural Centers, 144
Cybernetics, 185

Daly, Herman, 234, 235-236
Danobat co-op, 250
Danona, 254
Danona Litografía, 253
Daycare, 143, 148, 150, 158
Decentralization: *See* Centralization and autonomy
Decision-making process: of Caja Laboral Popular, 96-97; on capital contributions, 194-196; within co-ops, 18, 75-78, 81-82, 147; intercooperative, 10, 72-73; and Ulgor strike, 149-150; values of, 98-100, 170; on wages, 188-189, 190-193; *See also* Consensus; Democratic control
Democratic control: and Caja Laboral Popular, 39, 97; of capital, 160; of co-ops, 16-17, 158, 160, 169, 192; as guiding princiiple, 11, 66, 112; and organizational structure, 75, 79; of society, 114, 139, 240; and unions, 79
Democratization: of Caja Laboral Popular, 95; of capitalist firms, 47; through co-op groups, 201-202; within co-ops, 3, 10, 150, 191; during recession, 186; of society, 155, 226, 227-228. *See also* Decision-making process; Worker control
Descarte, Rene, 2
Devolution, 226, 231
Dialectical materialism, 156, 157
Dikar co-op, 255
Disability benefits, 19, 161
Discipline, 73, 74, 149, 174
Doiki co-op, 248
Domination, 63, 106, 230
Dualism, 2, 131

Eastern Airlines, 197
Echeverria, Toribio, 70-71
Ecological postmodernism: description of, 4-5, 20-21; and equilibrium, 238-239; idology of, 30, 55-56, 239; and Mondragon, 55, 153; potential of, 228, 230, 240, 244; process of, 30-32, 136, 204; values of, 185, 223. *See also* Equilibrio
Ecology: definition of, 4; and industrialism, 137, 220; in Mondragon practice, 30, 158, 162-163; as Mondragon principle, 21, 222; movement, 220, 228; social, 4, 20, 29, 112, 205, 220, 233; and socialist governments, 234; and technique, 25. *See also* Environmental destruction
Economic downswings: and Caja Laboral Popular, 94, 129-130; failures during, 174; Mondragon's response to, 128, 129-131, 174; successes during, 171-172. *See also* Recession
Economics, "science" of, 103-107
Economy, Spanish: and Basque country, 189-190; in 1960s, 51-52, 167; in 1970s, 52, 167, 175,
183; in 1980s, 52, 94, 114, 172, 175. *See also* Recession
Edelman, Gerald, 57
Ederfil co-op, 252
Ederlan co-op, 48, 210-211, 247
Education: Mondragon philosophy of, 12, 15-16, 140-141, 142-143, 215; Mondragon programs in, 143-144; in new technology, 208; for outsiders, 206; regional planning for, 203; for women, 146, 147, 151. *See also* Educational Co-ops; Schools
Educational Co-ops: description of, 13, 15-16; origins of, 46-47. *See also* Hezibide Elkartea; Research co-ops; Schools
Efficiency, 111, 224
Ego and His Own, The, 142
Eguna, 43
Egurko co-op, 251
Eibar, 70-71
Eika co-op, 252
Elgiobar co-op, 13
ELA-STV (Solidarity of Basque Workers trade union), 41, 192
Eliot, T.S., 225
Elkar co-op, 253
Ellerman, David: on Caja Laboral Popular, 92, 113, 118; on China, 229; and Industrial Cooperative Association, 261; on intervention, 129, 130; on marketing, 120-121, 122; on Mondragon accomplishment, 112
Ellul, Jacques, 83
Embega co-op, 252
Employment: Mondragon's commitment to, 173, 175, 189, 198; regional, 200; and retraining, 215. *See also* Job security; Jobs
Enara co-op, 248
Energy: and Mondragon, 163, 210; nuclear, 23-24, 28, 163; research, 214-215
Entrepreneurship, cooperative: early Basque, 70-71; efficiency of, 111, 131; and shared risk, 4; strengths of, 9, 109, 111-113; as tool, 61
Entrepreneurship, individual, 108-109
Entropy, 236-238
Environmental destruction: in Basque region, 162-163; and the future, 237, 245; from industrialism, 20, 139, 155, 221, 228, 243-244. *See also* Ecology
Equilibrio: components of, 23, 28-30, 55, 131; and cooperation, 62; description of, 4, 139; dynamics of, 30-32, 98, 156, 157, 239; of economics and values, 187; and the environment, 163; importance of, 112, 221-222; of individual and community; 10, 29, 30, 107, 184, 223; process toward, 22, 77, 150, 222-223; and social change, 228
Equilibrium, 237-238
Eredu co-op, 255
Erein Cooperative Group, 163

Index

Eroski, 144
Eroski co-op: and Caja Laboral Popular, 90, 96; and education, 143, 144; locations of, 13, 15; origins of, 48; relationships to other co-ops of, 161, 164; sales, 9, 143-144, 257; size of, 15, 143, 216, 257
Eroskide, 144
Escuela Universitaria de Estudios Empresariales, 143, 209
Eskola Politeknikoa: educational philosophy of, 215; educational programs of, 15, 143, 209, 212; location of, 87, 213
ETA: armed struggle of, 38, 149, 206; and co-ops, 152, 154; tax, 173
Etorki co-op, 253
European Common Market, 94, 128
European Economic Community, 172, 205, 206-208, 210, 226
European International Peace Communication and Coordination Center, 227
European Nuclear Disarmament (END), 206, 218n
Euzkadi, 36-37, 186, 205, 206
Export co-ops, 201
Exports: agricultural co-ops', 256; and Caja Laboral Popular, 115; industrial co-ops', 202, 210-211, 247-256; Mondragon, 170, 201, 206-207, 257; retail co-ops', 257; service co-ops', 257

Fascism, 36, 64, 107, 108, 145, 227-228. *See also* Franco, Francisco
Fagor co-op: capital distributions of, 81, 209, 210-212; description of, 81, 209, 210-212; economic fortunes of, 177-178; origins of, 117; strike, 148, 149; training, 143; transnationalism, 229; women at, 147
Fagor Clima co-op, 210-211, 254
Fagor Electrotécnica co-op, 210-211, 252
Fagor Industrial co-op, 210-211, 249
Failures: co-op, 126, 130, 172, 174; under capitalism, 179. *See also* Intervention
Falange. *See* Franco, Francisco
Feasibility Study, 120-121
Ferguson, Charles, 224
Feminine Vocational School, 146
Ferrer, Francisco, 141-142
Fire insurance, 162
First Young Navarrese, 144
F.I.S.O. *See* Fund for Intercooperative Solidarity
Flanders, Will, 263-264
Forming co-ops. *See* New co-ops
Founders' equity, 125-126
Francis Xavier, Saint, 42
Franco, Francisco: bureaucracy of, 47; demise of, 36, 145, 148, 149; economy of, 40-44; and Mondragon, 205; oppression of Basques by, 10, 37, 40, 42-43, 51, 141, 144, 146, 149; oppression of workers by, 10, 40; political fortunes of, 51; repression of, 3, 36, 71, 84, 231; in Spanish Civil War, 42
Frazer, James George, 107
Freedom: description of, 142; and community, 201, 220, 223, 224; and industrial modernism, 220, 233; in Mondragon, 139, 157. *See also* Individual rights
Freidman, Milton, 83, 103, 142
Freire, Paulo, 143
Freud, Sigmund, 107, 136, 138
Funcor co-op, 48, 248
Fund for Intercooperative Solidarity (F.I.S.O.): and co-op structure, 174, 201; description of, 19; formation of, 12, 72, 97, 161

Gaiko co-op, 249
Galbraith, John Kenneth, 87
Gandhian low-tech, 125
Gárate, José, 187
Gelb, Alan, 62, 74, 184, 193
General assembly: of Caja Laboral Popular, 96; function of, 18, 74, 75-76, 161; relation of, to organizational councils, 81; in recession, 192-193; in Ulgor strike, 149
General council, 20
General Electric, 216
General Motors, 122
Give-backs, 196-197
Global Market, 206-208, 225
Gogar co-op, 255
Goier, 15, 209
Goiti co-op, 13, 250
Goizper co-op, 252
Gomá, Cardinal, 42, 43
Gorbachev, Mikhail, 63, 227
Gorroñno, Iaki, 100
Gorroñnogoita, Alfonso: and Caja Laboral Popular, 85, 100; and Mondragon, 10, 47, 158; on solidarity, 160
Gouldner, Alvin, 27, 57
Governing council: control of, 79; and discipline, 74; in recession, 187, 190-191, 192, 193; role of, 18, 75, 76, 82
Graham, Robert, 39
Green Movement, 220, 222, 227
Greenberg, Edward S., 153
Greenwood, Davydd, 150
Griffin, Susan, 29-30
Growth: in capitalism, 27, 106, 138, 233; and co-op groups, 204; of co-ops, 51-53, 88-90, 117, 128-129, 167, 176; future of, 232, 235, 244; in industrial modernism, 27, 137, 232, 233, 235-236; Mondragon attitudes toward, 30, 100, 113, 235; risk to co-ops of, 49; in socialism, 27, 138; of Spanish economy, 40-41; value of, 138. *See also* Hiving off
Guardia Civil, 38, 149

Guipúzcoa Province: co-ops in, 13, 48, 205, 247-257; and Mondragon, 3, 6, 36, 38; mills of, 39; politics of, 42
Guria O.P. co-op, 249
Gutiérrez-Johnson, 150, 191

Hagel, Hansel Mieth, 219
Hagel, Otto, 219
Haltzari co-op group, 202
Harvard Business Review, 225
Havel, Vàclav, 230
Health and safety, 18, 75, 77
Health: benefits, 161-162, 203; care, 162, 233; insurance, 19
Health and Safety: decisions about, 18, 75, 77, 158; procedures, 162; at Toyota, 123
Herriola co-op, 254
Hertell co-op, 252
Hezibide Elkartea: description of, 9, 15, 46; origin of, 46, 140. *See also* League for Education and Culture
Hierarchy: in capitalism, 106, 107; and cooperation, 63, 157; and co-ops, 95, 150; and ecological postmodernism, 205; in industrialism, 25, 26, 66, 136, 137, 233; in Marxism, 157; opposition to, 205
Hiving off, 13, 48, 117, 127, 204
Hobbes, Thomas, 105
Hondarribia Consumer School, 144
Housing, 158, 164, 202, 221, 233
Housing and construction co-ops, 13, 15, 116, 164
Hugh, Thomas, 41
Human value, 184-185, 204, 208, 240

Ian co-op, 256
Ibárruri, Dolores, 145
Ignatius of Loyola, Saint, 42
Ikasbide, 16, 43, 206, 209
Ikerlan co-op: and cooperative congress, 161; description of, 9, 16, 87, 212-214; energy research, 163; and government support, 206; product development, 209, 212-214; training, 56, 143
Ikus XXI co-op, 255
Illich, Ivan, 138
Impreci co-op, 253
Independence: Basque 37, 38, 52, 67-68, 149; of cooperatives, 16, 17, 127, 169; and fueros, 45. *See also* Basque nationalism
Individual rights, 138, 223, 240. *See also* Equilibrio: individual versus community
Industrial Cooperative Association, 112, 187, 229, 261-262
Industrial co-ops: and Caja Laboral Popular, 116; criticisms of, 154; description of, 14, 247-256; formation of, 144, 146-147; number of, 13, 127; position in Mondragon system of, 3, 96; size of, 14, 53, 247-256. *See also*

Fagor; Ulgor
Industrial Design Center, 212
Industrial modernism: and co-ops, 3, 153; crisis of, 220, 243; elements of, 10, 24, 230; and hierarchy, 25, 26, 107; ideology of, 20, 22-28, 136-138, 239; origins of, 2, 226; price of, 20, 22-24, 28, 29, 221, 240, 244; and progress, 27; technique in, 25-26; transformation of, 223, 231, 232
Industrialism: and "freedom," 66; and growth, 27, 137, 232; ills of, 63-64, 136, 155, 228; limits on, 55, 61, 64, 157, 235; modern, 65; philosophy of, 106
Inflation rates, Spanish, 258
Institute for Community Economics, 263
Institute of Industrial Design, 15, 209
Instituto Nacional de Industria, 40
Insurance: costs, 189, 190; decisions about, 161-162, 203; development of, 18, 19, 158; and the government, 49, 206. *See also* Health insurance; Lagun-Aro; Unemployment insurance
Intercooperative relations: benefits of, 3, 19; commitment to, 173; and co-op groups, 201-204, 259-260; and shared profits/losses, 97, 126, 203; structure of, 16-17, 81, 82, 201-204; and unemployment, 121, 198, 200, 203. *See also* Caja Laboral Popular; Cooperative Congress
Interest: on Caja Laboral Popular loans, 94, 114, 186, 187; on worker accounts, 50, 92-93, 159
Investment. *See* Capital investment
Intervention: and Caja Laboral Popular, 116, 129-130, 175; in conventional companies, 130; during recession, 186-188
Iranskale Eskole, 15
Iranukor, 15, 143, 209, 212
Irizar co-op, 249
Investment, 47, 49. *See also* Capital investment
Iroquois Confederacy, 245
Izarraitz co-op, 250

Jackobs, Steven Curtis, 68
Jacobs, Jane, 184
Japan, 62, 99, 109, 122-123
Jesuits, 42
Job security: in conventional firms, 179-180; in co-ops, 160, 172, 173, 179
Jobs: new, 172-173, 175, 200-201, 202, 206, 235; number, in co-ops, 172, 247-257; and solidarity, 193
John Paul II, Pope, 44
Juntas de Ofensiva Nacionalista Sindicada (JONS), 51

Kamata, Satoshi, 122-123

Kendu co-op, 248
Kide co-op, 249
King, Martin Luther, 61

Labeko co-op, 126, 174
Labor Research Review, 262
Labor: as fixed cost, 118, 121-123, 174; sovereignty of, 11; wage, 64, 77, 185
Lagun-Aro: and co-op security, 174, 187; description of, 8, 19, 87, 161-162; relationship of to other co-ops, 161, 202; and unemployment, 198-200
Lana co-op, 68, 163, 256
Lankide organization, 201
Lan-Mobel co-op, 254
Larrañaga, Jesús, 47, 207, 208, 220, 240
Latz co-op, 248
Law, Spanish: and Caja Laboral Popular, 90-91, 115, 117; and consumer price index, 191; on co-ops, 17, 19, 47, 48, 49; and layoffs, 190, 196
Layoffs: avoiding, 118, 121, 130, 179, 200; co-op, 198, 200; in recession, 187, 188, 190; and share economy, 197; and Spanish law, 196. *See also* Unemployment
League for Education and Culture, 15, 46, 47, 140, 143. *See also* Hezibide Elkartea
Lealde co-op, 250
Legal department, Caja Laboral Popular, 115
Lembcke, Jerry, 152
Léniz Valley, 152
Lenniz co-op, 210-211, 254
Leroa co-op, 254
Leunkor co-op, 210-211, 253
Lévi-Strauss, Claude, 57
Levitt, Ted, 225
Liberalism, 223
LKS. *See* Caja Laboral Popular, Empresarial Division
Loans: to co-ops, 94, 114, 130; to early co-ops, 47, 49; to new co-ops, 120, 125; during recession, 186, 187; for U.S. co-ops, 261, 263
Logan, Chris, 89, 168, 174, 229
Losses, pooling, 97, 126, 203

Machines, 185, 215-216, 231, 233, 237. *See also* Technology
Madariaga, Salvador de, 40
Madrid, 86, 149
Maherco co-op group, 202
Maier co-op, 251
Maiak co-op, 254
Management, conventional, 196
Management, co-op: during economic crisis, 130; and governing council, 76; workers' relationship to, 18, 73-74, 215; training, 209; women in, 147, 150. *See also* Decision making process
Management council, 18, 75, 81-82

Manufacturing. *See* Industrial co-ops
Mao Tse Tung, 44
Maritain, Jacques, 142
Market, Spanish, 210. *See also* Global market
Marketing: and Caja Laboral Popular, 115, 120, 130; and cooperation, 122; and Eroski, 216; during recession, 187; strategy, 202, 203, 209
Marquina, 71
Marx, Karl, 27, 69, 83, 152, 154, 156
Marxism: and capitalism, 107; and class, 22; co-ops' revision of, 100-101; and critique of co-ops, 151-158; and industrialism, 157. *See also* Socialism
Mastnak, Tomaz, 230
Maternity leave, 150-151
Mathematics, 137. *See also* Counting
Matrici co-op, 248
Matrici Plásticos, 251
Matz-Erreka co-op, 251
Mendizábal, J.M., 160, 240
Miba co-op, 256
Michnik, Adam, 227, 230
Midwest Center for Labor Research, 262
Mill, John Stuart, 139, 154
Mill owners, 36
Mircea, Eliade, 132
Modern School Movement, 141
Modernization, 128, 130, 172
Mollner, Terry, 263-264
Mondragon, cooperatives: antecedants to, 70-71; and Basqueness, 45, 136; differences from U.S. co-ops, 9; failures of, 113-114, 126; and industrialism, 221; life cycle of, 117-118; locations of, 6, 13, 247-257; number of, 3, 8, 13, 51, 127; origins of, 3, 10, 15, 35-36; 41, 46-48, 231; security of, 86, 179-180; size of, 13, 31, 51, 53, 80-81; types of, 3, 8, 13, 247-257
Mondragon, town of: and co-ops, 6; location of, 36; politics of, 36, 43, 149; schools in, 15, 143, 209; social life of, 70
Mongelos, Javier, 201
Monthly Review, 151-152
Moscow, 145
Mounier, Emmanuel, 142
Múgica, Bishop, 43
Mumford, Lewis, 137

Nationalist movements, 226. *See also* Basque Nationalism
Navarra: co-ops in, 13, 248-249, 251-254, 260; geography of, 6, 36; politics of, 42
Neguri, 39
New co-ops: Caja Laboral Popular's support of, 19, 86, 94, 125-126; Empresarial Division's role with, 113, 116-121, 126; financing, 50, 123-124; Mondragon's support of, 66, 173,

Index 275

203; products of, 207-208; screening, 118-120; and unions, 79
New York Times, The, 216
Nicaragua, 151
Nisbet, Robert, 30
Nobel, David, 215
Nove, Alec, 169

Oakshott, Robert, 44
Ochandiano Talleres co-op, 48, 250
Oiarso co-op, 252
Oihana co-op, 254
Oinaker co-op, 250
Olarria co-op, 255
Ona-Press co-op, 251
Oñati, 143, 209
Ondoan co-op, 257
Opus Dei, 40
Orbea co-op, 255
Organizational structure, Mondragon: changes in, during recession, 186-188, 201-204; current, 16-20, 75-78; early, 48-49
Origin of Species, The, 27
Orkli co-op, 252
Ormaechea, José María, 47, 72, 99-100, 161, 203. *See also* Modernization
Orona co-op, 255
Ortubay, 47
Ortza co-op, 251
Osatu co-op, 253

Parental leave, 150-151
Pasionaria, La, 145, 165n
Pensions, 161, 233
Perestroika, 228-229
Personnel, 18, 77, 115, 147, 203
Pert, Candace, 58
Phillips, Wendell, 231
Philo of Alexandria, 68-69
Pink Floyd, 56
Plan de Relaiziationte Excepcional, 206
Plant closings, 190
Plaskow, Judith, 29
Plato, 30
Policía Nacional, 38
Pollution. *See* Environment destruction
Portugal, 149, 231
Poverty, 221, 225, 234, 236
Practice: of cooperative principles, 64, 77, 109; importance of, 204, 205; and social change, 20, 56, 84, 238, 245
Prigogine, Ilya, 237
Principles, Mondragon: basic, 10-12, 21, 65-66, 161, 239-240; and Caja Laboral Popular, 86, 97; on community, 173; formation of, 49, 72; and jobs, 173, 179, 198; and organizational structure, 75, 82; and social change, 153; on technology, 25-26
Product development: and Caja Laboral Popular, 114, 116, 119-120; and feasibility studies, 120-121; groups, 202, 203; and Ikerlan, 212-214; process, 130, 174, 198, 207-208, 209-210;

during recession, 187
Production: and capitalism, 139; decisions, 65; infinite, 235; organization of, 233; and socialism, 138, 139
Productivity, 111, 174, 180, 190
Products: co-op, 247-257; social, 233
Profits. *See* Surpluses
Progress: in capitalism, 27; in industrial modernism, 27; in socialism, 27, 157; versus renewal and balance, 5
Proudhon, Pierre Joseph, 142, 151

Quaker, 72, 73
Quality circles, 62, 190

Radar co-op, 210-211, 254
Recession: and Basque country, 189-190; and Caja Laboral Popular, 97, 114, 186-188; capital contributions during, 186; Mondragon's response to, 124, 128, 186-189; and solidarity, 188-189; wage cuts during, 188, 189-194
Reconversion plan, 175, 177-178. *See also* Modernization
Regional co-op groups, 201-204, 259-260
Regional planning, 203
Research, 115, 130, 210
Research co-ops. *See* Ikerlan
Reserve fund, 50, 93
Retail co-ops, 9, 13, 15, 48, 257
Retirement, 161, 195, 199
Revolutionaries, 145-146, 165n. *See also* Arizmendiarrieta, José María
Rich, Adrienne, 146
Risk taking, 4, 17, 50-51, 124, 126
R.P.K. co-op, 253

S curve growth pattern, 52, 128-129, 170-171
Saiolan, 15, 209, 212
Sakana, 248
Salazar, Antonio, 231
Sales: agricultural co-ops', 256; and Caja Laboral Popular, 89-90; growth of, 89-90, 176, 178; Fagor, 211; individual co-ops', 247-257; industrial co-ops', 247-257; retail co-ops', 9, 257; service co-ops', 257; total co-op, 8, 170-171, 175-176, 177, 257
San Isidoro Labrador co-op, 256
San Sebastian, 144
Schools, 46-47, 233. *See also* Educational co-ops
Schumacher, E.F., 127-128, 133n
Schumpeter, Joseph, 106, 107-109, 113, 138, 168
Scoiner co-op, 126, 174
Second-degree co-ops, 14, 18-19. *See also* Caja Laboral Popular; Ikerlan
Self-management. *See* Worker control
Service co-ops: description of, 13,

14-15, 257; growth in, 125, 148; Uldata, 14. *See also* Auzo-Lagun
Service sector, 214, 216-217
Sexism, 136, 144, 146
Share economy, 197
Size: Mondragon philosophy of, 80-81, 127, 204; Clamshell Alliance and, 133n; and Ulgor strike, 150. *See also* Growth
Smith, Adam, 32, 103, 105-107, 113
Social change. *See* Social transformation
Social choices: applications of, 4, 113, 160, 179, 214-217; and cooperation, 64-65, 82-84; creation of, 158; and education, 142; and the future, 228, 244-245; and Mondragon, 208, 222, 239-241; significance of, 59, 65, 157, 182, 235
Social council: description of, 18; role of, 75, 76, 77, 80, 200; role of, in recession, 191-193; strengthening of, 150; women on, 147
Social Darwinism, 26-27, 30
Social security. *See* Insurance, social
Social security co-op. *See* Lagun-Aro
Social structures, deep, 56-58, 137
Social transformation: as basic Mondragon principle, 12; co-ops and, 10, 21, 78, 112, 155, 222, 235; in Europe, 140, 226-227, 230-232, 240-241; potential for, 66, 153-154, 160, 234; process of, 83, 140-141, 156, 220, 238; and world politics, 206
Socialism: and centralization, 54; and control, 230, 231; and cooperation, 62-63; and co-ops, 228; failed businesses within, 114; and growth, 27, 235; ideology of, 139, 224, 233; and industrialism, 2, 23, 62-63; and progress, 27, 232; in Spain, 196; and state capitalism, 229; solutions for, 233. *See also* Marxism
Socially constructed reality, 56-57
Solidarity: Arizmendiarrieta on, 78; as basic co-op principle, 3, 12, 49, 77; between Caja Laboral Popular and co-ops, 92-93; class and ethnic, 160; co-ops' threat to, 152; and pooled resources, 203; transnational, 12; and unions, 79, 189, 193. *See also* Wage solidarity
Soraluce co-op, 250
South Korea, 151
Soviet Agro-Industrial Bank, 63
Spanish Civil War, 36, 42-43, 144-145
Spanish Labor Movement, 196
Spanish Socialist Party, 205

Stability, 179-180. *See also* Job security
Stalinism, 138
Steady state economy, 236-237
Stengers, Isabelle, 237
Stirner, Max, 142
Strikes, 39-40, 70, 150. *See also* Ulgor strike
Success, economic: pattern of, 178; durring recession, 171-172, 175-176; significance of, 139, 169-170
Success, social, 135, 136-137, 139, 168
Support co-ops. *See* Second-degree co-ops
Surpluses: allocation of, 50, 100, 158-160, 233; and Caja Laboral Popular, 19, 86, 92-93, 97; and charitable donations, 50, 66; and conventional companies, 122; Fagor group, 211; limits of accumulation of, 66; and new jobs, 172; pooling of, 93, 201, 203; in recession, 175, 177-178

Tajo co-op, 251
Technique, ideology of, 25-26, 219
Technology: decisions about, 25, 28, 238; development of, 9, 209-210, 212-214, 217; in industrial modernism, 22-23, 136; and job loss, 124-125, 179, 215-216; and liberation, 233, 238; new 124-125, 174-175, 200, 203; U.S., 224; and world market, 207-208
Théorie de lois civiles, 156
Thomas, Henk, 89, 168, 174
Tolsan co-op, 48, 248
Totalitarianism, 230-231
Toyota, 122-123
Trabajo y Unión, 10, 130
Training, technical, 143, 208, 209. *See also* Education
Transnational movement, 225, 227, 228, 229
Trusteeship Institute, 263-264
T.U. Lankide, 240-241
Txurtxil co-op, 250

UGT, 41, 141
Ularco Group: and capital, 194-196; description of, 51, 202; director of, 201; transfer policy, 200; and wage cuts, 189-194; women in, 147, 150
Uldata co-op, 210-211, 216, 257
Ulgor: and Caja Laboral Popular, 50; founder of, 10, 207, 220; hiving off, 117; origins of, 47-48; products of, 8, 254; during recession, 188-190; retooling of, 205; sales of, 254; size of, 13, 81, 127, 172, 254
Ulgor Strike: achievements of, 150, 154, 189; context of, 70, 148-149; description of, 149-150; and ETA, 152
Ulma co-op, 198, 255
Ulmatik co-op, 210-211, 216, 257
Unemployment: Basque, 52, 95, 124-125, 172, 173, 198; in capitalism, 121, 122-123, 221; and Mondragon, 172, 174, 184, 200, 203; during recession, 188, 189-190; role of high technology in, 124-125; structural, 198, 199, 206; threat to co-ops of, 198; types of, 198, 199; and worker training, 143
Unemployment insurance, 19, 52, 162, 184, 198-200
Union Carrajera, 2, 39-40, 46, 47
Unions: Basque, 41, 70, 78, 188, 192; in conventional companies, 78-79, 122, 197; and co-ops, 77, 79, 152; Franco's repression of, 36, 40; and Mondragon, 192, 193, 194; and worker power, 197, 220
United Auto Workers (UAW), 122, 262
Uraldi co-op, 254
Urban planning, 116
Urdaliz, 149
Urola co-op, 250
Urssa co-op, 255
U.S. Department of Energy, 210
Usatorre, José, 47, 207-208
Use value, 185
U.S.S.R., 63, 145, 227-228, 234, 231. *See also* Gorbachev, Mikhail

Values and economic choices, 82-84, 98-100, 112, 170, 182. *See also* Equilibrio; Principles, Mondragon; Social choices
Vanek, Jaroslav, 168, 170
Vitoria, 47, 48, 206
Viviendas y Contratas co-op, 256
Vizcaya: Basque province of, 6; co-ops in, 13, 36, 48, 248-257; mills of, 39; politics of, 42, 145; schools of, 141
Voting: in co-ops, 11, 47, 48, 193; Marx on, 154

Wage cuts: and give-backs, 196-197; in recession, 122, 123, 128, 188-193
Wage labor, 64, 77, 185
Wage solidarity: as basic Mondragon principle, 12, 65; decisions about, 72-73, 161; description of, 49-50; during recession, 188, 189-190, 193
Wages: in Caja Laboral Popular, 148; control of, 18, 75, 77; management, 74, 180; Mondragon, 33n, 50, 159-160; overtime, 195; during recession, 189-194; and unions, 196; withholding, 195; women's, 148, 160; and worker satisfaction,168
Watchdog council, 18, 75, 81
Wayman, Tom, 101
Webb, Ben, 231
Weitzman, Martin, 197
White-collar jobs, 200
Whyte, Kathryn King and William Foote, 28, 80, 112, 149, 163-164, 187

Wiener, Norbert, 185
Wildenhain, Marguerite, 219
Williams, Raymond, 23
Wittgenstein, Ludwig, 137
Women: in Basque culture, 144, 145-146; and education, 144, 147, 151; in Mondragon, 146-148, 150-151, 192; in Ulgor strike, 149-150
Women's co-op (Auzo-Lagun): 147-148
Women's Movement, 145
Work teams, 80
Worker control: as basic Mondragon principle, 3, 11, 49; of Caja Laboral Popular, 95; process of, 9-10; during recession, 187, 196-197; risks of, 152. *See also* Decision making process; Democratic control
Worker Owned network (WON), 262
Workers: Basque, 173; and capitalists, 100, 180, 196-197; number of co-ops, 8, 53, 247-257; satisfaction of, 168, 196; temporary, 121-122, 179; and training, 141, 143-144; Ulcaro group, 51; women, 147
Working People's Bank. *See* Caja Laboral Popular
World Bank, 62, 184
World Cooperative Congress, 206
Writing, 137

Zaragoza, University of, 47
Zertan co-op, 252
Zubikarai, Agustín, 43
Zubiola co-op, 187, 248